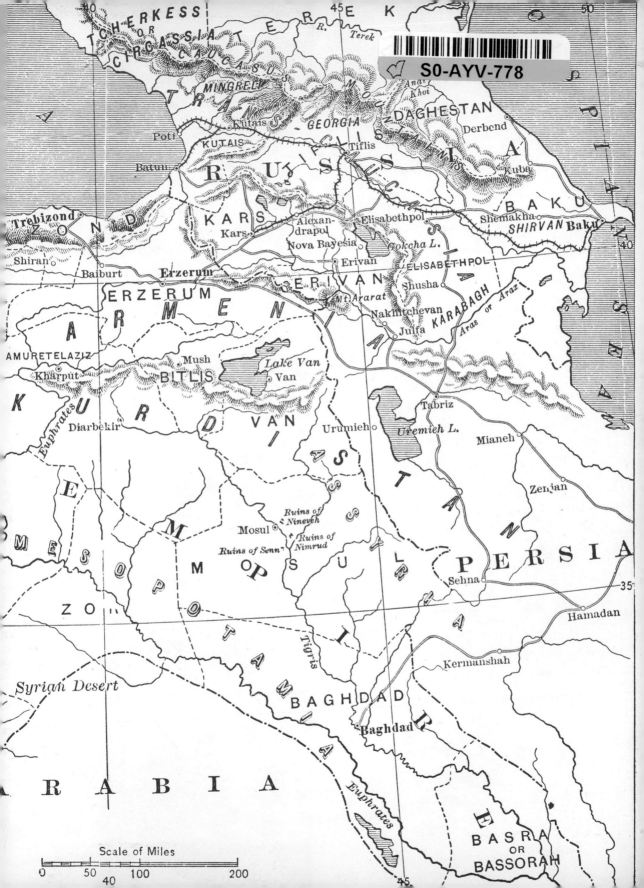

ORIENTAL RUGS

ORIENTAL RUGS

BY
JOHN KIMBERLY MUMFORD

Bramhall House · New York

Copyright © 1981 by Crown Publishers, Inc.
All rights reserved.

This edition is published by Bramhall House,
a division of Clarkson N. Potter.
a b c d e f g h

BRAMHALL HOUSE 1981 EDITION

Manufactured in the United States of America

Library of Congress Cataloging in Publication Data

Mumford, John Kimberly, 1863-1926.
Oriental rugs.

Reprint of the 4th ed. published in 1929 by
Scribner, New York.
Includes index.
1. Rugs, Oriental.   I. Title.
NK2808.M88   1981   746.7'5   81-32
ISBN 0-517-33935-8

FOREWORD

Until only two decades ago, John Kimberly Mumford's *Oriental Rugs* was one of the few scholarly works devoted to the subject. Originally published in 1900 during the first great wave of oriental rug importation and the peak period of commercial production, this classic has remained an invaluable tool for today's collector. A pioneer attempt to document and classify rugs and khilims, it now provides a unique insight into what was being collected at the time and into the problems of quality that have directly shaped and influenced the contemporary marketplace.

Oriental Rugs, the first book of its kind to be published, answered a distinctive need. From the 1870s until the Depression, oriental rugs were being shipped by the bales from the Middle East, and no other literature on the subject existed save brochures from rug-selling firms and publications on masterpiece items. Suddenly, oriental rugs covered the floors, walls, and divans of American homes, and very little, if anything, was known about them. They were instead shrouded with an aura of mystique and nebulous terminology perpetuated by Middle Eastern dealers, who were in control of the rug trade until recently and who profited from the public's ignorance.

Mumford's exhaustive research and method of classification, exemplified by his textile tables, were an important step toward the serious recognition of oriental rugs as a major art form and toward rendering the subject accessible to collectors, dealers, and auctioneers alike. With the exception of a few noted twentieth-century scholars, including Amos Thatcher, Rosa Belle Holt, and G. Griffin Lewis, the book was virtually unrivaled. Reprinted several times, it remained prominent in oriental rug literature after the Depression—the end of the great collecting period—up until the 1960s, when interest in the subject resumed with renewed fervor.

Although much additional research has been completed in the last two decades, *Oriental Rugs* is astonishingly relevant to the contemporary collector. Many of the problems concerning the rugs' quality, age, and dyes that were applicable in the early twentieth century have since become even more significant, thereby affecting the present price structure.

Of utmost importance to today's reader is Mumford's assessment of the commercialization and industrialization of the rug craft due to the increased commercial pressures of the late nineteenth and early twentieth century. The oriental rugs' overwhelming success in the West and the consequent shortage of genuine antique pieces strongly encouraged the occidentalization and degeneration of traditional designs and motifs, the production of machine-made carpets, as well as carefully devised "antiquing" procedures. The introduction of chemical dyes in the 1870s, far cheaper and simpler to use than the traditional vegetable dyes—particularly noted for their subtle and resonant hues—further debauched the craft, bringing brighter and often more garish colors to the fore. This revolutionary procedure has contributed to today's almost limitless demand and soaring prices for the dwindling supply of the old natural-dye pieces.

Fascinating to the contemporary reader is the realization that many of the present so-called antique rugs are the very subject of Mumford's criticism. Thus, he will perhaps become more selective in his own collecting habits and turn his attention to the good-quality pieces that maintained an integrity of color, texture, and design. Mumford singles out the geometrically patterned tribal rugs, then still woven outside the sphere of Western influence, and now among the most desirable and highest-priced pieces on today's market.

Of unquestionable historical value is the author's descriptive, albeit somewhat romantic, account of the traditional oriental rug craft that continued to resist

FOREWORD

Western commercial pressures when this book was first published. Mumford goes beyond a simple discussion of the various weaving and dyeing techniques still in practice at the time; he also provides an invaluable insight into the social and ethnic structure of the period based on his deep understanding and feeling for the craft. Fundamental in his discussion of the craft's hierarchical structure is the important role played by women, whose weavings formed a significant part of their dowry. However, they were seldom initiated to the complicated dyeing skill reserved for a chosen few. The complete secrecy with which the latter performed their craft led to the severance of ties with the past when the chemical dyes gained popularity.

No time is more appropriate for a new edition of *Oriental Rugs* than today. Indeed, now that the awareness and sophisticated knowledge of rugs have reached proportions Mumford probably would never have even fathomed, it is appropriate to assess the early beginnings of their collectible history. In addition to its invaluable documentary evidence pertaining to the Caucasian, Turkish, Turkoman, Persian, and Indian rugs, as well as to khilims, the book is an excellent guide for the contemporary collector intent on being able to recognize good from bad quality and making a sound investment. However unfortunate, timeless is the advice he offers the reader: only the highest prices will fetch the most desirable pieces.

ALIX PERRY
American Associate Editor
HALI, The International Journal
of Oriental Carpets and Textiles

PREFACE TO THE FOURTH EDITION

IN the fifteen years that have elapsed since the first appearance of "Oriental Rugs" momentous changes have taken place in the Orient. The past decade has witnessed in Persia the downfall of a dynasty, and indeed of the throne itself. The oldest of empires has been for a space the newest of republics, and is now beyond question far advanced toward the inevitable partition. While these lines are being written the Turkish forts at the gateways of Constantinople are trembling under the assault of Russian, French, and English guns, and the Ottoman power, after five centuries of guile and audacity, is turning its face again toward Asia, whence it stormed down upon Europe in the far-away day of its strength.

These and manifold other mutations in the Oriental countries cannot but have had their effect upon the rug-weaving industry, and even more obviously upon the rug-weaving art. But all these changes have tended in the one direction, which was foretold when the original edition of this book was published. Hand in hand with the political movements in Asia has gone the promised commercialization of weaving. By far the greater part of the rug making of

PREFACE

Turkey is now controlled by a trust, and the industry in Persia is rapidly coming under the same influence.

Since the avowed purpose of this book in the beginning was to describe, identify, and expound the old, native rugs of the Orient, there seems to be no reason why any measure of attention should now be given to modern "grades," which under corporate dictation have come to be manufactured in vast numbers and in standard commercial sizes, on contract looms, taking their inspiration almost wholly from Paris, London, and New York. With these Occidental inventions of the latter day this book has no more to do than with the new products of the Worcester and Philadelphia carpet looms. The one variety is as thoroughly commercial as the other, though the Oriental fabric, for divers reasons, is still made by hand.

Although a round dozen of books about rugs have issued from American presses in as many years, the author and publishers of this work are pleased to note that, concerning itself with the purely native rugs, it has maintained its status in public favor through all this time. Succeeding books have only amplified its outline. Several times since its first publication the book has been reprinted, and each fresh supply has encountered an almost undiminished demand. The present volume, in somewhat altered form and garb, and constructed with the aid of newer and less expensive manufacturing processes, is offered in the belief that it will meet the need of those who have been deterred by the necessarily high cost from possessing themselves of copies from the preceding editions.

PREFACE

The text, plate-subjects, textile tables, *et cetera*, are practically the same as those of the earlier imprints. An error, however, important to the student, has been corrected, and the story thereof is interesting. It has to do with the Soumaki, or so-called "Kashmir," rugs of the Caucasus, discussion of which will be found on page 119. Between 1896 and 1899 the author expended considerable time in an effort to trace the origin of the name Soumaki, and was forced to the conclusion that it was either an obsolete form or a corruption of "Shemakha," the name of a hill city in eastern Caucasia, in the neighborhood where these rugs were known to have been made for centuries.

In Batoum, Russia, on a subsequent journey, this question was discussed with the United States consul at that port, Mr. James C. Chambers, himself an amateur of rugs. Mr. Chambers scouted this derivation, insisting that he had seen an old map showing a khanate of Soumaki, which lay to the west of Shirvan, but which had been gerrymandered out of existence by the Russians early in the nineteenth century. A search of some months failed to discover the map, and other evidence not appearing, the book went to press perforce with this quite erroneous derivation unchanged. Three months later Mr. Chambers wrote to the author that in an old, unused desk in the consulate he had found the venerable map, and on it the more venerable province of Soumaki.

It is pleasant, after so long a time, to have an opportunity to rectify the mistake. The consciousness of it has been annoying, but a compensatory measure of amusement has been derived from the unanimity with which the blunder has

PREFACE

been adopted by later writers, some of whom have not acknowledged an acquaintance with this book in their copious bibliographies. For fifteen years I have persistently "winked at 'Omer down the road," and "'Omer" has never once "winked back."

Upon publication of this new edition of "Oriental Rugs," the author confesses a perhaps pardonable pride that a work done in good faith has so well withstood the test of time.

SHADOW LAKE, ATHENS, N. Y.
June, 1915.

PREFACE TO THE THIRD EDITION

THE belief, expressed when this volume first appeared, that there was need for it, seems to have found justification. Both the earlier editions were exhausted within a few months after publication; upon the first, indeed, collectors and dealers placed a three-fold value before half a year was past.

In the preparation of the present edition for the press, circumstances have made necessary a change in the illustrative scheme. The color plates, which, in the preceding issues, met with such general approbation, had become unfit for further use, at least mechanically unproductive of results such as proper illustration of the book required. For the making of new plates it would have been difficult, even if it had been desirable, to bring together all the rugs previously used. New selections have therefore been made, which, it is believed, will serve even better the broad purpose involved. A wholly new color series is thus presented.

By permission of the executors of the estate of the late Henry G. Marquand, five rugs from the collection made by that gentleman have been taken as subjects for color plates. Some of these ancient carpets are not to be ex-

PREFACE

celled, either in artistic quality or in rarity, by any fabrics to be found in the royal or public collections of the Old World, and that they can be shown here as examples of the weaver's work in a time when the East was greatest in wealth, power and artistic development, should be to the reader, as it assuredly is to the author, a source of great satisfaction. Admirable translation of the inscriptions in the chief of the Marquand pieces has been made by Dr. Richard J. H. Gottheil, of Columbia University.

Two pieces, which appeared as artotypes in the original book, are now reproduced in color, a promotion of which both are eminently worthy.

So far as the book has borne upon the rug industry there is apparent no change of condition sufficient to demand serious modification of what has been said, save, perhaps, in the case of the Indian weavings, in which, as is plainly enough remarked in the text, constant betterment has been visible from the day when American firms began to control labor in that weed-grown field of manufacture.

The writer cannot conclude this small foreword without expressing profound personal pleasure that the work, offered at the first with desire that it might be a means of uplift as well as of diversion, has been received with such unfailing favor, from those best qualified to sit in judgment.

New York, October 1, 1902.

PREFACE

THE volume here presented goes, the first, into a field as empty as it is extensive. It is the result of several years' study, and the author hopes that it will serve well the purpose which prompted its creation.

The maker of books of this sort is, after all, only a weaver. The sum of what he can accomplish is to produce a fabric sound, thorough in workmanship, grateful in design, and true in color. If it shall prove serviceable, survive the effects of wear and time, and perform throughout its term of endurance some office of æsthetic gratification as well, that is about all the weaver can hope for. His first concern, it would seem, is firm foundation. The warp and weft of fact are paramount. These the writer has sought assiduously, wherever they were to be found, including, naturally, the mysterious, contradictory East. It is only in the Orient, where these rugs are born,—that Orient which does not know itself or its neighbor, scarcely its resplendent past and certainly not its enigmatical future,—that one can understand how complex, how interlaced, how confused and confusing, is the subject which the writer has here attempted to systematize and present in comprehensive form. Only there does one see clearly why the labor was not undertaken long ago.

Out of the years spent in the work little time has been devoted to the fanciful or imaginative side of the subject. Its poesy and romance have been in a measure accepted as corollaries, assumed as among the reasons for the book's existence, and, therefore, perhaps neglected in the presentation. To those who have already come under the spell of the Eastern weavings this will not be felt as a lack. What of color has been distributed through these pages is of more moment to those who are still groping in the dark belief that rugs are — merely rugs. If too little of tingent has been employed, it is because the fabrics themselves, properly understood, provide it in plenty — far better than can any vocabulary or any thesaurus of poetic imagery. If foundation shall here have been laid for that understanding, the work will have been well done, and the worker will be content.

Acknowledgment should be made of contributions to the book and whatever of service it may render. From Mr. A. C. Denotovich was received much light upon Eastern life and manners, together with energetic coöperation in the collection and classification of technical details. His familiarity with the peoples and languages of the Orient, as well as with the various weavings, was of inestimable value during the author's sojourn in the countries where rugs are made.

Many facts regarding the Persian textiles were had from

PREFACE

Mr. Hildebrand Stevens of Tabriz, and, upon the subject of Caucasian and Turkoman fabrics, from Mr. James C. Chambers, United States Consul at Batoum, Russia.

In making the examinations requisite to accuracy it has been necessary, in this country, to resort to large trade collections, where many rugs of each variety could from time to time be compared. For such privilege the author is under obligation to Mr. L. B. Searing of W. & J. Sloane; Mr. W. Mansell Daintry and Mr. J. L. Parker of Arnold, Constable & Company; Mr. A. C. Van Gaasbeek of Van Gaasbeek and Arkell; Mr. F. B. Proctor of Gulbenkian & Company; Mr. A. H. Campbell of Wild & Company; Mr. W. H. Banta of the Oriental Rug Company; and Mr. A. Blumberg of Tellery & Company, Amritsar, India.

One further word of thanks must be said. Knowledge of rugs is best gained by the eye. Rug owners who have lent pieces for illustration have therefore added to the volume an element most essential to its usefulness.

With these comments the book is offered, in the desire that it may lead to a clearer knowledge of the subject, and stimulate a more exacting taste among patrons of an art industry which merits a better fate than to be perverted or destroyed.

NEW YORK, November 15, 1900.

CONTENTS

CONTENTS

MAPS

LIST OF ILLUSTRATIONS

REPRODUCTIONS OF RUGS

LIST OF ILLUSTRATIONS

LIST OF ILLUSTRATIONS

PHASES OF THE RUG INDUSTRY

PHOTO-ENGRAVINGS

DESCRIPTION OF PLATES

PLATE IV. FIFTEENTH CENTURY ROYAL PERSIAN

11.10 x 6.1

From the Collection of the late Henry G. Marquand

THIS is probably as near perfection as the woolen carpet of the East has ever come. It was a gift from the Emperor of the Persians, presumably to the Emperor of the Turks, for an authenticated record in the possession of its late owner set forth that the rug was among the effects of the Sultan Abdul Aziz of Turkey at the time of his death. The only pieces of this extraordinary character which have passed out of possession of the Oriental rulers and satraps who owned them are now locked in the treasure chambers of other princes, or displayed in the public or private galleries of Europe.

In point of design this piece is closely kin to that owned by Prince Alexis Lobanow-Rostowsky, a reproduction of which in colors was published as Plate XII in the Vienna Museum's work "Oriental Carpets."

Beginning with the matter of color, there appears here in the medallions of both centre and border the uncommon shade of wine red which is found in Plate XII. The green, instead of being used as a ground color for the border, is applied to the production of a higher and infinitely more artistic effect. Upon a black central ground is spread, after the fashion of the Sufi times, a bewildering but perfectly balanced and coördinate display of moss-green creepers. The parent stems, which are the framework of the vine structure, are in a deep shade of orange, outlined with more pronounced red. Even these are slender and curved in the most graceful manner; but the green branches, leaves, tendrils, and even flower shapes which grow out from them, are of incredible delicacy and profusion. Here and there, at regular intervals, and in corresponding positions on both sides and ends of the field, are tiny natural flowers, in glowing colors, similar to those seen in such plenty in the Ardebil carpet (Plate XXIII), save that in number and size they are reduced to a minimum in order not to distract attention from the more essential animal figures which inhabit the field.

In the centre is a medallion, with what for the sake of clearness may be termed "escalloped edges," and depending from this, toward each end of the rug, though with no pretense at actuality, are the temple lamps. Medallion and lamp simulacra are both grounded in what has been called the Ispahan red, and upon this, in pink—a faint, unobtrusive, but withal beautiful contrast— other fragile interwoven vine traceries.

This serves merely as a composite background for the superb arabesque design worked in silver thread, the pile yarns apparently having been omitted to allow the metal threads to be attached directly to the warp, in what closely resembles the Soumak or tapestry stitch. A very similar device is also found in the centre of the Ardebil carpet.

In the innermost space of the medallion, symmetrically grouped, are four birds, evidently of the hawk tribe, drawn with much skill and considerable veracity. Outside the medallion, disposed amid the green in the most lifelike attitudes of flight, pursuit, combat, etc., are the animals which play such prominent parts in the Moslem allegories, and which were, in fact, endowed with such large mythological significance by the peoples of Asia long before the rise of Mohammedanism. The profundity of meaning which attaches to these divers beasts, and even to their sundry attitudes and occupations, is hard to come at ; but it is impossible to overlook the difference in posture and relation to one another between the animals in the Lobanow-Rostowsky rug and this. It is quite to be credited, too, that these changed attitudes and relationships, coupled with the wholly dissimilar color scheme, are meant to convey a different meaning, to depict another state of feelings, another stage in the progress of the endless contest between right and wrong that the animal entities are supposed to typify.

Without endeavoring to expound the beliefs of which the animal kingdom provides visible symbols, it will suffice to repeat that the beasts of prey generally represent light, victory, glory, right ; and such as deer, gazelles, sheep, goats, and the like, the opposite. In the Lobanow-Rostowsky rug the central field is of a lighter color, verging on yellow, and corner spaces are formally set off, occupied by the heron and other birds. Here the corners are abandoned, and the birds included in the centre medallion, the heron, usually an emblem of long life, being omitted. It should be noted that the birds of the hawk tribe have been in all lands and ages suggestive of victory. The coincidences in color and design here are scarcely to be dismissed. They suggest much. The heron is left out; the hawks, which occupy the corner space in the other rug, are here transferred to the centre of the carpet. The backs ground is laid in funereal black, but traversed and overspread with the nascent green which is emblematic of renewal, perpetuity, and great spiritual joy.

Thus, without translating the inscriptions on the rug, which will be referred to later on, there is a suggestion of death, coupled at the same time with repeated symbols of victory, and a suggestion of fierce prosecution of the endless struggle between right and wrong, light and darkness.

But the contest as figuratively set down in this carpet seems to have progressed to the point of partial conquest, since the panther has captured the fawn and bears it down, whereas in the Lobanow-Rostowsky rug the movements of pursuit and flight among all the animals seem to have just begun. Jackals still follow the track of the deer; the leopard, a bold and fierce figure crouches in his thicket of green, ready to spring upon the he-goats, warring powers of evil. The huge red lion, Persia's own symbolical beast, an element not shown in the other rug, roars on the trail of the spotted stag, which turns, terrified. In deep thickets, close to the lairs of lions and leopards, the timid rabbit hides in dread, or elsewhere takes refuge in flight.

Yellow has in all ages been expressive of joy and victory. It is royally displayed in the broad borders of the rug, overspread with fine vine patterns in a monotone of orange. In the border of the Lobanow-Rostowsky rug there are, all told, six cartouches, grounded in black, of the same shape as those found in the Ardebil carpet, and joined by escalloped medallions in the same manner. But here there are twelve of these cartouches, instead of six, and they have a ground color of the Ispahan red, inlaid with pink vines, similar to the medallion in the centre. Again the idea of immortality is to the fore, as that is the ordinary significance of the cartouche.

Thus, from first to last, in spite of the black centre which suggests a mourning carpet, there is the note of triumph, joy, and immortality. In view of the intermittently hostile relations maintained between Persia and Turkey during the era when the rug was unquestionably made, all that is to be read in its design is most vital, and seems expressive of some phase of history, which was then making so vigorously.

Whatever temporal significance the carpet may have borne, as a gift from one monarch to another, the general interpretation outlined in the foregoing is amply sustained by the inscriptions in the border, a most sympathetic translation of which has been made by Dr. Richard J. F. Gottheil, of Columbia University. With his permission it is here given.

> O Saki, the zephyr of the Spring is blowing now;
> The rose has become fresh and luxuriant.
>
> The drops of the dew are like pearls in the cup of the tulip,
> And the tulip unfolds its glorious flag.
>
> Narcissus keeps its eye on the stars,
> Like the night-watch throughout the night.
>
> To sit alone in the desert is not
> Isolation with the company of wine.
>
> When Saki passes the beautiful cup around
> The rosy cheeks of the beauties become
>
> Violet for the love of the rose,
> And look like the purple robe of a horseman.

The lines, though it is difficult to locate them precisely, are, like nearly all the inscriptions found in Persian fabrics of whatever age, a quotation from one of the poets of that most poetical of all eras, and perfectly illustrative of the high artistic impulse which centuries of war, pillage, gradually waning power and swiftly increasing poverty and suffering have failed to eliminate from the Persian nature.—*From the Author's Notes as set down in the Catalogue of the Marquand Collection.*

INTRODUCTION

"Although we have every reason to believe that the art of carpet weaving dates back to the beginning of history, there is probably no industry about which we know less bibliographically, and the paucity of reference is more extraordinary as it is not confined to the works of remote ages, but is continued to our own time. A visit to any of the leading carpet merchants of the principal cities of Europe will illustrate and confirm this statement. Beyond such broad terms as 'Persian,' 'Turkoman,' 'Smyrna,' they know little of the old carpets in their stocks, whilst the exigencies of competition force them to conceal the names of the localities of manufacture of modern carpets, excepting certain well-known factories."—SIR C. PURDON CLARKE, *Formerly Assistant Director of the South Kensington Museum and late Director of the Metropolitan Museum, New York City.*

THE purposes of this book are: First, to consider the deep and enjoyable meaning of Oriental floor coverings; second, to throw light upon the life and work of the weavers; third, to dispel, so far as lies within the power of the author, the obscurity in which the subject has hitherto been involved, and place the reader in possession of such information regarding the rugs, both genuine and spurious, now generally offered for sale in American markets, as shall, in a measure at least, deliver him from the mercy of the decorator, the salesman and the auctioneer; fourth, to emphasize the superiority of the old vegetable dyes, the true Oriental coloring; finally, to give an idea of what constitutes true value, of the comparative worth of the various Oriental weavings, and the means of distinguishing them.

Prior to the appearance of this book, no work was obtainable which even pretended to the performance of this needful task.[1] Publishers and booksellers who many times in each year were compelled to answer

---

[1] Reference to subsequent publications will be found in the preface to the present edition.

no, to requests for such a manual, will confirm this assertion. In view of the enormous sales of rugs—those actually made in the Orient, both good and bad, and those turned out by millions from factories in England, Germany, and America, it seems incredible that there should have been nothing in form of print to tell the purchaser aught of the commodities upon which, whether as collector or householder, he expended large sums of money. Both upon artistic and hygienic grounds the use of Oriental forms of carpeting has become widely prevalent in the United States during the last twenty-five years; and yet, for a long time after the heavy importation began, no man might know more of the class to which his rugs belonged than his dealer or his purchasing agent chose to tell him.

The fact that the importation of Eastern fabrics on the one hand, and the manufacture of American imitations and substitutes on the other, increased so amazingly after the early eighties, is of much significance in connection with the dearth of definite published information upon the subject, during so many years. Rug dealers have always been unwilling to reveal the secrets or, in truth, any of the real working knowledge of their trade, and the guarding of the mystery has been distinctly worth the while.[1]

The only books treating of the subject, with practical intent of any sort, were the splendid publications bearing upon a few ancient and almost priceless pieces in the European collections, and the advertising *brochures* of rug-selling firms—pages fertile in word-painting and tempting in construction, but sterile in practical information. These dealt chiefly in the glamour of the theme, but they prospered in the thing whereto they were sent.

The sentences of Sir Purdon Clarke, cited at the beginning of

---

[1] Custom House statistics shows that while prior to 1892 there were brought to this country only $300,000 worth of Oriental rugs annually, the value of the importation has grown, even under the most deterrent tariff schedules, to many millions. The manufacture of American machine-made rugs has increased thirty-fold in the same time.

this chapter, were written of the European rug trade; but they apply as accurately to much of that of the United States. To illustrate: The writer saw, among five hundred fabrics in a New York establishment, a dark, stout rug, perhaps five feet by ten. The befezzed Oriental who was in charge urged its purchase.

"It is a fine rug, that," he said; "a very rare variety."

"Of what variety is it?"

"That," he responded with impressive gravity, "is a Lulé."

"Ah! A Lulé. And from what does the name come?"

"From the old city of Lulé in Persia," he answered; "my father was born there; it is a fine old town."

It was plain he was going on to tell the threadbare narrative, as venerable as the city of Lulé, and as fictitious, of how this particular bit of carpet was more than a century old—was, in fact, an heirloom in his family; of how his father had died just after bringing it all the way to this country, and it could now be had for the wretched sum of fifty dollars, because its associations made him so sad.

As a matter of fact, the name "Lulé" is a corruption of the French *roulez*, and is given by Levantine dealers, whose business is largely transacted in Gallic, to a class of carpets so thick, so tightly woven, that they cannot be folded, but must of necessity be rolled up for shipment.

But the part of this anecdote most germane, perhaps, to the present discussion is that the rug was not in the least a "Lulé," but a somewhat down-at-heel Kurdish product from the sand-hill districts of Mosul.

The ignorance of this particular vendor happened to be grossly patent; but the incident illustrated, as well, the too common custom of beguiling the buyer with egregious tales, a custom against which the average person is unarmed. There is probably no place in the world where a man with no leg of actual knowledge to stand on will prove so helpless as in the midst of a stock of a thousand or more Oriental rugs. The floors are carpeted with them, the walls and ceilings are hung thick with them. Those for sale are flashed before his eyes, often without classification, and with a rapidity of succession which is deadly, even to expert judgment. The swift kaleidoscope of diverse and unfamiliar patterns, coupled with an array and arrangement of colors the like of which is not elsewhere, produces a dazed condition akin to hypnosis; the faculty of selection is benumbed.

But, lest these observations be misapplied, it should be said promptly that in this maze there is much to confuse the most expert. There are rugs in every trade collection which defy identification. The elements to be considered are many and complex, since the people engaged in rug-making number into millions, all with wills and inspirations of their own.

Were it not for this, conformity to local habits of texture and design would establish a rug's origin; but both are apt, nowadays, to mislead. The weaver in a tribe whose fabrics have for centuries been built upon a woollen warp and weft may substitute cotton or goat's-hair for one or both, either from necessity or caprice. It is conceivable, too, that some wild leader in the North may on a day have revealed to him a new and extraordinary design. To the thousands of his clan he may issue an order to abandon the old patterns, and to fashion in their stead this new figment of his imagination, to his own glorification and their profit. A year later the bales will come to market, in place of the customary products of the tribe, and dealers will wrangle mightily over them. Scorn will be visited upon him who shall make bold to say that he knows these strange creations to be—let us say—Kazaks, even though he bought them from a Kazak, or, for that matter, saw them wrought.

The latitude for error is boundless, even to the best judges, since manufacture for market has become the rule instead of the exception, and European and American designs have been sent to the Oriental weaver for working. There is, perhaps, no art in which opinions as to the origin of products differ so widely, and with reason upon the side of all. Hence no writer, no authority so called, no dealer in rugs may lay claim to infallibility. Patterns, figures, designs are largely discarded as a means to identification. The designs are jumbled to suit a market demand, and it is, of course, impossible to identify a nondescript. Turkish, Persian and Caucasian elements are wrought into one and the same rug by prisoners in the East Indian jails. Many designs, too, have come into common use over a wide extent of territory. In a Persian bazaar I have heard two Hamadanlis disputing for half an hour as to whether a certain pair of runners came from Kara Geuz or Kengawar.

Nevertheless the craft is not wholly debauched; types are not yet wholly annihilated. It is with types that this book essays to deal, and with this understanding the textile tables and specific descriptions of various rugs are presented. They are formulated from the results of personal experience in the manufacture, collection, buying and selling of rugs, and upon the author's own studious examination, both in America and in the Orient, of many specimens of each class discussed.

The divisions are more minute than those ordinarily made by rug sellers. The significance of this is made plain in the quoted remark of Sir Purdon Clarke. The names here employed are those in vogue among the rug traders of Smyrna and Constantinople. Some are provincial; some indicate a town, oftentimes merely the market-place; some, a tribe; some have no discoverable origin. Others still are inventions of recent time, devised solely to mark a quality. Many of them all are wholly misleading, and not understood in the districts where the carpets are made. It seems best, however, to adhere to them rather than to bring about confusion greater than that which already exists. There are doubtless many names, adopted for purposes of trade, which are not to be found here. Hundreds of new and sounding titles may be advanced, so long as carpet firms invent novelties, or shepherd women weave upon their mountains, each as she wills, putting into their fabrics the glory of the sunset, the bend of the river where their flocks water, or rude depictions of the sheep grazing about the foothills.[1] But it is unquestionably true, as an English authority has said, that "the place of production can, within a wide area, be ascertained with sufficient certainty."

Something must here be said concerning the deterioration in Oriental fabrics, to which inferential allusion has already been made. In some districts the decadence in the present product, from the old standards of design, color and execution, is pitiful. The weavers seem to have learned from the West the demoralizing lesson of haste, and have developed, to a sad degree, the attendant vice of carelessness. At the same rate of retrogression that has marked the last two decades, the next generation will, perforce, have lost the magic of its forbears, and the fabrics which have delighted and amazed the

---

[1] For example, rugs, chiefly of Persian manufacture, are sold under the names Kinari, Sarpuz, and Sarandaz. These titles are of no significance as denoting any particular locality of manufacture. They are applied arbitrarily to rugs of a certain shape or quality. Kinari is the Persian name for the long strip carpets, the makatlik, or "runners," which form the sides of the triclinium ; Sarandaz denotes the wider strip which goes across the head of the room, and upon which the lord of the house sits. Sarpuz, when reduced to English in like manner, means simply a covering. The name may be applied to any soft, light rug adapted to the uses of domestic comfort.

An anecdote illustrative of the way in which new rug names are secured is told by Mr. W. H. Banta. It relates to the Bandhor rugs, which are known far and wide throughout this country as a heavy and rather low-priced quality of Asia Minor carpets. "Many years ago," he said, "there was ordered by a New York firm a line of stout carpets on the model of the modern Ghiordes, but with some variations in design. When the first one arrived a gentleman from Boston saw it, liked it, and offered right away to buy it. A price was named, double what we had really intended to sell it at, but he didn't balk. When he asked the name of the fabric we had no name to give him, so two or three of us got out the map of the East, and each selected a name. These, written on slips of paper, were placed in a hat, and I put in my hand and drew out the paper bearing the word Bandhor. So we called the rugs Bandhor, and they have been so known ever since.

world will have become mere matters of history. The patterns are being Occidentalized, if the expression is permissible; the colors are already, to a great extent, the product of the laboratory; the characteristic beauty and strength of the Eastern rugs are even now far on the way to extinction.[1] All the causes contributory to this condition can scarcely be enumerated, and it would be vain to enter upon arraignment of the many classes who lend their share of aid toward it. The question is essentially an economic one. There is involved the acquisitiveness of the several dealers through whose hands the fabrics pass, and even the weaver himself is not exempt from discredit, since he yields to the temptation to produce much, though of poorer quality, that his gains may be greater. Unless the human *fames auri* can be allayed, the evil will continue.

But aside from this phase, it must be seen that at the root of the matter lies the demand of the West for these fabrics, a demand born of the growing artistic tendency—or, possibly, the "Oriental fad"—of Western peoples. The centre of population changes. The races left in the Orient, mere remnants of the millions who swarmed there of old, are unequal, with their slow methods, to the task of carpeting the homes of the teeming West and yet maintaining the quality which prevailed when there was no demand save that created by their own necessities.[2]

There are industrious sales-gentlemen who will stoutly and unblushingly deny the deterioration. They will contend, whether sin-

---

[1] "Possibly there may be a resurrection of the Persian art, but in the meantime aniline dyes, tawdry European imitations and western models, without either grace or originality, are doing their best to deprave it."—*Mrs. Bishop: "Journeys in Persia and Kurdistan."*

[2] The popularity of the Oriental hand-made fabric has, it is now manifest, been the chief factor in destroying the art as it was practised in the olden time. The American demand, particularly for large sizes, became constantly greater and more insistent. The inevitable result was a more thorough organization of the industry, and finally a very large measure of actual centralization. This sounded the doom of individual inspiration.

cerely or not, that innovations have been solely in the nature of practical improvement. They may even defend the substitution of aniline dyes for the old vegetable mordant dyes of the East, upon the grounds of "facility," "brilliancy" and "scope." But such will hardly find solace or corroboration in a comparison of the antique and modern Feraghans, or make bold to place the old-time Ghiordes beside much of the rubbish turned out to-day from that ancient home of fine workmanship.

As to the precise meaning of the word "antique," as applied to Eastern carpetings, interpretations differ. For the purpose of the collector, an "antique" has been defined as a fabric which has not less than fifty years of actual age. But the number of these arriving in this country constitutes such an infinitesimal proportion of the entire importation of fabrics offered for sale by that name, and artificial methods are so efficacious in producing the appearance of age, that rug dealers, for business purposes, have come to count as "antiques" all fabrics which, in respect of dyes, materials, patterns and texture, are constructed in anything like similarity and equality to the rugs of half a century back.

The almost fabulous demand which has grown up in the last twenty-five years has in many lines cleared the market of antiques, and given rise to a reckless outpour of inferior stuff, such as can be thrown together in a minimum of time and sold for the lowest price. Working overtime, and with unlimited employment in view, the Oriental, happy that there has arisen such a call for his handiwork, does not dream how near is the "demise" of the goose which has laid him this golden egg.

But although the weaver's art has, under stress of temptation, become in a great measure an industry, pure and simple, it should not be judged by any extreme example. Wisdom seems not to have waned so easily in all parts of the Orient, for there are rug-producing neighborhoods where the standards of design and workmanship have been more scrupulously upheld. Whether, in adhering to ancient methods the weavers of these parts had foreknowledge of the penalty which waits upon retrogradation, may not be clear, but the logic of the matter is apparent in the prestige and the compensation which in every rug market wait upon this staunch devotion to classic models.

But even the best of modern products are forced to pay tribute to the infatuation of the West for what is or seems to be of great age. The astute vendors of the East, and undoubtedly some in this country, take shrewd advantage of every blemish in a rug, and employ unnumbered tricks of chemical and other treatment, to add the appearance of age, and consequent value, to fabrics which left the looms perhaps not more than a year ago. It may be that your "antique," which you brought home yesterday in all the proud joy of ownership, has within its brief twelve-month of existence been made to undergo many processes. It may have been treated with lemon juice and oxalic acid, for example, to change its flaring reds into old shades, or with coffee to give it the yellow of years. Its lustre may be born of glycerine. It may have been singed with hot irons. Its hues have perhaps been dulled by smoke. It may have been buried in the ground and then renovated, sand-papered back and front to give the thinness of old age, and for the sheer decrepitude of an almost sacred and invaluable antiquity, hammered and combed at the sides and ends, and on spots over its surface. There is no end to these devices, and not much cure for them.

On the whole, it is to be well considered whether, with these facts in view, the wisest course in selecting Oriental rugs, for all save the most opulent buyers—the "collectors"—is not to abandon the rather bootless search for genuine antiques, and purchase fabrics confessedly new, but which conform minutely to the highest standards; which have the requisite number of knots to the square inch, the colors of which will not run when attacked by water, the patterns of which are purely the patterns of the East—what may, to identify them, be called *practical antiques.*

The money paid for artificial age would secure all these merits in a new fabric; the amount of service and genuine comfort derived would prove greater in the end, and as heirlooms—for they will out-live the buyer by generations—they would be dearer than if they had come into the family with what may accurately be called a " doubtful past."

In any event it is best to recognize, first as well as last, the indis-putable fact, that you cannot now secure desirable old Oriental rugs for a song. Even though they be sold in the Orient at what we should consider most reasonable prices, it must not be forgotten that the duty upon them is fifty per cent. *ad valorem.* When transportation, the or-dinary expenses of business, profits of jobbers, *et cetera*, are counted, the foreign fabric necessarily calls for a substantial price; and it is safe to rest assured, generally, that who sells an Oriental rug *very* cheap, is selling a very cheap Oriental rug as well.

HISTORY

CARPET, as it has long been understood, is a narrow word. It has meant, at most, merely a floor-covering. It is only in recent years that the Oriental fabric, lying loose upon the floor, has been designated by any other name than rug, no matter what its dimensions, nor how nearly it covered the entire floor space of the apartment. In our terminology nails have always been required to make a carpet, even of a rug. Our multiplication of pieces of furniture has so subordinated the carpet that it has had merely the value of background.

In Eastern life this is not so. The carpetings, in strictly Oriental furnishing, have always constituted well nigh the whole equipment and adornment of the apartment. They cover the floor, they cover the divans, which, save for small inlaid octagonal tables, are about the only furniture ; they take the place of ceiling and wall paper, and their picturings have always been employed to do what paintings, engravings and etchings do upon our Western walls.

The reason for the last-named utilization of the carpet may be found, in part at least, in the embargo which the Mohammedan canons lay upon the use of pigments, and further, in the even more stringent rules of the orthodox portion of Islam, which forbid, as well, all depiction in art of the human figure, or even of birds and beasts. Thus the art of the East has been largely confined to textile fabrics, and except in Persia and parts of Central Asia, where the rigorous Sunnite doctrine does not maintain, its expression has not gone outside the realm of conventional and cabalistic designs. The Persians, belonging to the Shiite sect of Mohammedans—the " loose constructionists "—accepted with readiness the grotesque animal figures of the Chinese—many of them, like the deer, leopard[1] and dragon, having their own religious significance, and even carried to an advanced degree of perfection the representation of human figures and the sprites of their mythology.[2] But for the most part the Mussulman populations have heeded the prohibition, and restricted themselves to such results in depiction as are vouchsafed by wool and silk. It is small wonder, then, that the fabrics are rich and varied. They embody, perforce, all that the Oriental knows of color, form, symmetry, the exaltation of faith and the delight of living.

---

[1] The figures of the lion and deer, or leopard and deer, seen so often in conjunction in the central fields of Persian rugs, are of very ancient origin. Scholars' opinions vary as to their precise derivation ; while they are believed to have been brought from China, in the ancient religion of which similar portrayals had a definite significance, kindred shapes are, nevertheless, found in gigantic relief upon stone porticos in the ruins of Persepolis, so that their importation from China, if that be indeed their birth-place, and their inweaving into the symbolism of the old Persians, must have been accomplished at a very remote period. Aside from all doubts as to their origin, it is generally agreed among Orientalists that the feline shape represents daylight, and that of the deer, or antelope, or whatever species of the family it may be, darkness. Invariably, the lion preys upon the deer, and, by a figurative interpretation, has come to be regarded in this connection as symbolic of victory or glory. It is perhaps imaginative, but, for all that, not wholly without reason, to believe that here, in some sort, is the foundation of the story that—

> " The lion and the unicorn were fighting for the crown,
> The lion chased the unicorn all about the town."

This derivation is not unlikely, since in some of the ancient depictions the vanquished animal is plainly seen to have the single horn growing from its forehead.

[2] " The religion of the Prophet forbade any representation of the human figure. This prohibition does not appear to have been long observed, for we find that the walls of palaces and of the houses of the rich were covered with paintings. There was a school of painting at Basra [Bassorah, on the Shat-el-Arab], and a historian gives us the names of two painters of high celebrity in their art."—*Professor Stanislas Guyard.*

HISTORY

The custom, prevalent in the Orient, of removing the shoes be-fore entering the doorway of a mosque or the habitation of a fellow-being, warrants the construction of fine carpets, in delicate tints and of dainty texture, for domestic use as well as for places of worship. But it is by no means certain that the first use of these was to be trod upon. It would seem, rather, that they were, in the beginning, em-ployed as hangings.

How remote the time in which these strange textile devices were born is a matter for archæology to determine. In a dozen different families of Oriental rugs are to be found the patterns of the stone carvings on the ancient Maya temples in Yucatan, which, if students of Mexican antiquities are to be believed, were built when Egypt was a wilderness, and abandoned centuries before Confucius. These Mayas were the people whose missionaries, it is averred, crossed the Pacific to settle in the Deccan, and journeying over Asia taught to infant Egypt the fundament of the Mysteries, and handed down to Judaism and Christianity, for future use, the story of Cain and Abel, and even the older one of the tempted Eve.

There is needed no effort of imagination to believe that in the gay carpets of the East there lies written, though now probably un-translatable, the record of the universal mysticism. That they were made in prehistoric ages, and that their first value was religious or regal, rather than utilitarian, seems beyond doubt. Even in its rudest forms the art was sumptuary. It is coeval with the first up-lifting of one man above his fellows, whether the exaltation was reli-gious, pecuniary, or physical.

It is not the purpose here to transcribe the historical record of this branch of the textile art, save in so far as shall serve to suggest forcibly the deep significance of Oriental fabrics, as embodying the natural religions which preceded all known or recorded formulæ, the kinship of races now accounted alien to one another, and the trend

and tenor of Eastern life, which through centuries of invasion, tur-
moil, and wandering to and fro, has retained the forms which were
taught it in the morning of the world.

The skeptical—necessarily a synonym for practical—will be-
grudge to rugs this measure of dignity or import. It is not, however, claimed that these carpets relate in legible form the specific oc-
currences of history. They do not specify. They are not even
cuneiforms. They array no names, no dates. They do, nevertheless,
when studied collaterally, tell an edifying story of a widespread and
almost universal faith whose forms are lost, and of peoples of which, in
this age of atomics, there remains little save the names. It is the indubitable identification of modern rug designs with the solemn and
mysterious emblems of the "unrecorded time," the proven fact that
the archaic systems of weaving were the same as those in vogue in
the East to-day, that compels the thoughtful modern, of whatever
race, to view these fabrics, as Sir George Birdwood says, as "works
of art, and not manufacturers' piece goods produced at competition
prices."[1]

There is thus far, it seems, no means of establishing, positively,
an origin for these fabrics more ancient than the Egyptian. Certainty
halts there, perforce, until some new light shall rise to reveal clearly
an older civilization than that in the valley of the Nile. But there
the weaver, laboriously, as he does to-day, wove his threads into the
same mystical, universal shapes which come now in the rugs consigned
from Smyrna and Stamboul. And yet, Heliopolis is a straggling
ruin. Grass overgrows the foundations of the temples in which great

---

[1] This is in striking accord with the utterance of Adelbert de Beaumont, in his essay, " Les
Arts Decoratifs en Orient et en France." He says : " Cachemires de l'Inde, bijoux de Lahore, ivoires
et porcelaines de Chine et Ispahan, gazes et mousselines d'Agra, armes et tapis de Kurdistan, etc., sont
tellement supérieurs a ses imitations de fabrications modernes, par la qualité de la matière, par la beauté
des dessins, l'harmonie des couleurs, la solidité, le bon marché, que tout homme eclairé et de bonne foi ne
saurait un seul instant hésiter dans ses préférences, qu'il se place au point de vue de l'art ou à celui de
l'industrie."

tapestries once hung before the shrines of the Phœnix and the sacred Mneh. The glowing fabrics which made beautiful the altars of Isis and Osiris are dust, and in Cairo shrewd traders charge the Giaour travellers from Europe and the Americas ten prices for *sedjadeh* shipped over from Constantinople or Smyrna for the purpose, or for the scattering prayer-rugs and grave-cloths which come out from the districts beyond the desert. The Levantine merchants, if you ask them about the rugs from Damascus or Baghdad, will shrug their shoulders and shake their heads in negation;[1] but many skilful hands once labored at the looms in these cities, and the fabrics of Thebes, Tyre, Memphis, and Sidon were doubtless worth at one time almost their weight in gold.

Assyria and Chaldea stand next to Egypt as ancient homes of carpet-making, and though no specimens of the early Assyrian remain, the character of the designs is known from the wall reliefs found at Nineveh, which now have place in the British Museum. Professor J. H. Middleton, of Cambridge, says of these: "The stuffs worn by Asur-Banipal are most elaborate in design, being covered with delicate geometrical patterns and diapers, with borders of lotus and other flowers, treated with decorative skill. A large marble slab from the same palace is covered with an elaborate textile pattern in low relief, and is evidently a faithful copy of an Assyrian carpet. Still more magnificent stuffs are represented as being worn by Assyrian captives, on the enamelled wall tiles from Rameses II.'s palace (fourteenth century B. C.) at Tel el Yahudiyah. The woven

---

[1] There are made, in parts of the Baghdad district, and shipped from Baghdad, coarse nomad rugs following the lower order of Iran and Mosul designs, but Baghdad is not recognized as a home of carpet manufacture by the most of Levantine dealers. That its industry should have so fallen away is incomprehensible, since even down into the first quarter of the present century carpets were produced here which took rank with the best of Persian fabrics. They were, it is true, marked by many of the Chinese elements, an inevitable consequence of the long period of Mongol occupation. The textile product of the district nowadays takes principally the form of *djijims* or portières, and other embroidery, for which materials are abundant in the outlying country.

patterns are most minutely reproduced in their different columns, and the design, special to Assyria, of the sacred tree between two guardian beasts, is clearly represented, though on the most minute scale."

This paragraph contains much in substantiation of the claim that modern Oriental carpets are identical with the earliest fabrics produced in Egypt, for the "delicate geometrical patterns and diapers, with borders of lotus and other flowers," will be found reproduced with scarcely any modification in many Eastern rugs to-day. And touching the marble slab here referred to as "a faithful copy of an Assyrian carpet," it is agreed that many of the Babylonian designs are found in their completeness in the modern Persian pieces. "The preëminence of the ancient Babylonian weavers," says another writer, "does not appear ever to have been lost by their successors, and at the present time the carpets of Persia are as much prized and as eagerly sought after by European nations as they were when ancient Babylon was in its glory."

As for the "design, special to Assyria, of the sacred tree between two guardian beasts," referred to by Professor Middleton, it was found by the writer in New York City, no longer ago than December, 1899, in a Persian silk rug of beautiful workmanship and high value. The Armenian dealer laughed at it as uncouth, and said he had no idea of its meaning. Yet it linked the immediate present with the life of oldest Assyria, across the abyss of more than thirty centuries. Truly, "Mizraim cures wounds, and Pharaoh is sold for balsams."

Pliny speaks in highest praise of the skill of these Assyrians in weaving, wonders at their artistic blending of colors, and records the fact that all this sort of work had come, long before his era, to bear the name of "Babylonica peristromata"—the seal of its most perfect masters. To this day, among the peoples of the Levant, that old Greek name lingers, and the traders of the Mediterranean fully believe that the whole art of rug-weaving had its earliest beginning, as well as its greatest splendor, in Babylonia and Chaldea.

Of the Phœnician and archaic Grecian textile patterns the only knowledge to be had is in the designs of the pottery, which show in detail a multitude of patterns, both separate and consecutive, which appear in the rugs of Asia Minor and the Trans-Caucasus to-day, in perfect integrity. Professor Middleton refers to them in this wise: "Simple combinations of lines, arranged in designs obviously suggested by the matting or textile fabrics." He says further: "Some of the designs of this class seem common to all races of men in an elementary stage of progress, and occur on the earliest known pottery, that of the Neolithic Age."

As time went on, this primitive ornamentation grew more profuse. Greece and her neighbors borrowed the floral-geometrical patterns, chiefly the lotus and attendant shapes, from Egypt and Assyria, and made them part of their system of ornamentation, at the richest period of Greek predominance. This loan, it will be seen later, Greece and her pupil Italy repaid with interest to Persia, heir of the Assyrian art, centuries afterwards.

While, after the perfection of the floral forms, Greece was widening the field of her textile decoration, the far East, too, developed a newer richness in its weavings, the renown of which is so abundantly preserved. How prominent a feature the carpets were of all the life of the Orient, plain and hodden in its poverty, bright and sumptuous in its splendor, the literature of all its eras shows. The Bible, from Genesis to Revelation, is filled with allusions to them. Their colors brighten the pages of Homer. Herodotus and Strabo bear witness to the use of gold and silver carpets upon the floors in Persia. The chroniclers of conquest pause in their narratives to tell of the fabrics which were like a sunrise of gold upon a world strewn with blossoms. Every author of antiquity whose writings the hand of Time has spared has left record of those splendid weavings.

For centuries, down into the Christian era, the fame of the Persian carpets grew among the people of the West, and vessels plying the Mediterranean carried rich freights of textiles to golden Rome. Fortunes were lavished on them. Upon their conquest of Byzantium the Romans appropriated much of its civilization, but again receding, left its art almost unaltered by their presence. The East has remained the fountain-head of harmony. Even war and carnage had no power to quell the spirit of its art. The Crusaders came home with their wonderful stories, and wore on their shields as heraldic devices the dragons and griffins and nameless birds which Egypt had centuries before wrought upon the tapestries of its temples. The Troubadors sang, and the spirit of the East had entered into their singing. Europe went Araby mad.

The Saracens, swarming into Spain, took with them the Eastern looms and patterns and hues, and wove in Cordova and other towns carpets like those of the Orient. Through all Europe, in this fashion, went the famous "carpets of Baldechine"[1] and with them the legend and poesy and mysticism of the land where they were born.

While the influence was spreading along the shores of the Mediterranean, another track had been opened by which notions of this dyeing and weaving and other Oriental handicrafts had been making way overland as far as Scandinavia, leaving all the way a trail which is plain to the present time. There have been found in towns on the Norse islands coins which show that commercial relations existed between those parts and the Orient early in the Christian centuries, and the southern races, exploring the Norseland long afterward, were amazed at the skill of these snow-girt nations in the dyeing of wool and the weaving of carpets and coverings.

[1] Baghdad.

But the Eastern textile industry as planted in turn in Spain, Sicily, and Venice, retained better its characteristic form, for the Mediterranean merchants took to their cities the most skilful weavers from the looms of Persia, and, first from Cordova, then from Palermo in the twelfth century, and from Venice in the fourteenth, Europe was supplied with carpets of the true Oriental pattern and method, to spread in its cathedrals, in the throne-rooms of its royalty and the boudoirs of its great ladies.

So far had Italy progressed in the sixteenth century that the Shah Abbas, whose reign marks the climax of development in Persia, sent from his court, in order to demonstrate his antagonism to the Central Asian influence, so strong after the conquests of Genghis, Tamur, and their successors, a company of young men to study art under Raphael. It was in the lessons brought back by these that the seed was sown of the ornate, Italianesque touch in decoration, which is traceable in the rich Kirman and Tabriz rugs of the present time, and others made in imitation of them.

The same era marked the establishment of the French factories, for the manufacture of " Turkish carpets " at Arras, Fontainebleau, Tours, the Louvre, the Tuileries, the Faubourg de St. Antoine, and the Savonnerie, culminating in the setting up of looms at the Gobelins', Beauvais, and Aubusson by Colbert for Louis XIV.

With these we have naught to do, save to note that at Beauvais the tradition and theory of the Persian carpets were long lived up to. At Aubusson and the Gobelins' the Babylonian richness has given way to Gallic vanity, and the harmonious and meaning designs of the sixteenth century Persian have been replaced by the panoramic untruth of French classicism. The method in vogue at the Gobelins', known as the Gobelin technique, is not that generally employed in the carpet-making districts of the Orient. The closely trimmed pile, prettily termed "a mosaic in wool," is exchanged for the production of complex color effects by the working of dyed weft-threads across the warp in true tapestry fashion. The crude beginnings of this system are discovered in the hard, wiry coverings called khilims, made chiefly in Kurdistan, Merv, Sehna, Shirvan, and among the nomad population in Anatolia; a further development of it appears in the pileless Soumak rugs of the Caucasus.

Great Britain had its first real knowledge of the Oriental carpet for domestic use, from Eleanor of Castile and her retinue, who brought with them on their journey into England in the thirteenth century the splendid pieces which Saracen weavers had turned out from the looms in Cordova and Granada. James I. established looms at Mortlake in Surrey, but the Civil War put an end to their operation, and only after the Edict of Nantes, when French dyers and weavers skilled in the Turkish colors and patterns took refuge in England, was the work there resumed with any measure of success.

It was three hundred and fifty years ago that the "Turkish carpet" looms were set up in France, then leader in every art. Year after year, through the intervening centuries, spinners have spun and dyers have mixed their dyes, and weavers have labored patient at the loom in many lands. The iron age has contrived machinery to do the work of myriad fingers, and designers, the best the schools of two continents could furnish, have fed gorgeous patterns to the flying wheels, in hope to conquer the judgment and favor of the world. And still the dusky weavers of Daghestan, Kirman, Sehna, Kurdistan, and Tabriz are knotting before their rude frames the most splendid fabrics on the globe, and the Occident, coin in hand, waits upon their weaving.

III

THE RUG-WEAVING PEOPLES

IT is hard not to put questions to an Oriental rug when you are alone with it. What of this little web, which in its gay Eastern coloring seems so much more like a silent, smiling guest than a property? Was it born in a shepherd's hut in the pillared mountains of Central Asia, with the snow whirling about the door, and the sheep and camels huddled without? Or did the birds sing among the roses of a Persian village to the weaver as he tied the stitches in? From what far defile in Afghanistan did it journey on camel-back to the sea, swept by the sand-storms of the desert, scorched by the Orient heat? Was it paid to a mollah for prayers at the shrine of Mecca or Meshhed? Did it change hands in fair barter in the market-place, or did it pass over the dead body of its rightful owner to the keeping of the swarthy man who sold it to the dealers from Stamboul?

It has been maintained, in another chapter, that Oriental rugs, studied collaterally, tell much of bygone peoples and religions. Considered in the same way, they are even more eloquent of the character, customs and conditions of the Eastern life of to-day. They have an inestimable value in suggestion.

This volume cannot pretend to describe, even cursorily, the multitudinous tribes which populate the rug-making countries. They are spread over a great territory. Many of them are alien to one another in origin. Many have undergone changes in speech and habit, both by conquest and peaceful assimilation, which make them seem kin when they are not kin at all. Others have preserved character, customs and language, unaltered through centuries, and are to-day practically what they were in the time of Moses. Some there are, dwelling in far fastnesses which look down over all Asia, whose province the modern geographer has scarcely invaded. Their highways bristle with armed men, and almost the only knowledge got of them is from the fabrics which are sent through the merchants of the neighboring and more pacific tribes to the great trade centres and the fairs in the low countries.

Every populous district throughout the East holds fair, for the purpose of local traffic, one day in the week. Fair day is as much an institution with them as is the Sabbath among the people of New England. These fairs are rotatory. They are held in the different towns of the district, each having its regular day. The greater fairs are held once a year, and the traders of all the East journey to them. At Baluk-Hissar, near Broussa, Asia Minor, the fair is in May. August brings the famous gathering of Yaprakli, fifty miles north of Angora, in the vilayet of Kastamuni. A collection of log-houses is there, great, flimsy buildings reared only for the purposes of the fair, and during all of August they are packed with men and merchandise. The remainder of the year they are empty, and all the country round is unpeopled as a wilderness. Another big fair is held near Mosul, the mercantile centre of Mesopotamia.

These exhibitions are to the South, in a small way, what that of Nijni Novgorod is to Russia. But more significant, in the present discussion, are the great fairs farther to the eastward, in the Persian and Turkoman towns. There for weeks the life of every quarter of Asia and Asia Minor may be seen at its gayest and best. No distance is too great for the trader to travel to show his wares. Mon-gols and Tartars of the Central Asian hordes, Tekkes from Merv with a pigtail down each side of the head, men from Bokhara, clad all in white, with shawls swathed about their loins, and the many-tongued *kashbag* dangling from their waists, fierce Kurds, descended from the Medes and Chaldeans of old, who can trace their pedigrees back in unbroken lines for a hundred generations, wandering Ilats, bearded Kazaks from the Kirghiz wastes, timid, indolent, astute, mendacious, dreamy-eyed Persians, greasy Afghans and Beluches whose most ecstatic joy is in bloodshed, East Indians, in whose de-meanor is the calm of centuries, Syrians, Arabs with horses as proud as themselves, Anatolians, wheedling Armenians, resourceful Greeks and the inevitable Jew—they are all there, bargaining away for dear life.

All the ways leading to the great bazaar are dusty from the end-less procession of heavy-laden asses and camels. Even from distant China come the caravans, and almond-eyed merchants exchange their bales for print-cloths, clocks, and jewelry of the Mediterranean. Here one may learn how wide is the field of Oriental carpet manufac-ture. To this *omnium gatherum* are brought, along with other wares, the woven products of remote districts, and the rug trader who has brow-beaten the people of his own village sharpens his wits here against those of rivals as shrewd and heartless as himself. But with all this mixture of peoples whose promise would not stand for an hour with an American shop-keeper, every man's word, in a busi-ness transaction, is as good as yellow coin. Their dealing is almost all in the nature of barter, and obligations are held good by word of mouth until the vendor can collect his debt in some commodity he needs, from a third, fourth or fifth person who owes the purchaser. No checks are drawn, and little ready money passes.

At night, while the fair lasts, bonfires are lighted in the *hasar* or yard of the caravanserai—in Turkey it is called *avluh*—and in their

weird light jugglers and mountebanks perform. Wandering trouba-
dours, blind men as a rule, or Dervishes, contest in improvisation, as
singers were wont to do in Europe centuries ago. When their rhym-
ing is ended, both rise from the little rugs which they carry for use in
such engagements, and go about among the company, collecting coins
in their shells or great horns. These receptacles are rudely mounted
with silver, and are usually swung by a chain. Shooting, racing, mock
fights, wild music and such dancing as surely was never seen out of
Asia, make up the programme of the time's delights. Then the
camels, which came bearing Western trinkets, return homeward laden
with the carpets of Persia, Afghanistan, and the Trans-Caucasus.
Contracts have been made, and the middlemen from the rug districts
go away with orders tucked snugly in their girdles. Then follows a
new buying of wool, a new dyeing, and warps are stretched for a new
season's work, upon looms worn by the hands of many generations.

The whole business of rug-making throughout the East, except,
of course, where it is conducted by large firms, is controlled by the
head merchant of the town. This extraordinary person has a finger
in every enterprise. He is in many cases mayor, storekeeper, lawyer,
notary, farmer, and whatever else offers a margin of money and influence. Upon the verandah of his house are as many looms as there
is room for. The folk of his own household and the wives and
daughters of his neighbors find employment there. Early morning,
after the first prayers at the mosque, sees them skurrying to the
"factory." They work at so much a "pick" of twenty-seven inches—
or in Persia by the *arshin*, a somewhat larger measure, varying in
different localities—but the price is merely nominal, for the earnings
are invariably taken out in trade at the store. The local potentate
thus manages to hold them forever in his debt, and when a debtor
dies the obligation passes on as a legacy to the heir.

People who make rugs in their own homes are none the less in the *tudjar's* power. He provides them with wool, sees to the paying of the dyer, advances to them whatever groceries and other supplies they need, and keeping a studious eye on the progress of their work, appropriates the carpet when it is finished, and adds it to his store of merchandise to be taken to the next fair for sale.

Monotonous and profitless and hopeless as this system is, the Oriental people cling to it. They have a weavers' guild—*esnaff*, the Turk calls it—but it never undertakes to regulate wages. Its chief function is to protest—and that heartily—against any innovation upon this old method of procedure, to lift up its voice in rebellion when any mention is made of the importation of European machinery to aid in the spinning or dyeing of the yarn.

The burden of the rug-weaving, in all the carpet countries, save India, falls to the women. They are patient, nimble-fingered, and learn the patterns quickly. In some parts of Anatolia and Persia the great demand in Western markets has driven men to the loom, and in the cities of Persia where rug-making has flourished for centuries under the personal tutelage of royalty and nobility, the best artisans are men. But in the more remote sections, and among the nomads, the women do all the weaving. They are the designers, too. They invent from year to year all the modifications of the old patterns. The head woman, the traveller Vambery relates, makes a tracing upon the earth, doles out the wool, and in some of the tribes chants in a weird sing-song the number of stitches and the color in which they are to be filled, as the work goes on.[1] As little girls of six or seven years

---

[1] This "rule o' thumb" method of designing is not confined in the Orient to rug-making nomads. It is common throughout Asia Minor, even nowadays, to see builders, who are their own architects as well, tracing on the ground the plans for successive steps of the work they are engaged upon. No general plan is made in advance, except in the case of a great palace, bath or mosque, where a miniature made by the master builder himself is used. Ordinarily, he plans as he goes. The design drawn on the ground is carefully studied. If it bids fair to come out all right the quarrymen and stone-cutters are ordered to cut according to it. The only measure employed is the primitive one of the "hand's span."

the women begin to work about the looms, rolling and passing the yarn, then learning to beat down the rows of knots after the weft has been thrown across. The first actual weaving they do is on the broad central fields of solid color; and from that they work up to the handling of complex patterns. The borders are the final test of skill. The girl's first earnings are spent in self-adornment—the purchase of ornaments such as she must wear her whole life through. At sixteen she must be skilled enough at her trade to begin thinking of a husband. It would be harsh to say that the girl is sold into the servitude of providing this lord with food, clothing, and his modicum of tobacco and *raki*, but the terms of marriage make clear the purely business nature of the transaction. A *contre dot*, to phrase it mildly, is paid by the husband to the father of the bride. If her first spouse be called away by death from the enjoyment of such an arrangement, the next who weds her must pay more. Repeated bereavement only serves to augment her value. This rule is plainly based on the theory that with each new year of experience at the loom, she becomes able to earn more money by her weaving.

In some parts of Asia, notably in Kurdistan and Eastern Turkestan, and among the Yuruks of Anatolia, the women enjoy some measure of emancipation. They go abroad unveiled, and laugh at the slavery in which their sisters in other sections are held. But the Turkish or Persian woman of the weaving class is content. Her life mission is to work for her husband; she does it uncomplainingly. He helps her in the handling of the wool, and maybe in spinning and dyeing. In his spare time he tills a little land, raises some wheat and vegetables, tends a small vineyard or has a field of dye products.

This last was a famous occupation for men in the Orient, until the chemical dyes began to be imported. Since then it has declined until there is no longer any profit in it. With digging alizarin root in the winter months, when the sap is down, gathering the yellow seeds, valonias, and gallnuts in the fall, and the many flowering shrubs and berries in their seasons, the weaving woman's husband could fill in a good share of his year, and, if he was saving, add a pretty penny to her earnings.

But the old dyes, especially in the sections most accessible from the coast, are out of fashion. The anilines, which have been industriously pushed by invading agents, are about six-sevenths cheaper, and require no long process of compounding. Alizarin, when vegetable dyes were universally used, sold for twenty dollars a hundredweight. It has now fallen to three dollars or less ; and not only is it an unprofitable crop, but the land where it has grown is thenceforth ruined for any other purpose. The Oriental farmer spends, in clearing his fields of the tenacious roots, more than he has ever made by their cultivation. So the male of the carpet-making family idles, and is happy therein.

For education, there is little of it. In some districts the authorities, spurred on by the missionaries and by the Western cry for reforms, have in late years opened schools. But the work of instruction lags. Reading and writing are about the extreme limit of erudition. Besides these schools, the village priest, who is also village schoolmaster, teaches children to sing verses of the Koran. In parts of Persia learning is more prized. There is rather more inclination to educate the young than in Turkey. The low-class Turk seldom knows even how to read or write. Information of an official sort is conveyed to him not through the medium of newspapers or placards, but by the government herald, or town crier, who goes about clanging a lusty bell, and shouting, "*Bou gyun Allah couveti ilan*"[1]—the solemn formula introductory to his errand.

The Greek and Armenian populations are wiser in their day and generation. They make their lives and customs conform to progress.

[1] "To-day with the help of God."

They utilize every innovation, turn every invasion to their own profit. They are wedges which are helping, by slow degrees, to open Asia to the commerce, learning and freedom of the West. In the schools of their communities, found in most of the large towns, the pupils are taught the handicrafts, the making of embroideries, cushions, counterpanes and slippers from European patterns. This sort of kindergarten training has large practical value. It makes them apt at following strange designs, and secures them employment upon the high-priced *fantaisie* work which is all made upon orders, and which the Turkish women are unable to master.

In the mind of the Turk there is a deep-seated distrust and dislike of the European and his improvements ; among the even more conservative races farther East this antipathy is a passion. In the mountain regions there are tracts where safety for the " Frank "—as all Europeans are called—is a thing unknown ; where his life and valuables are almost certain to be taken by the first roving company that spies him, unless, indeed, he be held for ransom. His only absolute safety against molestation is in an Oriental escort, backed up by a passport and *tezkereh*, with instructions mandatory upon all officials along the line of his journey to see to it that he goes unharmed.

There is usually, however, a warm welcome for the native wayfarer from the Mediterranean coasts, and it is a red letter day when a traveller comes to one of the hamlets which, for the sake of safety from marauders, are formed by the huddling together of the farmers who till the fields for a distance of perhaps twenty miles about. The son of the *mukhtar* (mayor) holds the voyager's bridle. The *mukhtar* himself helps him to dismount, leads him into the house, and makes him the central attraction of the place, as long as the sojourn lasts. The foremost of the townsmen come to add their greetings, and, incidentally, to look the newcomer over, and see if he have not some new wonder to tell or show. It is an imposing ceremony, formal as a court function, and yet fraught with all cordiality. The host lights the fire in the *mussafir odasi*, or guest room, and spreads before it the hearth rug, proudest possession of the household. Chairs there are none. Along the sides of the room heavy felt divans are arranged, and over them are spread rugs of fine quality, with rich, rug-covered pillows for comfort's sake. At the head of the apartment sits the host, with the guest at his right hand.

When the salaaming is over and all are seated, the first of the callers takes from some recess of his raiment a little bag of raw coffee-beans. This he hands to the village dandy, an indispensable person on such occasions, who goes to the fire-place, and sitting cross-legged on the *odjaklik*, browns the berries in a long-handled pan, which he shakes over the fire like a corn-popper. This done, he places them in a wooden mortar, and with an iron pestle begins to crush them, droning a chant of welcome meanwhile, and beating time upon the coffee as he sings. Then he puts the *jezveh* or coffee-pot on the fire to boil. While this solemn proceeding goes on the guest, if he be versed in the customs of the country, passes his tobacco among the company, who roll cigarettes; and then the coffee comes. Thus amid the soothing fumes, and the even better-loved incense of talk, the night wears away. Each visitor in his turn produces a bag of coffee, and before the company disperses half a hundred cups may have been swallowed by every one of them, in case this traveller be what every good traveller should be, and what the Oriental loves almost as well as himself, a story-teller.

A session of Heidelberg examiners could not quiz him more industriously than does this room-full of villagers. Despite the stubborn resistance of these communities to industrial innovations, their interrogatories show the consuming interest they feel in the progress of the outside world. Steam, electricity, all manner of Frankish customs, inventions, agriculture and its mechanisms, methods of trade, prices—these are the things upon which their interest centres. But there is in their questioning, for all its closeness and persistency, naught of intrusion or discourtesy; they never pry into the visitor's religious, political, or family affairs. The comfort and safety of a guest are paramount. He abides there as long as it pleases him, eats his fill of the family comestibles—thin bread and sheep's-tail fat, *pilaff*, or whatever there may be—and goes on his way without mention of recompense from the host. A wrong done to him is a wrong done to the head of the house where he is harbored, and personal redress is tolerably sure to follow it. Not alone is this true of the more cultured part of the population. Even among the wind-swept habitations of the mountaineers, whose hoard is little, and to whom a human life is so much chaff, guesthood is sacred.

There are many Christian weavers in the Orient, yet there is an utter absence of rugs betokening the Christian faith, save that the Greek cross, doubtless without any religious intent, is worked in the body of the Kazaks and in some Tzitzis. It must be remembered that the Christian teaching is nineteen hundred years old, but with this single exception its emblems are not found in any Oriental rugs made for market, though Indian and Mongol have wrought their creeds in wool, and every sect of Islam has given its belief expression in its fabrics. The desire for money has, of course, lured them to sell these almost sacred things, and carpets inwoven with the Koran have been smuggled out in spite of the governmental prohibition, to be trod by the foot of any infidel who was rich enough to buy them.

In a letter to the writer, Mr. L. A. Springer, European correspondent of the United Press, who travelled all through southeastern Europe and the Levant during and after the Græco-Turkish war, has thrown light upon this absence of the Christian emblems from the rugs imported to America. He said:

"I have just come from Novi Varos, a little place in the Sanjak of Novi Bazaar. It offers a fair specimen of what the Mussulman policy is doing for Christian communities in the Turkish dominions. Years ago Novi Varos throve by the manufacture of curious rugs. They were sent to Paris and London, and found great favor with the amateurs. But Novi Varos was almost entirely Christian, so the Porte put a 'last-straw tax' on the inhabitants and ended their making of rugs for the trade. To-day the little town, straggling in the depths of its valley, has about half its former population. Houses stand vacant, and the Greek church, which was begun in more prosperous times, is unfinished. The Turkish law, fortunately for the Christian pocketbook, forbids bells, and the congregation is called to service by the clapping together of two boards. Every girl is still a weaver of rugs, but not for market. Her rug is her dowry. She spends all her girlhood weaving it, that it may cover her marriage bed.

"I went with the village priest into some of the houses. They are very poor and squalid, but in almost every one is hidden one of those superb rugs. Their beauty, as the women brought them out from the chests in which they are kept, made a striking contrast with the mean surroundings.

"The nap of these rugs is wool, but hemp is used for warp and weft. The people make their own dyes from barks. The designs are almost wholly of a religious character—the symbols of the church. Upon one was woven the figure of the Virgin, in the peculiar Byzantine style of the pictures in the Greek chapels. Another represented a priest in his richest robes. Others were a mingling of patterns from vestments.

"These people have absolutely no idea of drawing, or of form, as taught in schools; many of them have never seen a picture, except those in the village chapel, nor a rug made anywhere else than in Novi Varos; yet their weavings are all artistic, and the colors tastefully chosen.   The body of the rug is almost invariably white, the principal border red, relieved with tints of blue and green, and a deal of brilliancy is lent to them by the use of the most flamboyant yellow."

PLATE I.   BAKU RUG

15.1 X 4.8

Property of the Author

This rug might well be declared a thoroughgoing Kabistan, save for small discrepancy in the finishings.   Instead of the broad cotton selvage shown by the Kabistans the weavers of the old Baku Province just to the East along the Caspian coasts, affect a single cord edging, after the manner of Shirvan, which in turn adjoins the Baku district on the South.   In design and color the piece is almost perfect Kabistan, even to the birds in the corners, but a small streak of dull brown, probably camel's hair, thrown across the blue ground at the top, out of deference to superstition, immediately suggests the Baku weaving.

IV

MATERIALS

IT is pleasant to believe that warmth of temperament, deep love of nature, delicacy of feeling, and an inherent sense of harmony, coupled with monumental patience, are the causes of the long-continued supremacy of the Easterns in the making of textiles. But there is another reason, which must by no means be lost sight of. The venerable recipe for making rabbit pie, which involves as a primary ingredient the capture of the rabbit, is in point. Nature has indeed endowed the Oriental with all the essential qualities of an artist, but Divine generosity and consistency are more clearly displayed in the fact that there has been placed at his hand every material needful for the prosecution of his art. All the Eastern countries, which may be called in this connection the rug-making countries, reaching far north of the constantly advancing Russian border, and from the Mediterranean to the Great Wall of China, are natural homes of the animals which yield textile filaments.

One can easily understand, in this light, how the Caucasian, Turk, Persian and Tartar, equipped with the faculty and supplied with the means, have held their own, and more, against the artisans and designers of the West, and the unlimited machinery with which science has striven to outdo them. These lands of the West, com-

33

manding in altitude, benign in climate, in great part bountifully wa-
tered, seem to have been providentially mapped out for pastures.
Parts of the vast plateaus and sweeping foothill regions, distributed
over Asia Minor, the districts of Kurdistan, western and southern
Persia, Turkestan, Beluchistan and Afghanistan,[1] are in truth good
for little else but grazing, and for this they are peerless. Divided by
great water-courses, and laced by lesser streams, they are, save in
some few unfavored parts, not afflicted by trying rain periods, and
heaven tempers the winds, even of the Kirghiz steppes, to the lamb
whether shorn or unshorn. Sheep, goats, camels, vast herds of them,
roam these uplands, where they find a quality of nutriment for which
chemistry has not yet been able to devise a wool-making equivalent.[2]
There is no quarter of the world which has not heard the fame of the
goats of Angora and Kashmir. No country, save perchance the uplands of Spain, has produced wool equal to that shorn from the sheep
herding about the salt lake of Niris in Farsistan.

That there is something, either in the grass upon these plains, or
in the climatic conditions, which affects beneficially the growth of
wool, has been demonstrated by the utter failure to raise the animals
of these localities elsewhere with an equal degree of success, although

---

[1] The volume of the wool product of Afghanistan is enormous. Yule says that besides furnishing wool for the Afghan carpets, the flocks of these mountains and plateaus supply to a great
extent the demand of India, and in addition a great quantity of Afghan wool is exported to Europe
by way of Bombay.

[2] "In the manufacture of carpets, although all are made upon one general plan, certain peculiarities mark each country and each district. For example, in some places the foundation upon which
the pile is woven is of cotton ; in others, of wool ; and in others again, silk is used. In Kurdistan,
the foundation is usually made of wool, and the pile of goat's-hair or camel's-hair. Great differences
exist in the quality of these materials in different places. The wool of the sheep, as is well known,
changes its character according as the habitat of the animal is a warm, a cold, or a temperate climate.
In Kurdistan and Khorassan the wool is extremely soft, and in some parts very lustrous. This is due
in part to the breed of sheep, and in part to the pasturage on which they are nourished. . . . In many
places, also, the fleeces are of varied shades of color, deepening to actual brown and black, and are
used in the designs in their natural condition without dyeing. This is a circumstance of some technical importance, never as yet, so far as I am aware, much noticed."—*Robinson's "Eastern Carpets."*

effort has been made repeatedly, and at great expense. Long, fine wool for the nap is indispensable in the weaving of these knot fabrics, and a desperately small price is apt to be fetched in the Smyrna and Constantinople markets by rugs from districts where the pasturage is poor. In these places the weavers, to uphold the quality of their fabrics, are forced to use the fine pluckings from the goat's-fleece. These by lustre and softness, make partial amends for the quality imparted only by the fine lamb's-wool.

The availability of wool for textile uses is determined by the construction of the hairs. That which under the microscope presents the greatest number of serrations upon its surface lends itself most readily to weaving. In this regard much of the wool of Eastern Kurdistan excels even the famed Merino of Spain, or the equally praiseworthy Southdown.

For rugs of the heavier quality, such as the ponderous Oushaks and Anatolians, the sheep of the Asia Minor plains produce a wool that is adequate in length, and, while coarse, as it must be, is quite soft to the touch and very even.

The herding of the multitudes of sheep and goats over three millions of square miles of territory furnishes livelihood to numberless tribes of nomads, who pass a portion of the year in and about the towns and villages, and start out upon the ranges as soon as the season is sufficiently advanced. The shepherd, setting forth at morning with his flock, carries wool, spindle, and distaff, in addition to provender and his indispensable arms, and whiles away the hours of the long day, twirling his spindle and singing to his own delectation the "songs of Araby and tales of fair Cashmere."

Careful to single out the choice wool for their own uses, if they be rug-makers as well as flock-tenders, the shepherds pay strict attention to the combing of the young lambs, which, at one season of the year, shed a fine undergrowth. This, when the clearing up of the wool is made, is placed with the fleeces of lambs sheared for the first time and choice parts plucked from the wool of the older sheep, and usually retained for the tribal *chef d'œuvre*. In different parts of Persia this is called *pashim* or *pasham*, and is used in the making of the finest shawls and prayer-rugs.

May is the shearing-time. These Eastern shepherds are deft shearsmen, and even more deft at sorting the several parts of the fleeces, detecting small imperfections in the portions ordinarily accounted best, and so distributing every handful that the yarn, when it comes to the weaver's hands, shall possess the evenness only to be secured by infinite skill and care in the handling of the wool.

After the sale, which follows close upon the shearing, the preparation of the wool begins. It is a complex process, first and last, and one which requires experience and painstaking almost beyond belief. The inhabitants of the several sections have different notions concerning the treatment. Methods which centuries of experiment have approved in one district are condemned in another as ruinous. It is altogether likely that there is that in the wools of the different growths which demands for them just the handling practiced in the localities where they are produced.

The first step, after the sticks and other foreign substances have been dislodged, is the washing and scouring. As to the best way of doing this, too, opinions vary widely. In Asia Minor and throughout the Trans-Caucasus the wool is washed many times in cold water, without being allowed to dry between washings. When cleansed of dirt, and of the natural grease of the animal, it is placed in large granite mortars, called *tubecs*, and covered with a mixture of flour and water, or with starch. The men of the family pound and mix the mass thoroughly, with great wooden mallets. It is then taken out, placed in baskets, and in them washed again for two or three hours in a running stream, until the last trace of the starch shall have disappeared. This washing is of scarcely less importance, in the eyes of the Oriental wool-handler, than the delicate operations of the dyers themselves. Much depends upon the quality of the water, and the superiority of one stream over another has been so thoroughly proven by successive generations that it is acknowledged without dispute. Soft water, of course, is the thing sought. Hard water necessitates the use of potash, which cuts the wool in such manner that when rugs made of it are brought into service they endure for only a short space.

The washing over, the wool is exposed to the sun to dry. About this proceeding the Oriental is equally fastidious. A particular degree of warmth, a precise amount of sun, and wind from a certain quarter are relied upon to work a marked superiority in the carpet, and where the wool is intended for fabrics of the first quality, or is ordered for the execution of a *farmaish* (made to order), the wool-worker will wait for weather conditions to his liking. Even in the spreading there is a knack essential to the best results in the finished goods. The drying, besides being gradual, must be even.

Refined by all these processes, the wool is weighed up, preparatory to picking and carding. There is a sad difference between the weight of the fleece as it comes from the shearer and of the residue after all the days of washing, scouring, and drying. About thirty per cent. is lost in actual dirt and probably thirty per cent. more in animal oil, so that, though the average weight of a whole fleece, newly sheared, is about five pounds, it is a good one that nets more than two or two and a half.

The old devices for picking or loosing the wool from the mats in which it is left after drying are as simple as they are odd. That in most general use is merely a huge bow, a strong, hardwood pole, seven or eight feet in length, strung with stout gut. This formidable weapon, subdued to purposes of peace, is suspended by its middle from the ceiling, so that the cord just touches the heap of wool. The picker is armed with a bell-shaped mallet, which he plies with periodical staccato upon the bowstring, and by the vibration the wool is whipped loose and thrown on the opposite side, wisp by wisp.

Another invention consists of a solid block, or sometimes a heavy wooden frame, from which protrude upward, in close rows, stiff, perpendicular pins. The native, man, woman, or child, sits on the ground, Turk-fashion, and draws the wool again and again over and between these pins, a process which picks it apart and fits it for the spinning. This method is used only for wool which is of more than ordinary length. It was particularly in vogue until lately in those parts of Anatolia where the material is prepared for working in the heavy modern carpets. Europeans have now established two mills in Oushak, each of which cards about three thousand pounds of wool a day. They have practically done away with the old methods.

The yarn hand-spun by the shepherds, in the open air, as described, is in great favor with the manufacturers, but the supply is small, since, as we have seen, the herdsmen, using only the selected wool, keep the yarns of their spinning for their own carpets. In a few towns there are shops where many hands are employed, but even in these the machinery is all of the primitive sort. The old-fashioned distaff and spindle are preferred, and the use of a wheel for spinning is as much of a concession as the Oriental will voluntarily make to mechanical progress. Attempts have been made from time to time, by European firms or their Eastern agents, to establish steam mills in connection with their weaving interests at Oushak and in other places. The proposition has always met with a loud protest from the wool-workers of the district, and the government, in paternal regard for its infant industry, has refused to lend a hand.

The yarn, which is made in three grades, light for the weft, medium for the warp and heavy for the piling—though in very fine carpets the light grade is taken for pile—is usually purchased by the firms for which the carpets are being made, and its cost checked up against the master of the looms, to be deducted from the money due on the completion of the work. This refers only to districts where the entire output is controlled by the European and American firms or their native middlemen. In the small villages inland, the native storekeeper, of whom mention has been made, advances the money for wool, or the wool itself, to his less prosperous townsmen.

The use of goat's-hair in rugs is restricted by its wiry nature. It is apt to spin poorly, and packs unpleasantly when much trod upon. To the carpets made by the mountaineers, who employ it most, it lends a certain wild, shaggy appearance, thoroughly in harmony with their strong colors and crude patterns. Of late years, experiments have been made in mixing the goat's-hair with wool, but even thus the traditional obstinacy of the goat is not overcome, and the Kulah and Ak-hissar mohairs have not met with the success which such enterprise and ingenuity merit. The Angora hair, especially, is slippery and unworkable. There grows, however, on the goats raised in the lowlands of Asia Minor, the sand hills of Turkestan, and the highlands of Central Asia, a fine, silky fleece next the skin. It starts in the autumn, and if not cut falls out before spring.[1] Then, during ten days or a fortnight, the herd are subjected to the most thorough combing. With care and attention, perhaps half or three-quarters of a pound of this down can be obtained from each animal. From the best of it Kashmir shawls are made, and its use in carpet-weaving is

---

[1] "In Tartary, or Mongolia, the Saiga or yellow goat of Du Halde is found, the hair of which is much used in their rugs, and there also wander in flocks the argali or wild sheep (the *mouflon* of Buffon), producing the brown-gray wool of which the foundation is usually made, while the bactrian camel, whose habitat is in the wilds of Tartary, affords material for some of their most beautiful specimens. The camel sheds its coat annually, in the course of a few days, and its fleece is superior to that of any other domestic animal. The Usbek Tartars, moreover, have the finest wool of any people, those of Southern Persia only excepted, for they feed their sheep with great care and generally under cover, protecting them even when exposed, as we do our horses."—*Robinson's "Eastern Carpets."*

illustrated in the finer Tartar fabrics—Tekkes, Yomuds, and Bokhara prayer rugs.

Of the real, straight goat's-hair which can be utilized in piling carpets, by all means the best is the *filik*, known in European markets as *peloton rouge*, and sold in America for camel's-hair. It is of a light chestnut color, and is used without dyeing, to produce brown grounds, as, for example, in the Mosul and Hamadan rugs.

Only on the plateaus of Eastern Persia, Afghanistan and Beluchistan are camels found which produce a hair suitable for rug-weaving. They are shaggy beasts, but the undergrowth of their coat forms a sort of fleece, which, however, must be plucked instead of sheared. The processes through which this hair passes, to fit it for the weaving, are similar to those employed in treating wool.

Of silk, little need be said, since the fabrics made of it are not here considered. It is silk the world over. It is produced in vast quantity in many districts of Persia, Central Asia and parts of Asia Minor. In Luristan it is one of the chief exports. In some sections, especially in middle Asia, the mulberry trees upon which the silk worm breeds grow wild in forests of considerable magnitude. Among the products of Samarkand are rugs of raw silk. Trial was made at Oushak of like material for heavy carpets resembling the woollen fabrics in size, design, and colors. It met with small success. The plenitude of silk has led to experiments of this sort in other Asia Minor districts. The latest has been in Cæsarea, where great numbers of silk rugs have been turned out. They are copied from the Persian and old Ghiordes, or the conceits of European designers are used. The American market is as a result flooded with these copies. They can be detected oftentimes from the fact that the pile inclines toward the top instead of the bottom of the rug, showing that they have been worked from the top to the bottom of the design. In copying, the original is turned, back toward the weaver, to facilitate counting the number of stitches in each color. The pattern rug is turned upside down because, the prayer pattern being prevalent, the apex of the arch furnishes a central point to work from, and the weavers, many of them unskilled, wish to secure this as early as possible in their progress with the fabric. The best silk carpets of Persia, patterned after the renowned fabrics of two or three centuries ago, are wonderful, but, like other light silk rugs, they are meant and chiefly used for hangings, and deservedly command very high prices.

V

DYERS AND DYES

COLOR is the Orient's secret and its glory.

These dark-skinned peoples, lagging so far backward along the pathway of civilization, mastered long ago the chromatic mysteries lurking in the shrubs of their deserts, the vines, leaves and blossoms which make these lands radiant, and they have guarded this subtle knowledge from foreign participation with greater care and jealousy than they seem to have exercised for their bodily welfare, or their place among races. The royal purple of Tyre, which the Phœnicians by some magic won from the molluscs of their seas, is virtually obsolete now. Science has found, in the refuse of factories, gaudy hues to serve the purpose; but the old dyes of the East still boast a splendor and lastingness which chemistry cannot counterfeit—a permanence emblematic of the countries where alone the marvel of their compounding has been understood.

This preëminence in dye-working carries with it, in Oriental countries, a dignity almost akin to that of priesthood. As a tree is known by its fruits, the dyer has place among his fellows by his hues. In proportion as the color he excels in is valued in popular judgment, the dye-master is honored in his town; and even if there were a lotion which could obliterate from dress and cuticle the traces of his trade, he would scorn to use it. His color is the badge of his ancient and honorable calling, dear to him as the insignia of rank to the soldier, or churchly black to the ecclesiastic. He glories in being bedaubed, and the shades of his particular color, upon hands, feet and raiment, are earnest of his skill. He is a walking sampler of his dyes ; the proofs of his proficiency are upon him.

Traversing a village street in the East, you are aware of the dyer from afar off. Red, or green, or purple from head to heels, he challenges sight when he is yet half a mile distant. There is the pride of a sultan in his carriage, and in his soul, it is plain, a chromatic joy which religion cannot give. He is a fine bit of color against the tame background of the town. In baggy knee-nethers and white camisole, his head all swaddled in a mighty turban, and his fat leathern pouch for pipe, tobacco, knife, money and trinkets, belted about his middle, he is a type. But add to all these his dye, which in many values of the same color illumines him, from the crown of his turbaned head to the tips of his bare toes, and he is a radiant being such as Occidental civilization has not known, save upon circus days.

The mind of this worthy is pervaded by a profound and, in a way, justifiable belief that he is the saving clause of the whole carpet industry. The mainspring of his life is the conviction that he really lends to the fabrics of his bailiwick, and of his native land, for that matter, all they possess of high æsthetic value. In his own view, he is the uplifter of an otherwise slavish and mechanical craft. Through him weaving becomes an art, and all the processes, from first to last, are merely incidental to the main affair—his coloring of the yarns. So he dips and struts his complacent life away, and to be an *al boyaji* —a dyer of reds—is to be one beloved of the Prophet.

In great rug-weaving towns the dyers are many, but there is work for them all. In Oushak, the carpet centre of Asia Minor, there are probably one hundred and fifty, each with his specialty. If a place be blessed with a stream possessed of the magic solvent property upon which the excellence of Eastern colors so largely depends, the dye-houses are ranged close beside its banks, for the quality of water is even more vital in the mixing of dyes than it has been shown to be in the washing and scouring of the wool. The superiority of one water over another has been established by empirical processes continued over many generations; and tests of other waters, for the solution of the Oriental dyes, in European cities, for instance, have resulted in an utter loss of spirit in the color.

But this must not be construed as detracting from the marvellous skill of the dyers. The profession is hereditary in the East, and the tricks of it are handed down as almost sacred legacies from father to son. Each dyer, or, better, each family of dyers, has some peculiar and secret method of producing different shades, and there was sharp rivalry until the European came upon the scene, with his coal tar and his chemical formulæ.[1] Since that time the native dyers have been a brotherhood, of which the pride of every member, and his more than reverence for his colors are the bond and the creed. Each

---

[1] "Aniline blue first appeared in 1860. Less than a year afterward it took ten manufactories in Germany, England, Italy and Switzerland, to produce this material.

"Whilst the manufacture of aniline colors thus became European, their consumption spread still farther, and now could be observed this unique fact in the history of commerce : the West supplied the East with coloring matter, sending its artificial dyes to the confines of the globe, to China, to Japan, to America and the Indies—to those favored climes which up to the present time had supplied the manufactories of Europe with tinctorial products. This was a veritable revolution. Chemistry, victorious, dispossessed the sun of a monopoly which it had always enjoyed. . . .

"This reduction in the price of aniline colors is such that all manufacturers who use coloring matters have found it worth while to replace their former tinctorial products by these artificial colors. Besides this, the employment of these products has greatly simplified the formerly very complicated and costly operations and processes of dyeing, so that an apprentice can obtain as good shades as a skilled workman ; this facility of application has certainly not less contributed to the success of coal tar coloring matter, than the richness and variety of the shades. . . .

"Everything, therefore, leads one to imagine that ultimately the natural will yield entirely to the artificial coloring matters. This revolution, the influence of which will be most important, since it will liberate for the production of food many hands now employed in industrial operations, would already have taken place *if the artificial colors hitherto discovered were as solid as their rivals.*"— *Reiman's " Handbook of Anilines."*

knows that the aniline dyes of the West are no match and no substitute for his; that many of the glaring hues of the coal tar have no durability, that in a carpet thoroughly wetted they will run and ruin the fabric, while his own handiwork will pass through a lifetime of exposure to sun and snow and rain, and grow in beauty as it nears the end of its usefulness. He believes, too, that the European is thoroughly awake to this difference. The great fear of his life is that by craft or subsidy the intruder will learn the secret. It amounts to a mania with him, and in all likelihood has some ground. This dread has a parallel in the anxiety felt by the managers of foreign carpet establishments, who lie awake at night in fear that the native weavers have stolen or are planning to steal the newly imported European designs. It is a perfectly reasonable fear, like that of the Oriental on behalf of his colors, for the Western patterns have great vogue among the natives, and the floors of the best houses in many towns, in Persia as well as Turkey, are covered with nightmares of Western color and device, to the exclusion of home-made fabrics.

The colonization of the dyers just referred to is solely to secure water facilities, and not for the purpose of defense against intrusion. Where the town water supply is not of a sort suitable for dyeing, systems of earthern pipe bring water from some more or less remote stream in the hills, and discharge it into a giant basin in the middle of a square set apart by the municipality for the purpose. On the four sides of this square—*boya khaneh*—the dyers have their shops, with the all-important water in plenty just outside their doors. Dirty, ill-scented establishments they are, too—long, low buildings, with front rooms which do duty as offices and sometimes as bazaars for the vending of small articles. In the rear rooms, in long rows, stand twenty-five or thirty huge earthern jars, for the dying solutions, and a few deep copper kettles, in which the boiling is done.

Passing from jar to jar, the dyer and his helpers, if his trade be extensive enough to require more than one pair of hands, dip the great skeins into one after another of the solutions, hanging each on a hook above the dye-jar to drain, before it is passed on to further immersion. It is an axiom that to secure the best results dye should never be wrung from the skein, as this causes uneven distribution. This system of successive dippings in several colors is one of the dye-master's secrets—the overlaying of color upon color, a blending, accomplished in the wool.

The great display of skill, after the actual decocting and mixing of the fluids, lies in accurate estimation of the length of time that a yarn should be subjected to each solution. It is upon precisely the same principle, and altogether as delicate and important a task, as the timing of a photographic plate. Away at the back of each shop is a ladder leading from the dye-room to the roof, where the yarns are hung to dry. How long a dyed skein should hang in the sun is another question of moment. Passing through the square, on a bright day, you may see the dyers, sitting on the roofs of their establishments, staring at the suspended skeins. As long as the yarn hangs there, the master stands sentinel. There is a particular instant when the sun's work is done, and done properly. When it comes, it finds the dyer on guard, and he hurries the skein to cover in a twinkling. A minute too soon, or a minute too late, and the rest of his professional existence would be "fast gray."

All these complexities of his craft this accomplished artisan carries in his head. He keeps no tell-tale book of recipes. In a frame in the outer room are displayed the different tints of which he is master. The number of them is bewildering. It is not unusual for an *al boyaji* to be skilled in some hundreds of shades of red, any one of which he can set about compounding at a moment's notice, without thought of reference to any "aids" or "authorities."

The price he sets upon his work is small enough. The country people pay the dyer's charges in wool, but where money is the medium, the cost of dyeing in the most expensive red is only about twelve cents to the pound, for blues seven or eight, and other colors as low as five. The dyer of blacks is at the foot of the craft. The prices are stationary, and competition never takes the demoralizing form of "cut rates." When employed upon salary, a competent dyer receives about ten dollars a month and boards himself. An assistant —not by any means a tyro at the work—can be had for half that sum. Women seldom take any part in the dyeing.

It is apparent from the condition of the pile in old rugs, that some dyes corrode and rot the yarn, and others preserve it. An Eastern dyer, if blindfolded, can "read" the pattern of an antique carpet by the touch, as accurately as a blind man reads his raised-letter Bible. Blacks seem to be most corrosive, and red, of all the other dyes, most preservative.[1]

The basic elements of the dyers' "materia" are known to almost every Oriental, for they grow in the home fields, and great work is made of their cultivation, gathering and sale, though the new generation is being educated to use the dyes of Vienna and Berlin. The shepherds and other inhabitants of remote districts make for themselves the few simple colors needed in their rough carpets, but of the methods of compounding for more delicate and fanciful shades, the every-day Oriental knows nothing, and there are hundreds of materials, growths of their own localities, which the dyers gather and convert into coloring agents, the precise value and use of which are, to the common herd, among the mysteries.

The distinctive feature of the old Eastern dyeing system was that nearly every tingent was of vegetable or animal origin, and that

---

[1] In parts of Persia and India dyers habitually wash the yarns in a solution of lime before applying the dyes. The object of this is to increase the brilliancy of the colors, but its principal effect is to make the yarn brittle and materially lessen its wearing quality. Where this treatment has been employed, an expert can usually detect it by feeling the pile of the rug.

similar ingredients were employed for mordants or fixatives. The treatment of the yarn with borax, saltpeter, tartar, copperas and the like had not been known. The native dyers held to the merits of the old-fashioned mordants—valonia, pomegranate-rind, sumac, divi-divi, and the barks of different trees, from which they had for so long obtained such renowned results.

In some newly made fabrics, notably those from out-of-the-way parts of the East, the dyes are found to be thoroughly up to the old standard, but in most quarters they have been sadly debauched. The introduction of the chemical mordants was the first fruit of increased foreign demand, and first step in the decline of quality. The Eastern governments warred energetically against it. In one part of Persia it was ordered long ago that a dyer convicted of using aniline preparations should have his right hand cut off by way of punishment. The mandate seems, however, not to have made a very deep impression. The loud, flaring, unnatural colors continued to appear in plenty in rug consignments, and passed in this country for vegetable with all save the few who could detect their falsity. In spite of this, mendacious salesmen declared, in guarantee of good faith, that the law was enforced to the letter.

Here is what may, I think, be considered good authority for declaring that it was not obeyed at all. It is an excerpt from the edict issued by the Shah of Persia, on January 1st, 1900. The necessity for wide distribution of the law throughout the realm and for its enforcement upon the notice of foreigners as well as natives, resulted in its being printed in French as well as in the Persian dialect. It prohibited several things. I have translated and transcribed, from the copy given me in Tabriz, only such portions as bear upon the matter of rugs.

In the name of the Merciful God!
Let thanks be given to that Supreme Being, and praise to His Sacred Prophet, to the Holy Family and to their Companions.

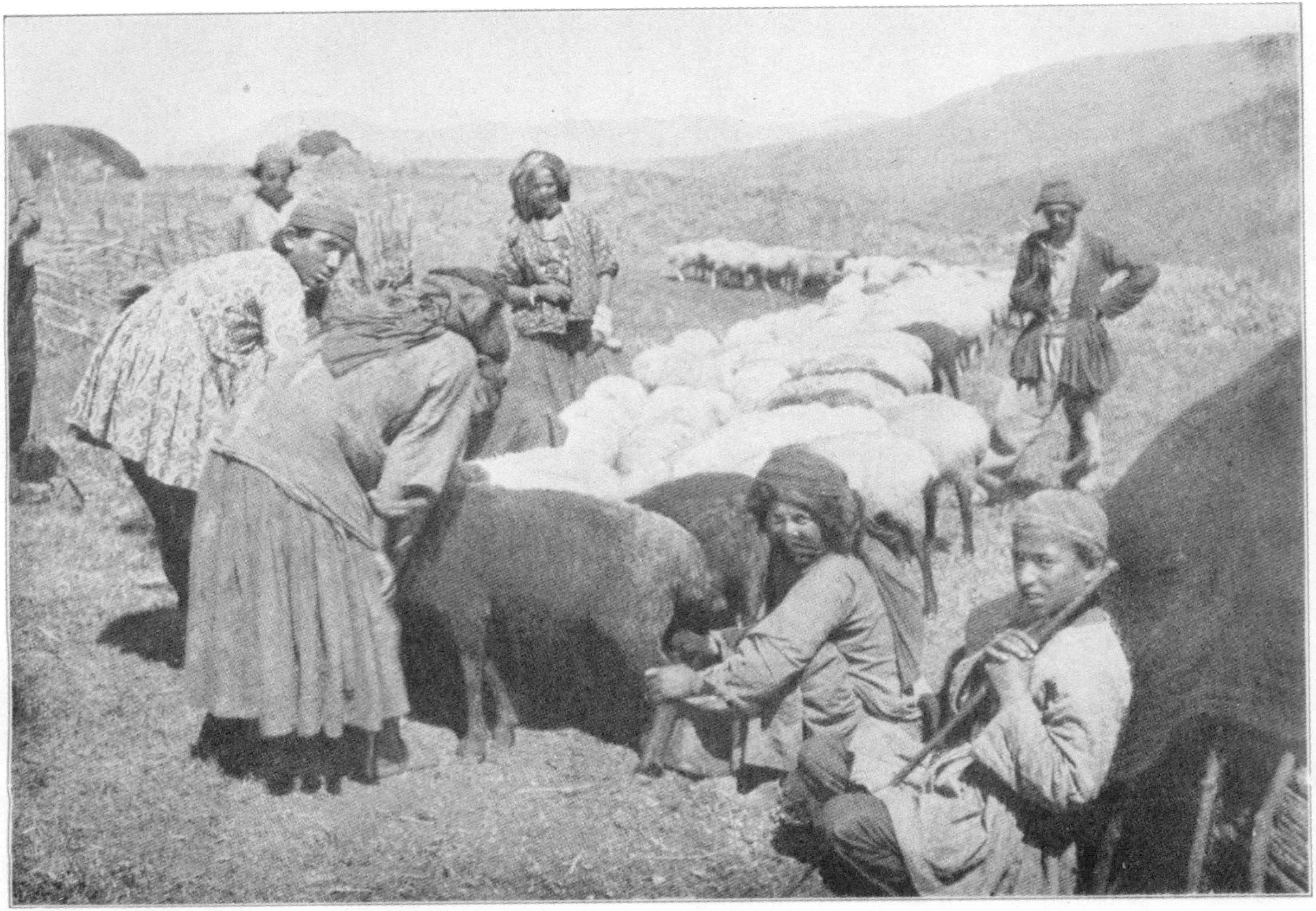

Shepherds of Northern Persia

ANATOLIAN WOMEN WASHING WOOL

DYERS AND DYES

We, Mozaffer ed Din, King of Kings, Absolute Sovereign of the Empire of Persia,

Whereas upon different occasions Our Glorious Father, Nasser ed Din Shah, whose memory is illustrious and revered, desiring to maintain the fine quality of Persian carpets, the fame of which is universal, forbade the importation of aniline dyes, which certain persons use to give a meretricious coloring to carpets.[1]

And whereas it has come to Our knowledge that these prohibitions, as well as some others, are frequently disobeyed by Persian subjects as well as strangers, and since it is necessary therefore to restate them, and at the same time give power to punish whoever shall violate them hereafter. For all these reasons We utter the present law:

ARTICLE I

It is forbidden to bring into the kingdom:
Aniline dyes, whether in dry or liquid form, as well as all coloring materials, whether dry or liquid, into which aniline enters as a component.

ARTICLE IV

Any importation, likewise any exportation or attempt at exportation, made either in violation of Article I of this law, shall be followed by seizure and confiscation of the goods.

Furthermore, if the goods prohibited from entrance or exit have not been declared or regularly presented at the office of customs, or if the said goods have been hidden among other goods, or concealed in any manner, the persons transporting them shall incur jointly and without any reference to their claims upon one another, a fine equal to the value of the goods, independently of the seizure and confiscation of the prohibited articles, as well as of those which have served to conceal them.

In case of importation or exportation by routes not running to a custom house, or at a point upon the coast where no office of customs exists, the fine shall be double the value of the merchandise, and the means of transportation, ships, boats, beasts of burden or vehicles, also the other goods imported or exported at the same time, shall be confiscated. Furthermore, the persons,

---

[1] " The importation of aniline colors, whose insidious brightness was tending to seriously damage the trade, has been prohibited, but it is still advisable for an intending purchaser to apply a wet cloth to test the fastness of the colors before concluding the bargain."—*E. Treacher Collins : " In the Kingdom of the Shah."*

whether authors or accomplices, sharing in the offense, shall be punished by a year's imprisonment.

ARTICLE V

The means of transport, ships, boats or beasts of burden, which have been used in the importation or exportation of prohibited goods, are specially liable and subject to seizure as security for fines incurred by virtue of the preceding article, and in default of payment of the said fines within thirty-one days after the discovery of the offense, they shall be sold for the purpose of obtaining the sum due.

ARTICLE VI

Persons against whom it shall be proven, in any way whatsoever, that they have participated in the importation or exportation of prohibited goods, whether in ordering, buying or selling such goods, or arranging for their transportation, or in any other way, shall be subject to the same penalty as those who have directly violated the provisions of this law.

The value of the confiscations and the amount of the fines thus incurred may be levied upon the movable or immovable property of the offenders.

Proceedings taken under this act must be officially brought to the notice of the defendants within two years, at latest, from the commission of the offense.

ARTICLE VII

Articles of merchandise seized or confiscated by virtue of this law shall be sold for the benefit of the Imperial Treasury, with the exception:

1.—Of aniline colors. . . . Such articles shall always be burned or destroyed publicly no later than the day following the seizure, in the presence of the chief of customs, of the governor or his representative, and of such other persons as it shall be possible to gather together. A certification of the destruction shall be made immediately and signed by all the persons present. A copy thereof shall be sent to the person upon whose complaint the seizure was made, and another sent immediately to the chief of the customs service at Teheran.

ARTICLE VIII

Any agent or employee of the government, any collector of customs or employee thereof, who shall be convicted of having permitted, tolerated or favored in any manner whatsoever the importation or exportation of prohibited articles, shall be punished by imprisonment for a period not less than one and not more than three years, according to the gravity of the offense; and, moreover, he shall be liable, by his goods and chattels, movable and immovable, for the payment of a sum equal to or double the amount of the fines and confiscation provided in the preceding articles against the authors of frauds of this sort.

ARTICLE IX

Rewards in money, to be deducted from the amount of fines and confiscations, may be given by the Central Administration of Customs to agents and employees who shall have discovered or furnished proof of violation of this law, and also to any person who shall have given to the administration information leading to the discovery of such violation.

ARTICLE X

All violations of this law must be established by an authentic certificate drawn up with all possible promptness, by at least two employees, and this proof shall be forwarded with all possible haste to the office of the customs bureau, which shall have power to collect the fines, the amount of confiscations, and to exact the corporeal penalties incurred. One of the copies of the *procès verbal* shall be sent to the chief offender, who must sign it or acknowledge its receipt, and the other copy shall be sent as soon as possible to the officer of customs, who alone shall have power to grant a reduction of penalties, if there be circumstances which warrant measures of clemency.

ARTICLE XI

This law shall take effect three months after the day of its signing by Us.

We order that it be printed in all the newspapers of the Empire and that copies be sent to the Ambassadors, Ministers or Chargés d'Affaires accredited by Us, and further order Our Sadr Azame to take the measures necessary to assure its execution.

Given at the Palace of Teheran, the 15th day of the month Ramazan, in the year 1317 of the Hegira, Jan'y 1, 1900.

MOZAFFER ED DIN.

By the Shah, The Sadr Azame, AMINE SULTAN.

How great a supply of Persian rugs, dyed with anilines, remained to be disposed of, it is impossible to say, but the Persian government, through its Belgian custom-house officials, at whose suggestion the edict was said to have been issued, enforced the prohibition to the letter. After the law took effect, several large consignments of anilines were seized and destroyed.

The government's step was a radical one. That it was deemed necessary is made plain by the fact that this law was the first promulgated by the Shah Mozaffer after his accession.

The best expression of the dyer's skill is undoubtedly found, as has been said, in reds. In what apparently contradictory colors the yarns are dipped, to lay a foundation for the ultimate shades of red, is past finding out. Madder, the root of *rubia tinctorum*, ground and boiled, is a basis for a multitude of the reds of the Eastern carpets. Its flowers, too, are steeped, and the liquid made from them fermented, to secure some extraordinary shades of this color. The red most common in Persian fabrics is made by combining alum-water, grape-juice and a decoction of madder, and drying the yarn in a particularly moderate sun. Many degrees of redness, from pale pink to intense and glowing scarlet, can be made from madder alone, by different treatments, and in combination with other materials it plays a part in half the hues which appear in Eastern carpets. One of the oldest of Oriental dyes is sheep's-blood, from which, by secret method, a rich and enduring vermilion is obtained.

Another material for deep red is kermes, a variety of coccus insect found upon oak trees about the Mediterranean. The normal color produced from it is a rich carmine. It is one of the oldest of

Oriental dyes, but it has been supplanted, in a measure, by the Mexican cochineal, which, after the conquest of Mexico, and the importation of its product into Spain and thence into the Orient, took its place as an Eastern dye. This is used for the most flaming reds, as well as in combination with other materials to give quality to tamer shades. It is more brilliant than the native kermes, but the Eastern dyers say, not so permanent. With the old vegetable mordants, it produces a comparatively fast dye. In dilution with madder it provides scarlet, cherry and various degrees of pink. There is a mineral kermes, an artificial sulphite of mercury, which borrowed its name to fit its brilliant color, and is not to be confounded with the insect dye. In recent years, many reds have had for basis the dyewoods—Campeche wood, Brazil wood, and others—which have been engrafted upon the Oriental system. Rich pink shades are often had from the rochella or orchil, a lichen which grows on the rocks around the Eastern seas. Singular reds are also obtained from onion skins, ivy berries, beets and a multitude of other plants, of which only the dyer knows the secrets.

The great majority of Eastern blues have for a basis indigo, which for the hundreds of shades used is compounded with almost every other dyeing material known in the Orient. In Persia, dyeing with indigo is accounted as high an art as is the science of reds in Turkey and Bokhara.[1]

The principal yellows are obtained from Persian berries, which although they are indigenous to Asia Minor, attain a greater size and

---

[1] "It seems strange that processes should be lost for producing articles, by a people who actually continue to manufacture without interruption the very objects into which these processes enter. Yet we repeatedly find such a result occurring in the history of civilization. There never has been a time, for ages, when the Persians have not been manufacturing rugs, during all which period they have been manufacturing their own dyes; and yet within forty or fifty years the secret of making the superb blue color which distinguishes the finest examples of old Persian tiles, illuminated manuscripts and rugs, has fallen into disuse, and no one seems now able to reproduce it."—*S. G. W. Benjamin: "Persia and the Persians."*

a more pronounced yellow color in Persia; from turmeric, the extract of the East Indian root curcuma, and from saffron and sumac roots. The turmeric yellow is not of itself a thoroughly fast color, but imparts a life to other shades when used in combination. It serves as a mordant for certain dyes, and owing to its instant change to brown, when brought into contact with any alkaline substance, is used in chemistry as a test for alkalis. Some yellow shades are produced also by combination of the wood dyes and saffron roots and flowers and a variety of ochra plant.

Indigo, in combination with the yellows, furnishes most of the greens used by the old native dyers. With the buckthorn, or rhamnus, it produces the Chinese green, and with turmeric and the Persian berries, a wide range of intermediate greens, both bright and dull.

The deepest shades of brown are obtained by dyeing with madder over indigo, as the deep Persian blue is secured from applying indigo over pure madder. Wood brown and camel's-hair brown result from the use of madder with the yellows. In Anatolia, this has been accomplished lately by use of the orange aniline colors. Gallnuts also enter largely into the making of the browns.

The densest blacks, which are little used except for outlining patterns, and defining border stripes, are made chiefly from iron filings, with vinegar and rind of pomegranate and sometimes with the addition of Campeche wood. Gray shades are secured by the use of Smyrna gallnuts.

The schedule of purples is one of the richest in the whole realm of Eastern dyes. The different red ingredients mentioned above are used in combination with indigo, and the dye woods and the *rochella tincturus* play a large part. The thoroughness with which the Oriental dyers have canvassed the whole field of substances to discover a new material for establishing or modifying colors is shown in the combination for a popular shade of violet. It starts with a mixture of milk and water, in exact proportions, then madder is added in certain dilution, and lastly, the whole is converted by sour grape juice. A great many shades of purple, heliotrope, lavender and the like are secured from the bodies of marine insects and molluscs.

This outline will serve to indicate the honesty which dominates the old Oriental coloring. It can only suggest the great variety of materials employed, and the consummate skill required in the blending. Vine leaves, mulberry leaves, myrobalans, laurel and angelica berries, artichokes, thistles, capers, ivy and myrtle—all things that grow within the ken of the dyer—have been tried to their utmost as possible color-makers and color-changers. Many of the growths are cultivated by the dyers upon their small acreage, in the intervals of their momentous labor in the shops.

VI

DESIGN

RUGS are written pages. In their maze of design is a symbol language, the key of which, in its ceaseless transmission through the centuries, has unhappily been all but lost. The variation of its forms, in the different classes of fabrics, may be looked upon as dialectic; and it must be believed, so far as the very ancient figures are concerned, that none of the dialects is understood by the weaver who employs it at the present day.

"Whatever their type of ornamentation may be," says Sir George Birdwood, "a deep and complicate symbolism, originating in Babylonia and possibly India, pervades every denomination of Oriental carpets. Thus the carpet itself prefigures space and eternity, and the general pattern or filling, as it is technically termed, the fleeting, finite universe of animated beauty. Every color used has its significance, and the design, whether mythological or natural, human, bestial or floral, has its hidden meaning. Even the representations of men hunting wild beasts have their special indications. So have the natural flowers of Persia their symbolism, wherever they are introduced, generally following that of their colors.[1] The very ir-

---

[1] "The colors white, yellow, green, blue, red, and black, in cases of the dominant color of deities and sacred animals, of the Sun and Moon, were not chosen haphazard, but according to the symbolic significance which the Egyptians were accustomed to attribute to each color—the idea of joy was connected with white and green."—*Brugsch: "Mythology."*

regularities, either in drawing or coloring, to be observed in almost every Oriental carpet, and invariably in Turkoman carpets, are seldom accidental, the usual deliberate intention being to avert the evil eye and insure good luck."

This utterance, which, coming from so profound a source, may be looked upon as revelation rather than poetic license, enables the lover of Eastern fabrics to weave for himself, from the curious and seductive shapes and the soothing harmonies which they embody, a bright and altogether exalted picture of the mental and spiritual life of the Orient. Abhorring a vacuum, the Eastern, at his highest mark of artistic capability, filled the blank space which was his bit of eternity with a fulness of warmth and beauty which spoke for him then, and as an enduring fabric speaks for him now, as a man whose intimations of a glad immortality never ceased until his fingers grew weary at life's loom, and the earth claimed him.

But study of the Oriental of earlier times, by the carpets which he made, must needs be mainly a study of the upper class, of the nobles in whose palaces and by whose designers and weavers the finer pieces were produced. Exhibition, publication, expert analysis and comparison of the oldest and most perfect of these carpets, which in any country and any era must have taken rank as art productions, have shed invaluable light on the course of artistic impulses in the East, three or four centuries ago. They have revealed in its most impressive phase the high seriousness of Eastern races. They have opened a field of study which becomes wider and richer with every moment of consideration.

In view of the teachings of these famous fabrics it must for the more popular purpose be accounted a misfortune that time has left few if any authentic examples of the commoner rugs of extremely old date. Actual comparison, therefore, of the fabrics exported from the East and sold in American markets to-day, with those made for every-day use hundreds of years ago, is practically out of the question; but so closely do the very fine modern rugs, particularly some of the Persians, preserve features of the wonderful old carpets in the European collections, that it is fair to presume that the rougher and more common varieties cannot differ greatly, in color and design, from those of the olden time.

There was, authorities declare, a period of climax in the highest order of Eastern carpets; and with equal candor they concede that even prior to the decline noticeable in our own time, there had been a marked degeneration, extending possibly over centuries. It was first manifest, they say, in the decadence of the pure curve, in a tendency to leave broad surfaces of ground color, in an abandonment of the perfect coördination which had given poetic unity and a delightful atmosphere of completeness. Then, from many of the carpets disappeared the central design so essential to artistic composition. Rectilinear drawing of the vines and creepers banished the softness which had been the chief charm of the Persian fabrics. The floral patterns gained in geometry as they lost in grace. Over all was evident a relapse from exalted artistic conditions, a barrenness of life, a decline of ambition. The exact period of climax has not yet been fixed. For most of the superfine antiques which remain in existence, the critics hesitate to assign a date, or even to point out definitely the locality of manufacture.

It seems safe to conclude that decay in art, if it was decay, was contemporary with national decline: that when the Eastern nations passed out of apogee the record of the transition was written on their fabrics. But there are those who deny the decadence who maintain that the perfection reached in these weavings was foreign, not Eastern; that it was the sacrifice of native truth and originality to strange artistic tenets. They hold that the standard was meretricious, and that what is termed decadence was only a natural and wholesome reversion to older and more authentic Oriental types; a return from Italian schooling to the ancient spirit and designs.

Commenting upon a piece displayed at the Vienna Exposition in 1889, which showed in a marked degree the tendency to rude rectilinear treatment, while preserving much of the Persian richness, a celebrated European authority said: "Have we in the peculiar floral design before us, which is so different from the Persian style of the fifteenth century, an example of ancient or modern industry? Is it the coarseness of an early style, or is it the weakness of decaying art, which meets us here in a garb of so little attractiveness?" This halting of one so thoroughly informed illustrates the tantalizing doubt which pervades the whole study of textile design, and which constitutes perhaps its greatest charm. But if it be true that "symbolism goes out as art reproduction increases," that the Persian masterpieces, beautiful though they be, are false to Oriental theory, are merely imitations of the ornate Italian method, supplemented by all of grace and richness that the Persians could bring to it, then the return, evident in later fabrics, to rude masses of color, and bolder and older designs, must be looked upon merely as a final triumph of the inherent over the acquired. And it must give to all the ruder Oriental fabrics a value which has been overlooked in them, if not denied to them, by the apostles of the "high school." If the general declaration that there is a symbolic meaning in all carpet designs be well founded, the fabrics of the commoner class must share in it. And if it be also true that what the critics who measure all values by Western standards call decadence is really a reversion to genuine, though perhaps "semi-barbaric," Oriental forms, then the rugs made by the native for his own use, necessarily free from the influences which invaded the art of the palace, must be considered a pure type, and expressive of Eastern meanings. It is this class of rugs that we get to-day, or rather did get, before the West began its mercantile invasion of Asia.

Freest of all from outside modifying influences are, we must believe, the carpets made by the nomads. Far below the high-class Persians as exponents of artistic status, the products of the mountain districts and steppes outrank many of those in point of consistency, and are to be prized as truthful reflections of the native life and character. Perhaps less of credit is to be accorded to the nomad weavers for having adhered stubbornly to their distinctive colors and patterns, since, inhabiting the deserts and waste places, courting and knowing no contact with society other than their own, they have met with no temptation to vary the character of their handicraft, or to stray into the fields of strange design in quest of some device better calculated to attract the notice of buyers. They are races which do not change from decade to decade. Their life is the same grim routine century after century, varied only by periods of strife and perfectly welcome bloodshed. Therefore their product, being, at least until very recently, made for their own uses, and not to fit the tastes or purses of Western decorators and housekeepers, has remained unaltered. The designs are, or were, tribal property, almost as unmistakeable as an accent.

Despite the roughness of these peoples, despite their ignorance of artistic precept, there is manifest in their work an æsthetic realization of the consistencies, an accurate, intuitive sense of color value, which makes them, where bold, intense color effects are required in decoration, useful as the dainty and intricate Persian can never be. There is admirable harmony in their arrangement, in spite of what strikes us instantly as garish and eccentric. Gaudy they may be called, even astounding, but the genuine examples, in which the old dyes have been used, are never inconsistent, never shocking; and they have the merit, rare nowadays, of being simon pure.

DESIGN

In these carpets of the nomad races may be distinguished one characteristic sign—the filling up of vacant spaces in the ground with small, disjunct figures. This is, according to the best authorities, a mark whereby the nomad influence may be traced in rugs which in general pattern and coloring conform to more urbane models. The accomplished Persian weaver of the high school, with a blank space to fill, would traverse it with continuous trailing vines and creepers, of Greek, Chinese, or Arabic derivation, adorned at intervals with delicate flowers, perhaps until his deep red or Persian blue "eternity" was a veritable garden plot of posies. Not so the nomad. When he employs flowers for such a purpose, he first robs them of stem, and hurls them upon his ground as if next moment they were to be trampled under foot. He is no artist, but his vigor is tremendous, and record of it is left in wool-yarns upon the carpets of his making, as well as in stout strokes upon the skull-piece of his adversary.

Consistency is as decisive a virtue in an Oriental rug as in human conduct, and the lesson to be read so plainly in some of these nomad rugs is one that may well be borne in mind in judging the merits of the finer varieties. Any really good fabric should stand the test of consistency. Those which do not are those which fail to interest as soon as they have ceased to be new. Only long and careful study of the forms of design can supply the knowledge requisite for making this test thorough, but the briefest acquaintance with a few good specimens of the various groups should enable any person to detect the utter incongruity of the unrelated patterns which so often make war upon each other from the ground and from the border of one and the same carpet.[1] Rug designs need not be complex to be

---

[1] Among very old fabrics are found examples made without border and consisting of a diaper or some complete design, bounded only by the edge of the carpet itself. These are oddities, and are most rare. A piece is occasionally found from which, for some inexplicable reason, the borders have been cut away. Examination of the edges will show whether it is an original "all-over carpet" or a haggled fragment.

good, but they should preserve their types to take rank as worthy or desirable examples.

The derivation of many of the ornament forms is a matter still so much mooted that this warning against incongruities should not be too strictly construed. It is impossible at this day to select any number of rug patterns from the multitude in use, and classify them as belonging exclusively to any single group of fabrics, or to any locality. The decorative art of the East is of too old a growth. Its beginnings are too deeply hidden in the shadows of an earlier age, its journeyings too manifold. In some learned quarters there is a tendency to derive from a common source all figures known to pure ornament. Professor Goodyear maintains that every decorative device had its birth in the lotus, that the figures in modern rugs, as well as all the forms of architecture, are descended from the lily of the Nile, emblem now, as in the old Egyptian days, of regeneration and immortality. Such a proposition is too thoroughly archæological to come at all within the province of this book. It is certain that unquestionable lotus forms played a large part in the Assyrian system of ornamentation, and that they appear with the selfsame treatment, almost without modification, in many Persian rugs. That transmission is entirely within the view of history. And with sometimes more and sometimes less of alteration the same arrangement is found in numberless rugs made in districts remote from the present boundaries of Persia. It is not to be wondered at. The whole Eastern country has been a highway for race movements, and well nigh every decorative design has in the mighty interchange become universal throughout the East; but the intense conservatism which has until now repelled the advances of Western art has served a useful purpose in this matter. The peoples of different parts of Asia and Asia Minor have developed characteristics—treatments, modes of drawing, arrangements—which for the time at least pass as essentially their own; and wherever the old figures have wandered, they have been modified, adjusted to local theories, and made to conform to the local color scheme in such manner that they are practically part of the system into which they have been adopted. Where this has not been done the carpets are mere bald composites, and have lost much of their artistic charm thereby.

In any endeavor to classify the various fabrics, even tentatively, on a basis of similarity of ornament forms alone, sight must not be lost of the fact that much of the territory where these rugs are made has quite recently changed hands, and while therefore some carpets are sold under new classification, the character of the people and the fashion of their workmanship remain as if they had not passed from one rule to another. Perhaps the best that can be done in the way of broad characterization is to say that the Caucasian, Turkish, and Tartarian or Turkoman fabrics are geometrical, while those of the Persians, and the Indian whose impetus and education are Persian, are realistic and floral. This general distinction will serve as a premise to consideration of the rugs of commerce. It is by no means meant that the floral element is absent from the Caucasian, Turkish, and Turkoman fabrics. On the contrary, they abound in flowers, but the genius of these countries has made the blossoms largely rectilinear. Caucasia and Turkestan have converted the forms of nature into geometry. The Anatolian weavers have conventionalized the Persian flowering vines and the flower and tree forms. Save for the distinctively Persian "pear" or "crown jewel" device, in the filling of some Kabistan, Tzitzi and Mosul rugs in the Caucasian class, and the pure forms in the Herati,—which is, as a matter of fact, Persian,—the designs have lost their Persian character upon crossing into Anatolia or over the northern or eastern borders.

Remarkable ingenuity has been displayed in the conversion of many of these features. To preserve the swaying vine effect found in the borders of the Persian, for example, the designers of the Ghiordes and Kulah rugs have utilized the stems of their leaf patterns. The direction of these is alternated so that a perfect, although somewhat angular undulation is produced. So delicately is this effected that quite protracted study of the rug may be made before the arrangement is noticed. Nor does distance seem to have stood in the way of this interchange of patterns. To all the Mediterranean coasts Asia Minor taught the form of textile art which it had learned, and took in return whatever notions they had of decoration. To this day little Turkish children sleep under coverings which had their patterns long ago from Morocco.

It is not strange, again, that Chinese fretted patterns should be found scattered over the central fields and ranging in the borders of the rugs of Samarkand, Kashgar and Yarkand, and in the borders of some other Central Asian carpets. These regions, situated in the direct line of travel across the continent, have always been affected by the Chinese influence; they are in large part populated by tribes speaking Mongol dialects. But it is more puzzling to find that the Chinese fret is intimately related to the Greek key, which is in the border of many old rugs made in Asia Minor, and which in carvings, frescoes, and every other form of ornament, is recognized the world over as a distinctly Hellenic property. The apostles of common origin in decoration make the way clear of such annoyances. For example, Professor Goodyear declares that the Chinese fret and the Greek meander alike, wherever found, are only rectangular exaggerations of the curling leaves of the lotus.

Owen Jones says that Chinese art is in essence Mohammedan, that it is Chinese only in treatment; that the Moors of the present day decorate their pottery under the same instruction, and follow the same law as do the Chinese in their vases. Chinese pottery, he adds, suggests the Persian both in flowers and creepers. As indicating the

PLATE II.   SHIRVAN RUG

6. x 5.2

Loaned by Mr. Reginald H. Bulley

In shape, design and coloring, this is a most singular Caucasian product and an unusually good one.   It has not, of course, the fine texture of some of the Persians, but in every respect of craftsmanship it is admirable.   It is a town product, without any of the nomad *grotesquerie*. The animal creation, so much drawn upon for patterns by Caucasian weavers, is represented, but not in the laughable, realistic manner common.   A decorous procession of orderly scorpions ranges through the outer border. and for guard stripes about this, small tarantula shapes thoroughly conventionalized.   Inside this appears the wine-glass border, and inside this again, the well-known "reciprocal" device in blue and red.   Then we have what would ordinarily be called the field, covered with a peculiar diaper design—white on a red ground—but there is a panel in the centre of the rug, that converts this outer portion into another border.   Little can be divined of the origin or significance of these inner patterns except the tree of life, and the presentment of this is thoroughly Turanian.   The rug resembles the Bergamo and certain Turkoman fabrics in its extreme width, but in character it is Caucasian throughout, and the finishings mark it as of Shirvan or Eastern Karabagh.

extent to which archæology must be consulted in the endeavor to trace the journeyings of the rug patterns from one part of the East to another, the following, from the same author, is eloquent:

'Buddhist art, and contemporary Hindu art, ornamental and otherwise, date from a time when Greek influences dominant in the Punjab and Indus countries, spread to southern India, and these were preceded by Persian and Assyrian."

And further: "At a later date Hindu art became saturated with Mohammedan lotus patterns. These were all originally borrowed in the countries conquered by the Mohammedan Arabs during the seventh century A.D.—Syria, Egypt, North Africa and Persia. The Arab art was, therefore, ornamentally based on the Sassanian Persian, and these systems, again, drew their lotus patterns from Græco-Egyptian and Egypto-Persian sources."

Professor Jones does not sustain the claims of the lotus to the universal parenthood of all ornamentation, but, doubt though we may that interesting contention, the origin of the lotus as a carpet pattern, and much of the traveling by dint of which it came to be impressed upon the art of every country in the Orient, are here made sufficiently clear. And in spite of the changes which centuries have brought, the lotus forms have been more faithfully preserved in Persia than in any other part of the East. It was in Assyria and Babylonia that, having been transmitted from Egypt, perhaps by the Phœnicians and Hittites, whose palaces were copied by the Aryan kings, they seem to have been first crystallized in ornament, and there they have lived, almost in their original purity. In a few typical forms the lotus is found in present day Persian carpets. There seems reason for classing the palmette, so called, and the rosette among these, though the palmette is held by some authorities to be a Greek form, and to have had its derivation from the human hand with all the digits extended; by others it is derived directly from a palm growth. The closed bud which in old wall-tiles, as well as in modern rugs, alternates with the rosette or the palmette, forming a variation of the "knop and flower" pattern, is merely the nascent form of the lotus. It is significant that the forms which show indubitable kinship with the lotus are chiefly used in border designs, thus binding and unifying the life story told in the body of the carpet, with an unbroken succession of the emblems of eternity and renewed being—the bud, signifying birth, and the full-blown flower, the completeness of age ; the creeper typifying the long repetition of the life process which separates and yet unites the two.

The life idea finds expression, too, in the tree forms, which seem, viewed as Aryan creations, to have had their origin in the lotus ; though the versions traceable to Turanian sources would appear to represent some other growth. "From the earliest antiquity," says Doctor Rock, "a tradition came down through Middle Asia, of some holy tree, perhaps the Tree of Life spoken of as growing in Paradise." [1] According to Birdwood, "it is represented on the commonest Spanish and Portuguese earthenware, by a green tree that

---

[1] The diversity of tree forms found in rug designs is almost limitless, and animal figures are presented in connection with the trees, in all the manifold fashions born of varied mythological and religious beliefs. A recent writer, borrowing from the pages of Washington Irving, has thus described the "tuba," the tree of paradise, representation of which is frequent in the more pretentious of the Persian rugs :

"On the right hand of the throne on which Allah sat, his face covered by twenty thousand veils lest the brightness of his countenance should annihilate the beholders, was a tree whose branches extended over a space greater than that between the sun and the earth. About it, angels were more numerous than the sands of the seashore or the beds of the streams, and rivers rejoiced beneath its shade. The leaves resembled the ears of an elephant and immortal birds flying amidst the branches repeated the sublime verses of the Koran. The fruits were milder than milk and sweeter than honey, and all the creatures of God if assembled there, would find sufficient sustenance. Each seed inclosed a houri provided for the felicity of true believers, and from the tree itself issued four rivers, two flowing from the interior of Paradise, and two issuing beyond it and becoming, one the Nile, and the other the Euphrates."

There is often found, too, what is by some called the tree of punishment, with an animal's head at the end of each branch.

There is 'another tree, representing a feature of the first of Mohammed's heavens, in which angels, in the form of animals, intercede for the animals upon the earth.

looks exactly like a Noah's Ark tree." "Sometimes, on Persian rugs," he adds, "the entire tree is represented, but generally it would be past all recognition but for smaller representations of it within the larger. In Yarkand carpets, however, it is seen filling the whole centre of the carpet, stark and stiff as if cut out of metal. In Persian art, and in Indian art derived from Persian, the tree becomes a beautiful flowering plant, or simple sprig of flowers, but in Hindu art it remains in its hard architectural form, as seen in temple lamps and in the models in brass and copper of the Sacred Fig as the Tree of Life. On an Indian bag it is represented in two forms, one like a notched Noah's Ark tree, and the other branched like the temple candelabra."

As showing the tenacity of the old forms, consider what is known in rug design as the Herati pattern, or more commonly the "fish" pattern. It is found in perfect purity still, in the rugs of Herat, some of them so new that they still bear the odor of the wool-pen; also in the Sehnas, Feraghans, Khorassans and Kurdistans, and in rectilinear form in pieces from Afghanistan. Its feature is a rosette between two long, curved leaves, in which some imagination has discovered the resemblance to fishes. This has given the device its name, though it has by some authorities been traced directly to very old Chinese heraldic emblems. The pattern is in any case an ancient one, and whether or not, in some older day, the fish, sacred to Isis and later to Venus, was intended in these lancet-leaf forms, is open to question; but the presence here of the lotus, emblem of fecundity, suggests such a possibility. The fish pattern is not found in the body of the rugs unless it be in comparative purity, as a diaper covering all or a considerable part of the central field. In this diaper it alternates with a square or diamond-shaped rhomboidal arabesque device in such manner that the "row" effect is perfectly maintained. There are two forms, *rizeh* and *darisht*, fine and coarse. In the Herat carpets the coarse form is used. In the Feraghans, Sehnas, and Khorassans the diaper is most compact.

There are other elements equally enduring. Take, for example, the "pear" pattern. For this device, which has been so widely employed throughout the East as to be almost universal, Professor Goodyear also claims a lotus derivation, but the foundation of the claim is not so clear as in the cases of some other figures. The "pear" seems to have intimate and original association with Persia, since it is in the Persian fabrics that it is most freely used. There is, indeed, hardly any variety of Persian or Kurdistan fabrics which does not display it. In the Sarabands and some Shiraz examples it covers the whole field. In the Khorassans it is used in most complex arrangement. Adopted into the rugs of other countries it follows a rectilinear form which shows that it is anything but indigenous.

There are many theories concerning the precise origin of the pattern; to some it is known as a "palm," to others as a "river loop," supposed to represent the bend of the river Jhelum in Kashmir, or, again, the Ganges. This meaning is chiefly accepted where knowledge of the device is obtained from Kashmir or India shawls. In these the figure is much elongated, which adds greatly to its grace; it is an exaggeration of the long forms found in the rugs of Khorassan, and is adorned after the Khorassan manner, though with far greater elaboration.

The popularity of the shawls in America antedated that of Oriental rugs by something like a century; hence the pear shape, which in connection with shawls is still called the cone, has popularly been supposed to be purely Indian. There is little doubt, however, that the pattern, like the shawl itself, is Persian, and was carried into Kashmir by the Iranians when they went thither in the seventh or eighth century, taking with them their arts and their ancient Zoroastrian faith. This is further borne out by the fact that the manufacture and use of shawls, of a sort similar to those made by the people of India and Kashmir, are still common among their kinsmen in Kirman, in southern Persia.

The "river loop" theory, therefore, seems to be without warrant, and wholly local. An explanation more plausible and consistent, and from a source which invokes credence, is that given by Iskender Khan Coroyantz, Imperial Commissioner for Persia at the Chicago World's Fair, and interpreter to the late Shah, Nasr ed Din, during his travels in Europe. He declares that the device represents the chief ornament of the old Iranian crown, during one of the earliest dynasties; that the jewel was a composite one, of pear shape, and wrought of so many stones that, viewed from different sides, it displayed a great variety of colors. If this explanation be correct, it is easy to understand the ornamentation of the pattern, which in the shawls, and to a certain extent in the rugs of eastern Iran, reaches such perfection. But it is not to be supposed that the shape was chosen for such perpetuity without symbolic or religious reason. Taking into consideration the deep devotion of the ancient Persians, there is no room to believe otherwise than that the crown-jewel shape represents, in its first meaning, the flame which they worshipped and which is worshipped to this day by their posterity in India and southern Persia. This view is born out by Sir George Birdwood in his "Arts of India," where he calls the device the "cone or flame."

I have selected, from the names applied to this figure, that of "pear" pattern, not because it has any historical or symbolical accuracy, for it has none; but because the image it conveys is more clearly apprehended by the Western mind; it is what the shape suggests, throwing meaning out of the question.

Efforts to fix the derivation of the fretted ornaments have been many. Some of them have been disregardful of the universality of symbolic patterns, for insisting upon which there seems now such abundant reason. Ch. T. Newton calls attention to certain coins from Priene, as indicating that the Greek key pattern symbolized the river Maeander. Birdwood, again, says in his "Indian Arts": "I believe the swastika (卐) to be the origin of the key pattern ornament of the Greek and Chinese decorative art." Support is given to this theory by a Chinese diaper pattern exhibited on pottery in the British Museum, and reproduced in Hulme's "Principles of Ornamental Art." It is a mere multiplication of the swastika in its simplest form, no other element appearing. Agassiz, in his monograph, says: "The original motive of the *Mæandrina Phrygia* is given us by leptodea, and many species of madrepores. The leptodea of the Persian Gulf show the patterns which ornamentalists call Greek—the wave patterns which surround Chinese, Persian and Arabic manuscripts." A remote derivation, and one, it seems, hitherto unsuggested, is the device used so freely in the carvings of the Maya temples in Yucatan and other parts of southern Mexico. It is there construed, by men who have spent years in the study of these extraordinary ruins, to be of serpent derivation, but its kinship to the Chinese and Greek forms is too plain to require argument. The claim made for Yucatan, that it, and not any part of Asia, was the cradle of the race, has startling substantiation in many of the ornament and architectural forms, and traces of religious belief which have endured there to this day.

Colonel Thomas Wilson, of the Smithsonian Institution at Washington, has published a scholarly and interesting monograph on the "swastika," in the introductory pages of which he says: "No conclusion is attempted as to the time or place of origin, or the primitive meaning of the swastika, because these are considered to be lost in antiquity. The straight line, the circle, the cross, the triangle, are simple forms, easily made, and might have been invented and reinvented in every age of primitive man and in every quarter of the globe, each time being an independent invention, meaning much or little, meaning different things among different peoples or at different times among the same people; or they may of had no definite or settled meaning. But the swastika was probably the first to be made with a definite intention and a continuous or consecutive meaning, the knowledge of which passed from person to person, from tribe to tribe, from people to people, and from nation to nation, until, with possibly changed meanings, it has finally circled the globe."

A multitude of authorities are quoted in Colonel Wilson's book, each attributing what he conceives to be the swastika's significance, and a multitude of illustrations show the forms this mysterious, prehistoric sign has taken, and the variety of objects it has adorned, in different parts of the world. It has been found in nearly all prehistoric ruins, in the temples of Central America, and the Indian mounds of the United States, as well as on the stone ware of Europe and the buried ruins of all the East. It has passed out of use in modern times among nearly all Christian nations.

Colonel Wilson says further: "The swastika mark appears both in its normal and ogee forms in the Persian carpets and rugs. While writing this memoir, I have found in the Persian rug in my own bedchamber, sixteen figures of the swastika. In the large rug in the chief clerk's office of the National Museum, there are no less than twenty-seven figures of the swastika. On a piece of imitation Persian carpet, with a heavy pile, made probably in London, I found also figures of the swastika. All the foregoing figures have been of the normal swastika, the arms crossing each other, and the ends turning at right angles, the lines being of equal thickness throughout. Some of them were bent to the right, and some to the left. At the entrance of the Grand Opera House in Washington, I saw a large India rug containing a number of ogee swastikas; while the arms crossed each other at right angles, they curved, some to the right, some to the left, but all the lines increased in size, swelling in the middle of the curve, but finishing in a point. The modern Japanese wistaria work-baskets for ladies have one or more swastikas woven in their sides or covering.

"Thus it appears that the use of the swastika in modern times is confined principally to Oriental and Scandinavian countries, countries which hold close relations with antiquity; that, in western Europe, where in ancient times the swastika was most frequent, it has, during the last one or two thousand years, become extinct. And this in the countries which have led the world in culture."

Discussing its prehistoric existence over such wide area of the earth's surface, Colonel Wilson builds wholly upon the theory of migration. He says: "The argument has been made, and it has proved satisfactory, at least to the author, that throughout Asia and Europe, with the exception of the Buddhists and early Christians, the swastika was used habitually as a sign or mark or charm implying good luck, good fortune, long life, much pleasure, great success, or something similar. The makers and users of the swastika in South and Central America, and among the mound-builders of the savages of North America, having all passed away before the advent of history, it is not now, and never has been, possible for us to obtain from them a description of the meaning, use, or purpose for which the swastika was employed by them. But, by the same line of reasoning that the proposition has been treated in the prehistoric countries of Europe and Asia, and which brought us to the conclusion that the swastika was there used as a charm or token of good luck or good fortune, or against the evil eye, we may surmise that the swastika sign was used in America for much the same purpose. It was placed upon the same style of object in America as in Europe or Asia. It is not found upon any of the ancient gods of America, nor on any of the statues, monuments or altars, nor upon any sacred place or object, but upon such objects as indicate the common or every-day use, and on which the swastika, as a charm for good luck, would be most appropriate, while for a sacred character it would be most inappropriate."

Thus the emblems of the older faiths are popularized in the ornament systems of the whole world to-day. Their very endurance speaks their fitness to endure, and to become universal, even in imperfect forms. The harmony of which they are an expression has in some mystical way seized upon the imagination of the West, and taken the place of later conceit, which finds in ingenuity alone its claim upon the fitful fancy of mankind. All that is not ephemeral in design, all that does not lose vogue in a season, seems to be directly traceable to these old, symbolic devices of the East, which have outlived the passing of nations and of creeds.

Allusion has been made elsewhere to the manner in which rug designs travel from one part of the Orient to another. Until one has been among the weavers and rug dealers of Persia, it is impossible to realize how thoroughly established and universally recognized the great majority of designs have become, how much more of a trade than an art is most modern weaving. The native designer copies and modifies. His originality stops with the petty changes in drawing or color made in some old design. In the first place the parts of the design have names, which are known to weavers everywhere. The main ground, for instance, is *metnih*; the band of solid color on the outside of the rug, *tevehr*; the narrow stripe just inside that, *zinjir*, or chain; the small border stripe, *bala-kachi*; the middle or main stripe is *ara-khachi*; the corners, *lechai*; the lines dividing the stripe, *su*, or water; the outlines of all designs, *kherdeh*. These are only terms used to indicate parts of the rug. Then with each complete design known by a name, the Oriental might, if he only would, order the most elaborate carpet without the expenditure of more than fifty words. It is necessary to dictate colors only for the principal parts of the design. The color of the smaller elements is usually left to the weaver's judgment, except in big factories. There the European or Levantine manager controls the distribution of colors even down to the smallest vine and leaf forms.

The Perso-Turkish word for design is *tereh*. An echo of the days when the weaving was done under viceroyal auspices is found in the names by which many of the standard *terehs* are known. There is, for example, the *tereh* Shah Abbas, one of the most beautiful and at the same time simplest of the ancient designs. While floral in character, it is a complete departure from the complex flower and vine masses common in fine Persian fabrics prior to the reign of the Great Shah. Its flowers, laid broadly in yellow, red and blue, and with only the smallest display of connecting vines, were of good size and in a way conventional, and stood out clear and fine upon a plain ground of the richest blue. They are really modifications of the alternating palmettes and rosettes found in the old borders. There still remain in the possession of some fortunate collectors, in this country as well as in Europe, old Shah Abbas pieces, worn to the woof but with the abiding vestiges of color still luminous. I have known a Persian who paid thirty dollars—and gladly—for a fragment of one of these old Shah Abbas rugs, not more than fourteen or fifteen inches wide, and perhaps two feet long. He drew it tenderly and with indescribable pride from his strong-box, and turned its velvety surface back and forth in the dim light of the bazaar, saying : " Now I have a real model. I shall see if the weavers of to-day are failures or not." The Shah Abbas pattern is still made in rug factories, but in most cases it bears the name only by courtesy. It is merely a jumble of disjunct floral figures in coarse weaving and usually execrable colors, crowded into the field of some huge carpet in a fashion that seems little short of mockery after one has looked on the chaste beauty of the old fabric.

DESIGN

Another design, which has so much of the decorative quality of the Shah Abbas that some of its floral figures seem like a plagiarism, is the *tereh* Mina Khani—named for Mina Khan, long ago a ruler in West Persia. In this the flowers, alternate red, yellow and particolored red and blue, are joined by rhomboidal vines of rich olive green, so as to form a diamond arrangement. In the old versions of this design there is left an abundance of the blue ground. The main borders also carry large flowers in soft colors. The narrow stripes often show the reciprocal figures of the Karabaghs. In the moderns the figures are crowded as in the Shah Abbas, and the lustrous quality of the colors has given way to the loudness of the anilines, which when years have passed over the carpet become dull and worse than unattractive.

The Sardar Aziz Khan, once a governor in Azerbijan, was also parent to a design, which still bears his name—*tereh* Sardar—but reflects no particular glory on his memory. It is common in the present day carpets, and is particularly adapted to the modern requirement in heavy design. Its principal element, by which it can be distinguished instantly, is the use of ridiculously long, narrow leaf forms, united by vines and relieved by bold floral shapes. The designer seems to have taken his first inspiration from the Shah Abbas, and added the great leaves, in place of slender vines, as a sort of sign manual.

The favorite substitute for the fish pattern in the fine old Feraghan rugs was the kindred *tereh* Guli Hinnai—or Flower of the Henna design. Henna is the plant with the extract of which the Persians dye their beards, hair and finger-nails in such extraordinary shades of red. The Guli Hinnai design presents a small yellow plant shape, set in rows, and with profuse flower forms uniting them in diamond arrangement, something after the manner of the fish pattern. The treatment of this in the Feraghans makes it resemble the

Herati diaper, though it is richer by reason of the predominance of red.

Turunji means "like a sour orange." It is the name given to all pronounced medallion rug designs with curved outlines. *Tereh* Sihbih—apple pattern—is a Kurdistan design, in which conventional elements bearing only the remotest resemblance to fruit are arranged in perpendicular rows in the ground. These are only a few of the names in vogue, but they will serve to show how thoroughly stereotyped the carpet designs of the East have become.

Before leaving this subject attention should be called to one salient feature of Oriental carpets, which may otherwise be misunderstood to the discredit of many a desirable fabric, and the loss of many a collector. In some admirable rugs faults of design will be noticed, departures from the evident scheme, which would ordinarily be unexplainable except upon the ground of carelessness of workmanship. These are the "irregularities" referred to by Sir George Birdwood, and though incomprehensible, as he elsewhere says, to the formal Western mind, their significance, so cogently pointed out by him, should in many instances lend value to the carpet in which they occur, instead of going to condemn it.

Perhaps the most remarkable case of divagation in design that ever found its way into this country was a rug which once passed through the hands of an importing firm in New York. Where it went, or who became its possessor, I do not know. This extraordinary carpet, which is so erratic that it defies classification, has perhaps a history which would be well worth the writing, if it could ever be learned from that distant East out of which it made its way hither. It is some four feet wide by seven in length, of extremely heavy, firm and admirable workmanship, and though it has the appearance of having been made by sewing together scraps of rugs of widely different varieties, was found upon examination to be one piece, and perfect in every way save one. It is begun after the pure **Sarakhs** design, in fine harmony of field and border. About eighteen **inches** from the beginning, the field pattern is abruptly changed to the **most** perfect Feraghan; the Sarakhs border is continued. Then, as suddenly, after ten inches more of progress, the inner stripe of the border is abandoned, cut off short, to make more room in the field, and for the Feraghan body is substituted a great and gaudy design upon a pale ground, which cannot be recognised as belonging to any type. In this last pattern the carpet is finished.

Whether this eccentric composition is a work of more hands than one, each succeeding weaver having put into it the pattern which seemed to him or her noblest; or whether it is a witness to the ability of some versatile Oriental to work well in several designs; or whether, again, it tells of a task taken up by a second weaver, after the death of its beginner, and, the second having been removed, another undertaking the labor of its completion, who can tell? It may be a pattern piece for several designs; it may be a "hoodoo" rug, or it may, on the other hand, be an extreme example of the irregularity of which the learned Englishman speaks, a carpet which some superstitious Persian has made to cover the grave of his progenitor, hoping that its exaggerated oddity would indeed "avert the evil eye" and vouchsafe an undisturbed repose.

There is one more trick of design in Eastern carpets, which to many will necessitate a word of explanation. Of Western apartmental arrangement the weaver of the Orient had in the beginning, little or no conception. The topography of his own home, to fit which his carpets were created, was of an unvarying order. It is this, by the way, which explains the prevalence of long, narrow shapes in so many varieties of imported rugs—the shapes which are called "runners" in our market, and are used chiefly for stair and hall coverings. The floor of the Eastern room is mapped into four sections, and for these four pieces of carpet are constructed. In the middle a wide strip, two narrow strips along the sides of this, and a fourth across the end, upon which the master of the house sits at meat, with room at his right hand and left for the guests of honor, or perchance his favorites, while persons of lesser importance occupy places upon the divans at the sides.[1] Knowing no floor scheme save this, the Oriental, when the dealers in Western markets called upon him for carpets of great size, wrought all four strips into a single piece; and in the large trade collections these vast and extraordinary objects are sometimes found. Historically, they are of value, for they are the *triclinia*, or (later) *triclinaria*, upon which the ancient East lay at its feasting. But they have no place in our scheme of furnishing, and, though they are woven, oftentimes, in the most skilful fashion, and are bought at great cost by persons in quest of the eccentric, they look to the novice like so many bits, sewn together with a purpose not altogether rational.

Confronted with these archaic creations the Western firms were forced to take the designing of the whole-carpet sizes into their own hands. There were needed indeed fabrics which, while they covered the requisite space, should, at the same time, preserve the completeness of design and color scheme which marks the smaller rugs. With this in view they provided sketches of what they wanted, and contracted with the Oriental agents for the making of the big, heavy pieces, the production of which has now grown to such vast proportions in different parts of the East. It was first tried in Asia Minor, and

---

[1] Occasionally there are found, principally in modern coarse Hamadans, what are known in Constantinople as *keosseh* (corners). These are merely quarter sections of large designs, woven as complete fabrics, and for oddity, more than aught else, used in small rooms, where two sides are taken up by divans, canopies, and other adjuncts or that modern hodge-podge, the "cosy corner." They are well adapted for this purpose, since the quarter of the central medallion common to the Hamadans covers the floor under the canopies, and the rich borders are displayed outside. Of late, also, some round pieces have been produced, in silk, chiefly if not altogether from the looms of Tabriz. They are meant, of course, for table covers, and some of them are well designed and deftly wrought.

proved so successful that Western designers are now stationed at weaving centres in Persia and India, as well as in Anatolia. The conceits of these gentlemen, following in general the theory of the East, but combining the designs of the various types or supplying Occidental features, in such manner as to please the Western fancy or accord with other Western decorations, are registered as the property of the firms. It has been the custom of the native weavers to appropriate them, but the governments, after long insistence and the invocation of consular influence, have decided that the registration shall protect the design, and that to violate it shall be a punishable misdemeanor.

VII

WEAVING

NOW for the weaving, the patient, painstaking labor at which so many hundreds of thousands of swarthy fingers are flying, and have been flying since the days of the Pharaohs.

Measured by results it is a wonder work; watched, in its tireless repetition of three simple processes that a child can master, it seems no more of an art than the constant turning of an hour glass—which, in fact, to myriads of these Eastern people, it is. The whole thing is simple, to look at, to read about; but there is, nevertheless, some peculiar spirit, some mental drift, some inherent and mysterious fitness pervading and governing their work, which makes these Orientals the best weavers in the world. Peoples of other races have reared looms, and dyed yarn, and, borrowing the tricks of color and of stitch from Turkey and Persia, have striven to work out upon the warp a harmony as rich and full as theirs. But they have failed. The English scholar has perhaps hit upon the truth when he says: " Antiquity, from its being nearer than we are to the divine origin of things, was ever mindful to symbolize in its sublime art the truth of the conviction that the green circle of the earth and the shining frame of the out-stretched heavens are but the marvellous intertexture of the veil dividing between the world we see, and the unseen, unseeable world beyond.   This is the reason of the vitality, the dignity and power of giving contentment, possessed by the arts of the world of antiquity, with which the arts of the modern world of the West will never be indued until they also become animated by the spirit of the pristine faith of every historical race in the old world. . . . . . For all the technical instruction which may be given, and all the luxurious illustrations of typical Eastern examples that may be published, no truly great carpet will ever be produced in Europe until the weaver's heart is attuned to sing to the accompaniment of his whirring loom, in grateful unison with every voice in Heaven and earth :

> " Holy, holy, holy, Lord God of Sabaoth ;
>
> " Heaven and earth are full of Thy glory. Glory in the highest."

Unlettered as are the great majority of the Oriental weaving class of to-day, there is little doubt that the religious element here referred to makes up a recognizable part of their existence.   At no moment, even of their working days, is the consciousness of their faith absent from them.   A race, every being of which, whether learned or ignorant, has prayers five times a day, no matter where he be, must, in the very nature of things, have an abiding faith in the nearness of the Deity.   While not daring to question the infinite value of such inspiration, it is difficult, for one who accepts the Mosaic doctrine of Divine retribution, to understand how any Oriental weaver, under these circumstances, has survived the substitution of the modern enormities for the conscientious work he was wont to do.   However that may be, it is not to be disputed that there is some faculty which to this day enables the Orient to excel the West in hand-wrought fabrics, even with uncouth appliances such as that same West has long ago outgrown.

Any lad, with a knack for carpentry, can make such a loom as that upon which the Eastern does his weaving.   Plain, absurdly primitive, it endures for a lifetime, or many lifetimes, and its timbers are often adorned with carvings done by hands long since still. **It** is in essential principles the same old-fashioned structure that is pictured on archaic tiles and vases ; the same that we know to have been used for thousands of years in the weaving of coarse cloth and canvas. The method, too, is the same in its rudiments, with the addition that instead of throwing the weft across the warp compactly, to make a thin, firm web, the knot upon the warp is employed to form a surface, and the weft becomes merely a binder, holding each row of knots close-pressed to its neighbor. This addition of the pile to the primitive web is believed to have originated with some of the tribes of Central Asia, where severity of weather made warmth a desideratum.

Some looms are plain, stationary, oblong frames. The majority of those in use in Asia Minor consist of two upright beams of wood, heavy or light according to the weight of the fabric to be woven. They are fixed parallel to each other, and the distance between them limits the width of the rug. They support at the top a roller, the ends of which turn in holes bored in the beams of the frame, or in deep notches across their upper ends.

To this by a rod which fits in a groove upon it, are fastened the warp-threads, forming the basis of the fabric. Ancient looms are represented as having a weight attached to the end of every warp-thread to hold it taut, in which case the weaving must have been begun at top. It is said to be so done in obscure hamlets of India and of far northern Europe to-day, but in Persia, Turkey,—in fact generally throughout the rug-weaving countries,—the primitive system is reversed and the rows of knots begin at the bottom, for which purpose, and to insure firmness, another roller or crossbar is placed there.

Several methods are in vogue for arranging the warp upon its frame. They are all upon one of two general principles : First, that of having the weaver shift position, mounting higher abreast the loom as the fabric grows; second, having the work pass downward before the weaver, by aid of the rollers at the top and bottom. In the first method the crossbars are, of course, immovable, save that to the lower one a little play is given so that as occasion demands the warp may be tightened by the aid of wedges.

For the second system, again, two methods are employed. The first is to wind the warp-threads on the top roller, and unwind them as needed, rolling the finished carpet up on the bottom roller as the work progresses. The second is to have the carpet pass over the bottom roller and up again at the back, the warp being a continuous thing, like a belting.

These looms upon which the warp moves to meet the weaver are used in a horizontal position in many parts of the East, notably in Sehna and about Bijar, and the weaver sits at the end. In these the carpet is regularly rolled along as it increases. The Bijar weavers actually sit on the finished part of the carpet as they weave. The nomads in Luristan, Kurdistan, and other grazing districts, when they have turned out the sheep and goats upon the range and pitched camp for the grazing season, erect stationary upright frames to endure until winter drives them from the place. Rude things these nomad looms are—mere trunks of trees, roughly trimmed, with the shanks of the lopped-off branches left to support the rollers and the flimsy scaffolding upon which the tawny women of the tribe sit at their weaving. Sometimes a ladder is placed perpendicularly at each side of the loom, and the plank upon which the weavers perch is moved upward from rung to rung as the work goes on. The looms built indoors for use in winter reach from floor to roof-timbers.

The warp in real antique rugs is, or was, in most varieties, woollen. The exceptions to this rule were the fine fabrics, especially Persian, where silk or cotton was used for flexibility, and those made by the nomads in districts where goat's-hair was plentiful and was, therefore, taken for the groundwork, while the wool was saved for the piling, or for sale. In these latter days cotton has come to be used much in the webbing, mainly because it is cheaper. In the old-time rugs the material of warp and weft was one of the chief means of determining the locality of fabrication. This was most useful, since, as is elsewhere explained, many patterns were so widely adopted that only by the character of the ground-threads, oftentimes, could the fabric be identified as the product of any particular town or district. Nowadays even the most thorough experts are deceived by the frequent substitution of cotton for warp or weft in localities where formerly only wool was used.

In India, owing to lack of wool, hemp is much employed; linen also plays a noticeable part. In America, where " Turkish " and " Persian " rugs alike are made, cotton, linen and hemp are put into the foundations for thrift's sake. The evil of a hempen groundwork is that under stress of wear and wetting it rots, and from a little break in the web the entire fabric is apt to go pieces speedily.

It is the custom among weavers of many localities to dye the ends of the warp-threads for some distance, so that the carpet may have for finishing at the ends a web of red, or blue, or both. This dyeing is done after the warp is complete. When the colored ends of the threads are dry the whole warp is fastened upon the loom and drawn taut by the wedges supplied for the purpose, above the ends of the lower rollers. Where stationary and rollerless looms are used, the jointure of the lower cross beam—known as the "piece-beam"—with the side-beams is made in an elongated slot, so that this tightening can be accomplished without difficulty.

It becomes needful, when the weaving is fairly under way, to separate the warp into two sets of threads, front and back. For this purpose two rods are used; one, about an inch and a half in diameter, to which every other thread of the warp is attached, but not so tightly as to prevent its being moved upward along the warp-threads, as the carpet goes on toward completion. The second, flat, and about three inches in width, rests between the front and back threads. The use of these rods will be explained further on.

Preliminary to the weaving, the weavers, or children who are learning the rudiments of the art, undo the big skeins in which the yarn comes from the dyers, and wind it into balls. These are hung in a multicolored row, upon a cross-rod fastened to the warp-beam overhead, and the ends hang down within the weaver's reach. In the factories in the weaving centres of Persia, spools are used. In remote districts, when yarn of a certain color is exhausted before the piece is done, the nearest shade that can be got is used to complete the figure. Sometimes, when no material at all like can be obtained, the pattern jumps abruptly into some other color. In large towns, where dyers are many, this never occurs, for the master weaver, foreseeing the lack, hastens to the dye-shop and has the supply replenished.

The patterns from which the fabrics are copied, among the country weavers, are usually old rugs, one or two of which each family, whether among the wandering shepherds or the home-staying folk of the town, keeps for that praiseworthy purpose. As much store is set by these as by the family plate in Western lands, and so familiar do these swift-fingered women become with the design by reproducing it year after year all through their humdrum lives, that a skilled weaver goes deftly along with it, supplying unerringly, as if by unconscious cerebration, the proper color in its proper place, even though it be only a single stitch in a tangled mass of utterly different hues. Her fingers seem to know the pattern, and half the time her eyes are not upon the work at all.

For beginners, the old rug is hung within arm's length, with the back of it exposed so that every knot and its color may be easily discerned. Thus a design, border and all, is gradually ingrained upon the young weaver's memory, never to be forgotten.

In towns where weaving is conducted on a large scale, when new patterns are to be used they are wrought out, sometimes upon great cardboards, on which the stitches are indicated by squares, each painted in its proper color; sometimes upon cheap cloth, the design of the whole rug being mapped there by sewing threads of the different colors upon the knot spaces. Then the whole is cut up, and distributed to the weavers. This is always done in making the silk rugs of Kirman and Tabriz. In most of the great rug-weaving

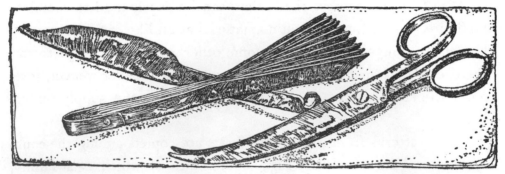

THE PERSIAN WEAVER'S TOOLS

centres, the European and American firms keep skilled hands, known as "scale-makers," whose business it is to weave small sections of any new design, and these are given to the workmen and women for patterns. In Ghiordes and Demirdji especially this custom is in vogue. The weavers there are unable to work from a painted pattern. They must have the actual fabric before them. Not so in Oushak. There they have pieces of the pattern framed. In many localities the number of knots of each color to be tied in by each weaver is called or read off by the loom-master. The patterns for borders and corners are made upon separate pieces, and as the work upon them is more difficult than that of the centre, the most accomplished weavers sit at the ends of the plank before the loom.

Armed with a little knife and a pair of curved scissors, the weaver sits down before the virgin warp and starts the fabric. There is some preliminary weaving of warp and weft threads together to form a web at the ends. Then the actual work of tying the pile yarn begins. Except for the Soumak fabrics and the khilims, which will be spoken of hereafter, Oriental carpets are confined to two systems of knotting. The first is termed the Turkish or Ghiordes knot, and is in vogue throughout Asia Minor, the Caucasus, Kurdistan, and in some localities farther East.

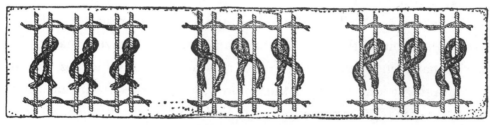

GHIORDES KNOT.   SEHNA KNOT; RIGHT-HAND SYSTEM.   SEHNA KNOT; LEFT-HAND SYSTEM.

The second is the Persian or Sehna knot, which, though better calculated to produce a close, fine, even, velvety surface, has in many parts of Persia been abandoned for the Ghiordes, which is a trifle more easily tied.

The difference may be understood by a glance at the illustrations. It is very simple. In the Turkish system the knot-yarn is twisted about the warp-thread in such fashion that the two upstanding ends of the pile alternate with every two threads of the warp. The Persian knot, on the contrary, is tied so that from every space between the warp threads one end of pile yarn protrudes.

In the number of knots which can be tied to the square inch the advantage lies with the Sehna method. The Ghiordes brings two ends of the knot yarn together, and leaves consequently a wider space between the knots than does the Sehna. But each tuft is larger by half, and if the pile is not very closely clipped—as it is not in most rugs where this knot is used—the spreading of these ends gives an equally compact surface. In the Kirman, Tabriz, Sehna, old Turkestan and Kabistan rugs, however, it is the custom to trim the pile exceedingly close, which brings out more clearly the minute color variations of the design. In Tabriz and parts of Kurdistan a special system is used. The rugs are woven in the Turkish knot, but the arrangement of the warp-threads is such as to secure extraordinary compactness in the pile.

The Ghiordes knot took its name from the old city of Ghiordes, where years ago the Turkish method had its greatest perfection, but nowadays, though the knot is the same and the weavers many, the fabrics have changed sadly. The art is not lost in Ghiordes, for at discouragingly long intervals there find way to market from that town dainty prayer rugs or some bits of *sedjadeh*, so fine of texture, so true in color, so traditionally perfect in design, that experts, knowing well how far the Ghiordese have fallen from workmanly grace, swear by the beard of the Prophet that they have been made in Sehna, after the Ghiordes patterns of long ago. Of all the fabrics of to-day the Kabistans of the Caucasus will be found, perhaps, most faithful in adherence to the old models, and in them are best shown the fine, velvety effects which may be come at with the Ghiordes knot, when tied by masters who have not proven recreant to the tradition of their craft. The Ghiordes knot is always one and the same thing. The Sehna, being more of a running knot, is sometimes reversed and worked from left to right. This is classed by some authorities as an entirely different system. In all these knottings two strands of yarn are frequently used, thus doubling the thickness of the pile.

The loosest knotting in distinctly modern Eastern carpets is found in Kulah, Oushak, Ghiordes, and the latter-day Feraghan. The most closely tied are those made in Saruk, Sehna and Kirman, and in some of the better Turkomans, and for the rest, Kabistans, Tabriz, and Serapis.[1] The number of knots to the inch is determined, of course, by the closeness of the warp-threads and the number of weft-threads thrown across after each row of knots. In Sehnas and Kirmans, where the warp is of silk, the weft-threads sometimes lie so close together that the weaver is compelled to put the stitches in with the needle.

It is the custom of expert weavers not to work straight across from one end of the row to the other, changing the yarn as often as the pattern calls for a change of color, as tyros do, but to put in all the stitches of one color on the row, wherever they are required, before taking up another yarn. This saves, in the making of a rug, a total of time well worth consideration. Where the pattern is a familiar one the weaver can determine at a glance on what warp-threads the knots of each color belong, and even in strange patterns a clever hand does it almost without error.

When a knot is completed the weaver cuts the yarn with a knife, and it is one of the tests of skill to cut so nearly to the intended length of the pile that a minimum of material shall be lost in the trimming with scissors, which is performed as soon as the row is complete. An inventive agent of a Smyrna carpet establishment once tried to compel the weavers engaged on the firm's work at Oushak, Kulah, and Ghiordes to use a small steel rod, which was fastened across the face of the warp, and around which the yarns must be car-

---

[1] "Various tests for ascertaining the quality of a carpet have been described. One is to drop on it a piece of red-hot charcoal; then, if the carpet is a good one, the singed part can be brushed off without leaving any trace of the burn. Chardin says : ' The Persian rule to know good carpets and to rate them by, is to lay the thumb on the edge of the carpet, and to tell the threads in a thumb's breadth ; for the more there are the dearer the work is.' "—*E. Treacher Collins: " In the Kingdom of the Shah."*

ried continuously in making the knots. On the outer side of this rod was a groove running from end to end. When the row of knots was finished a knife was run along the groove, cutting the yarn as it went. So closely did half the circumference of the rod approximate the ultimate length of the pile that the loss of yarn by subsequent trimming was reduced to about two per cent. It is ordinarily twenty-five per cent. when the cutting is done by guess, for by no amount of effort or experiment has a profitable means been devised for utilizing the refuse. The weavers rejected the rod angrily, for its use occupied time, and that was their loss, whereas the waste of wool from the old manner of cutting came out of the pockets of the firm.

Trimming the pile is one of the most important and difficult parts of the weaver's work; so difficult, in fact, that Americans, working upon imitation " Turkish " or " Persian " carpets in the factories of New York are unable to do it at all satisfactorily, and a machine has been constructed, on the lawn-mower or planing-mill principle, to take the place of the Oriental weaver's scissors. Uneven trimming of the pile is a fault found, strange to say, in some Eastern rugs which otherwise are of distinguished merit.[1]

When a row of tufts has been trimmed to even lengths, the threads of weft are thrown across, from one side to the other of the warp and back again. It is in this process that the rods before mentioned, the flat one between front and back threads, and the round one to which the back threads of the warp are fastened, come into service. By drawing the round rod out a little, the warp-threads are separated, back from front, so that the weft may be passed

---

[1] Experiment was made in Anatolia with what were known as raised patterns, produced by clipping the pile of the grounds close, and leaving that of the patterns longer, grading the length so as to form a comparatively accurate relief of whatever object the pattern was supposed to represent. A number of these singular and unpleasantly overdone fabrics came to this country, but they were so plainly at variance with the Eastern theory that they were justly neglected, and further making of them was abandoned.

across readily, over and under. Then, reversing the direction, and separating the threads by turning the flat rod down to the horizontal, the weft is carried back again, passing each warp-thread on the opposite side from that embraced by the preceding shute. Thus the row of knots is bound firmly, and the tufts kept upright, securing an even pile. In coarse fabrics of the *barchanah* order the Kazak custom of tnrowing four threads of weft across after each row of knots is much followed. Time and the effort of tying knots are saved. On the other hand, it is the habit among the Sehna and Tabriz weavers to carry the weft one way and then put in another row of knots before carrying it back. This makes the pile wonderfully compact.[1]

The next step is to beat down both knots and weft with a comb or "batten." In the Turkish countries this implement is of wood, but the Persians prefer it to be of steel. Unskilful use of this comb, beating one part of the row harder than another, will often produce unevenness in the completed rug, for which, in extreme cases, there is no cure except to cut it and sew it together again. Clumsy weaving causes the same imperfection. Some of the Mosul Kurdish rugs illustrate this.

When all this knotting, clipping, and inweaving of the weft-threads has been repeated to the end of the design, there remains only the finishing of sides and ends to be accomplished. This varies widely in the different localities, but in any one district very seldom, though there are some sections where two or even more styles are in equal vogue. In nearly all rugs there is left at the end a thin, hard

---

[1] The method of preparing these weft-threads is of almost incalculable importance. In many tightly woven fabrics made in newly established weaving communities the sides begin to curl after the rug has been in use for a time. The cause of this is that the weft-thread, which is carried on a shuttle and thus passed back and forth is too tightly twisted in the effort to give it firmness. A simple experiment, the doubling of a twisted cord, will show what happens. To guard against this curling it is the custom of skilled weavers to use two separate threads for the warp and have them twisted in opposite directions, that the tendency of the one may counteract that of the other.

web, sometimes scarcely long enough to be visible, woven of warp and weft, usually dyed in some solid color or with a stripe. Sometimes there is a thick but narrow selvage outside the web, across one or both ends. The loose ends of the warp-threads are then made into a fringe, short in most rugs but in many of the nomad fabrics left long for the effect, which is most striking. The forms which this warp fringe takes are many—knots, twists, and even in some cases braids, such as form the lariat of the Mexican herdsman. The warp-threads, again, may simply be cut loose, and left to make a rough finish. In others only one end carries a fringe, the other being stoutly finished by a singular doubling back of the warp, and in-weaving of it with the weft-threads. A few of the antique prayer rugs of Ghiordes have sewed on at the ends a silk fringe of the sort used in the finishing of so many European and American curtains.

The sides of the Eastern carpets are for the most part either selvaged or overcast, sometimes with wool, sometimes with cotton, and occasionally with camel's-hair or goat's-hair yarn, either dyed or in the natural color. The selvage is formed by simply working the weft, which is often dyed, around the last few threads of the warp, at both sides of the rug. Sometimes, as in the Daghestans and old Ghiordes, extra threads, colored, are used to form a fine selvage at the sides. In the Ghiordes these are of silk. The principal finishings are here enumerated in the briefest manner. An account of each, where it chances to have any striking characteristic, will be found in the chapters descriptive of the different fabrics, and the textile tables will show the typical finishings of all the standard rugs of commerce.

The most impressive touch a weaver ever gives a rug is to sew fast upon it, at some central point, when it is partly finished, a single blue bead, a clove of garlic or a tiny scrap of print-cloth. All these are held to be talismans, and to find any one of them on a rug you have purchased is to know that the weaver, in whatever place he wrought, gave personal and particular benediction to his fabric, and wished it good treatment during its little journey in the world. Oftentimes, when the bales of rugs are opened in Smyrna and Constantinople, pieces are found with scraps of paper fastened upon them, on which the weaver, or some one on his behalf, has written in the Eastern characters a petition "to all to whom these presents may come," that they use the rug kindly and pray now and then for the maker of it.

These eccentricities and superstitions which attend upon rug-making are without number. If, while the rug is in process of construction, a neighbor coming in exclaims at its beauty or promise, he is implored, in the name of the Prophet, to spit upon the fabric for luck. No instance is known, in the lifetime of the oldest weaver, where this observance was withheld. Should the guest go away without paying any tribute of praise he is counted to have bewitched the carpet, and incense is burned in the room forthwith to avert the blight of misfortune which needs must follow.

A marvel to Americans and Europeans at the great international exhibitions has always been the double-faced carpet, woven with a pile on both sides and in altogether dissimilar designs.[1] Many people have been at a loss to understand how this singular effect could be produced, and are loath to believe that the piece did not in reality consist of two carpets, fastened together back to back after their completion. The warp is tied on a frame, which works on pins at top and bottom, turning to the weaver first one side and then the other. Having finished a row of knots on one side in its design, he turns the frame over and works a row on the other, with different colors and different figures; then passes his thread of weft across to bind them both. It is a simple process, after all, but the effect is startling.

---

[1] How old this trick of weaving is it is impossible to say. Pliny speaks of having seen these ἀμφιμάλλα when he was a lad.

ORIENTAL RUGS

In all Oriental countries rugs were, until lately, made for specific personal purposes, and never put to any other use than that for which they were first destined. Although among dealers and purchasers alike in this country these classifications are little known, each class has its distinguishing name, and from passing through Constantinople and Smyrna as distributing points they have retained the Turkish use-titles, rather than those of the Persian, Tartar, or local dialect. These are:

Namazlik, or prayer rug.—This is the one piece of property which every faithful Mohammedan must own, and he clings to it devotedly as long as he lives. Throughout all the Moslem countries the *namazlik* preserves its significant feature, the point or niche at one end, representing the niche of the mosque. The colors and decorative character of the prayer rug vary in different localities. In some districts it is severely rectilinear; in others, the lines verging to the point may be curved. But the one-end configuration can never be mistaken for anything else. The *namazlik* is the Oriental's constant companion. When the call to prayer comes, he spreads his rug upon the ground, with the apex of the niche toward Mecca, and prostrates himself in reverence, his head resting in the angle. Thus bowed, he prays.

Prayer rugs do not vary greatly in size. The width is from two and a half to four feet, and the length from four and a half to six. The prayer rug made for personal use has, as a rule, the name of its owner worked in the wool, and is of the very best weaving.

Hammamlik, or bath rug.—This is usually presented to the bride on her wedding day. Her parents are the donors, but there is a certain humor in the fact that the rug, in nine cases out of ten, is woven by the girl herself. It reveals accurately her skill as a weaver, and the limit of her artistic taste, for it represents the thought and labor of years. The *hammamliks* are used to spread upon the floor in the baths and their constant contact with soap and water gives them a peculiar lustre. Their shape is unique. As a rule they are almost square.

Sedjadeh, or floor covering.—This name is given to carpets of medium size, say more than seven and less than ten feet in length. The specific name for the larger floor fabrics is *hali*, in Persian, *kali*.

Yestiklik.—These are known in America as Anatolian mats, and may be found in profusion in any good stock of Oriental rugs. They serve a multitude of purposes in our furnishing, but in the East, the best ones are made to cover the divan pillows. They are ornate, and gay in hue, since the pillow, with the Oriental as with us, is ornamental as well as useful. The Anatolian mats are more fully described in the chapter on Turkish fabrics.

Makatlik, or "runners."—These are what we know as "hall" or "stair" rugs. In the East they do duty as covers for the low felt divans along the sides of the room. They range from two and a half to four feet in width and from ten to twenty feet in length.

Hehbehlik, saddle-bag or saddle-cover.—Wherever there is a rug-making district there are saddle-bags peculiar to it. All the East rides, and the *hehbehlik* lends all sorts of splendor to caparison. It reflects, as indeed all rugs do, the general character of the people. Among the nomads it is rough in texture and astounding in color. The more polished races observe better artistic tenets in design, but the *hehbehlik* is always made substantially and with more freedom in the matter of brilliancy than any of the floor coverings except the *odjaklik*. In America these saddle cloths are used for pillow covers.

Odjaklik, hearth or fire rug.—This is the most precious of all Eastern family treasures. It is always spread before the fireplace on the arrival of a guest. It is wonderful in color and most elaborate in workmanship, and may be recognized by the pointed formation of the central field at both ends.

Turbehlik, or grave carpets.—The custom of spreading rugs, as the Occidental strews flowers, on the graves of relatives or friends, seems to have prevailed more generally in Persia and regions immediately adjoining it than in other parts of the Orient, though it is practised to some degree among almost every Eastern people. The *turbehlik*—from *turbeh*, a grave—is the combined handiwork of all the members of the household. Even the children tie knots in it, that it may be expressive of the sorrow of all. It was through the priests that the grave-carpets first came to be dispensed to the West. Now they are made for export, like other fabrics. The designs—cypress, willow, and myrtle—are eloquent of the *turbehlik's* character. The whole appearance of it is funereal, but there are flowers and other bright bits of color, which speak of a blissful hereafter for the dead whose bones it was meant to cover. This floral element, indicative of hope, is so essential that even the geometrical Daghestans relax their rule and use tree and flower forms. In Persia there is no limit to the decoration employed in these rugs. Trees themselves embody the idea of perpetual life.

Berdelik, or hangings.—These are the fabrics made, not for floor covering, but wholly for the adornment of wall space, or for portières and curtains. The shape, and sometimes the finishing, will suggest a particular intent, but all rugs which are of extreme fineness and lightness, especially those in delicate colors, may be counted as belonging to this class. The Oriental seems to have been endowed with an intuitive notion of the law of gravity in decoration. He never makes the error of placing on the floor a fabric intended for the walls. The top-heavy, upside-down effect, so apparent in many American rooms, is thus avoided.

In general, it may be said that the silk fabrics are to be classed as *berdeliks*. There are persons of lavish leanings, to be sure, who employ them on floors, but it is not a custom, least of all in the East.

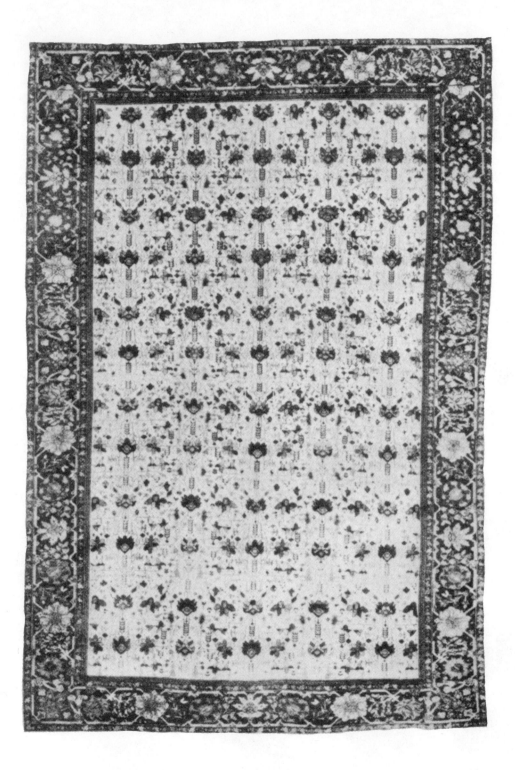

PLATE III. SARUK RUG

6.9 x 4.6

Loaned by Mr. F. B. Proctor

This is one of the best of such Saruk products as reach this country. In design it differs widely from the generality of the output. The row effect, which is common in middle Persia, is here, but the usual Feraghan devices are not used. The workmanship is very thorough, and in fineness and accuracy, particularly of the border, compares favorably with the weaving of the olden times, but the effect is lost, in a measure, by reason of the dark colors which are Saruk characteristics. Lost, for the same reason, is the fine shading of the colors in the border flowers. These resemble the Kirman work, while the floral elements of the centre are laid in solid colors, such as are in vogue farther to the north. The feature of the carpet, outside its general excellence as a fabric, is the delicate vine tracery of the centre, which is in a vernal shade of green and forms a perfect coördinate diaper design. The vines, however, do not follow the natural curve, found in the old South Persian carpets, but are more in the broken fashion of Herez.

A mark of modernity is the excision of several inches of border design at the top of the rug, probably because the warp proved shorter than that of the older fabric from which this was copied. The cut is even made through the very middle of a flower, to allow for the insertion of the corner device so that the ends may seem to be alike.

where there are only stockinged feet to press them. They are, furthermore, only fine editions of the woolen fabrics of the same localities. The silk is capable of far more minute color effects, and more perfect shadings, and has a natural lustre which no known treatment can impart to wool.[1]

But they are not essentially floor coverings. Silk rugs, therefore, are not considered in this volume.

---

[1] " Silk produced at Resht is brought here [Kashan] to be spun and dyed. Then it is sent to Sultanabad to be woven into carpets, and is brought back again to have the pile cut by the sharp instruments used for cutting the velvet pile, and the finished carpets are sent to Teheran for sale. They are made only in small sizes, and are more suitable for portières than for laying on the floor. The coloring is exquisite, and the metallic sheen and lustre are unique. Silk carpets are costly luxuries. The price of even a fairly good one of small size is £50, the silk alone costing £20."—*Mrs. Bishop: "Journeys in Persia and Kurdistan."*

VIII

CLASSIFICATION

IN the chapters which follow an attempt is made so to set forth
in description the principal types of Oriental rugs that a clear
and comprehensive idea may be formed, in the mind of the
reader, of the general quality, appearance, color, design, texture and
usefulness of each.

Attention is called to substitutions which are continually practised by vendors—substitutions made possible only by the general
lack of knowledge, among purchasers, of the points in which one rug
differs from another. Many names, sufficiently legitimate in their
way, but which are not included in the recognized nomenclature of
the trade, are attached by dealers, of their own fancy, to particular
grades of rugs. I have taken, as stated in the opening chapter, the
names in use among rug men in Smyrna and Constantinople. No
American buyer who has ever run the gauntlet of the Levantine
traders in these great markets has come away accusing them of stu-
pidity, and their fertility in new and fetching Oriental titles for what
are in all essentials established varieties of rugs, and thoroughly
localized, has long ago been proven. It is believed, however, that the
classifications here made include all the standard fabrics.

I have found upon inquiry in the rug centres of Asia that in some cases names given in Constantinople as indicating the town or province where the fabrics bearing them were made are erroneous, and have come into use merely through the fact that the rugs were taken to these towns for market. Persian dealers, receiving orders from Constantinople, are often at a loss to know what is wanted, as the names given do not comport with those in use where the rugs are made and marketed. To substitute here in the headings the names by which the fabrics are known at home would cause endless confusion. Therefore the trade titles are used, correction, where it is of importance, being made in the body of the text.

The running descriptions bear more especially on design and coloring, and the extreme difficulty of making these in any wise clear, in so small an allowance of space, must be apparent, since the conditions leading to infinite variation in both have already been touched upon. The whole aim has been to arrive, by inductive process and exclusion, at the true type in each class, group and variety.

Details of the texture—the knot employed, the material of warp, weft and pile, the length of the pile, the number of knots to the inch, measuring horizontally for the warp and perpendicularly for the weft, and whatever special peculiarities may belong to each variety—are set down in their respective columns in the tables which will be found at the end of the book. Where the texture of a certain weave is at variance with the tables I make bold to believe that it is because the fabric is not true to its type, but is either degenerate or capricious. In many points the tables are amplified by the descriptive matter. It is necessary, in order to give a clear idea of the classification, to present here a skeleton table comprising all the classes.

ORIENTAL RUGS

CAUCASIAN

DAGHESTAN-
1. Daghestan Proper.
2. Derbend.
3. "Kabistan" or Kuba.
4. "Tzitzi" or Tchetchen.
5. Tcherkess or Circassian.

TRANSCAUCASIAN-
1. Karabagh.
2. Soumak or "Kashmir."
3. Shirvan.
4. Kázak.

MOSUL-
1. Mosul Proper.
2. Turkman or Genghis.
3. Western Kurds.

TURKISH

KONIEH-
1. Konieh Proper.
2. Kir-Shehr.
3. Kaba-Karaman.
4. Yuruks.
5. Anatolians.

SMYRNA-
1. Ghiordes.
2. Kulah.
3. Demirdjik.
4. Oushak.
5. Bergamo and Ladik.
6. Ak-Hissar.
7. Meles or Carian.

PERSIAN

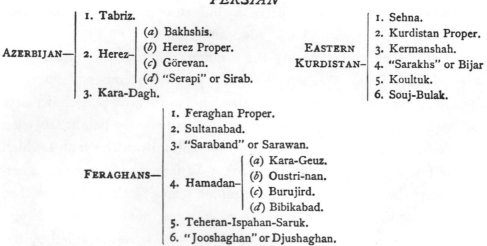

AZERBIJAN—
1. Tabriz.
2. Herez-
  (a) Bakhshis.
  (b) Herez Proper.
  (c) Görevan.
  (d) "Serapi" or Sirab.
3. Kara-Dagh.

EASTERN KURDISTAN-
1. Sehna.
2. Kurdistan Proper.
3. Kermanshah.
4. "Sarakhs" or Bijar
5. Koultuk.
6. Souj-Bulak.

FERAGHANS—
1. Feraghan Proper.
2. Sultanabad.
3. "Saraband" or Sarawan.
4. Hamadan-
  (a) Kara-Geuz.
  (b) Oustri-nan.
  (c) Burujird.
  (d) Bibikabad.
5. Teheran-Ispahan-Saruk.
6. "Jooshaghan" or Djushaghan.

KIRMANIEH-
1. Kirman Proper.
2. Shiraz.
3. Niris.

KIRMANIEH-
4. Mecca.
5. Khorassan.
6. Meshhed.
7. Herat.

TURKOMAN

1. "Bokhara" or Tekke.
2. Yomud.
3. "Afghan" or Bokhara.
4. Beluchistan.
5. Samarkand.
6. Yarkand and Kashgar.

CLASSIFICATION

There are manufacturing towns, such as Ghiordes and Oushak, in which several grades of rugs are made, and each grade receives its special name as a guide to a knowledge of its quality. These classifications have not been set down in the summary table, but in the textile tables details of the texture of the most important of these fabrics are given, and in the account of the products of each town or district other differences between the grades are indicated.

In several places, as a result of Western enterprise, and for that matter, of native ambition, large rug-making interests have been established recently, where some old and well-known varieties of fabrics are used as patterns. To these products no place has been given in the tables, but they have been mentioned in connection with the originals from which they have been copied. Many of them are of signal merit, and it is not on account of inferiority that they are excluded from the tables, but solely because they are only industrious reproductions, and analysis of them would be superfluous.

No tabular classification of the Indian rugs is given, nor is any attempt made to set forth the details of their construction in the textile tables, for the reason that, as now woven, they are not the original products, but are made in grades arranged merely upon a trade basis. The details, therefore, are much alike in all. The chapter on Indian carpets contains sufficient indication of the nature and comparative merits of the staple output.

IX

CAUCASIAN

THE region lying on both sides of the Caucasus Mountains and bounded on the west by the Black Sea and the Turkish frontier, on the south by Persia and on the east by the Caspian, has been an undisputed Russian possession for almost a century. Prior to that parts of it had changed hands from time to time between the Turks and Persians, and in the early stages of rug importation to America its fabrics were known as Turkish textiles. They were more widely used than those of Persia or the Anatolian Peninsula, and are still often referred to, in a general way, as Turkish rugs. This is due partly to the tenacity of custom and partly to the unwillingness of the dealers to sacrifice any whit of the fascination which clings to a purely Oriental name. "Caucasian rugs" unquestionably sounds cold, bleak and Russian. There is in it no suggestion of the warm, languorous Eastern life of which the word Turkish is so eloquent, though these Caucasian fabrics have in them perhaps more of pure Oriental decoration than many which rejoice in more luxurious titles.

But there is about the fabrics from this section so much that is distinctive, and their kinship is so plainly traceable, that they merit a more modern and more accurate classification. They are essentially as well as geographically, Caucasian rugs, and have a character of their own, wholly different from that of most of the fabrics now made in Turkey proper.

The Caucasian marks have, too, been so communicated to the rugs of the district lying to the west, in old Armenia and Mesopotamia, that I have felt compelled to class the so-called Mosul products as of the Caucasian order, despite the fact that the Mosul territory is on the Turkish side of the boundary, and, further, that in design many of the Mosul rugs present Persian elements in a coarse form.

The general groups comprised in the Caucasian class are, therefore, the Daghestan, Transcaucasian and Mosul fabrics.

DAGHESTAN FABRICS

For thorough workmanship, harmony of color, and adherence to traditional design, some of the floor coverings grouped under the general head of Daghestan are unexcelled. The district from which they are named is a three-cornered bit of country east of the Caucasus, wedged into the angle which the mountains make with the Caspian Sea. The many tribes which once maintained their autonomies, small and great, within the confines of the region had different languages, or in any case different dialects, and some of them, it is recorded, had no written forms. The vigorous Russification to which they have been subjected since the conquest—conquest against which they warred long and sturdily—has given them a common language and a spur to industry. It has shown them the road to market, but, save in that increased production has been attended by something of the universal decline in quality, it has not changed in any important particular the character of the weavings.

The Daghestan rugs have, in fact, shown closer adherence to old standards than those of almost any Eastern provinces. In their work these Daghestan weavers are patient and painstaking. Among the mountaineers, sometimes, the leisure of two or three years is spent in the making of a single rug. The region is one of the few which have not changed the whole character of their industry, under the inducements which recent years have offered. As in Persia, towns and districts which are only a little way apart follow altogether different models in their rug-making, and show no inclination to depart from their respective customs, although communication is much easier now than it was before the Russian occupation.

Daghestan Proper.—The proper Daghestan rugs can be singled out from all the fabrics of the East, almost unerringly, if one fact be borne in mind—that they are made in imitation of jewels, or, some maintain, of mosaics. They show it at a glance. They have all the brilliancy, accuracy, and clean cutting that either idea suggests. Their whole effect is one of geometrical cleanness and clear atmosphere. They are illustrative, to the last degree, of the pure ornamental forms of the Mohammedan East. The geometrical finds its best expression in them. Only occasionally, to adorn the border stripes or to break up some annoying expanse of ground color, is the floral form resorted to, and then it is severely conventional. The colors, too, are positive; the transitions and contrasts are pronounced. There is no shading off from one hue to another. All this would result in harshness were it not for the masterly adjustment of color values and areas. The completeness and perfect balance of the Daghestan are its charm.

While the designs vary much in detail, the class character is plain in them all. Beyond the geometrical nature of their figures, it may be said that their common feature is the universal use they make of the angular hook, which may be called a "latch-hook," and which seems to be an outgrowth of the Chinese fret. In different forms it appears in all the Daghestan fabrics, and in some of the Asia Minor and Turkoman rugs as well, but in the Daghestan proper its development is probably more complete than in any other rugs, with the possible exception of some Yomuds and the Shirvans and Soumaks, which so far as design is concerned are of the same general family. In the Daghestans this hook is used for every purpose. It is attached to almost every figure by way of finish; it serrates the borders of large geometrical shapes, and softens the contrast between two adjoining fields of color without making its hard self apparent. It is a well chosen agent to produce the delicate, harmonious effect which maintains in the Daghestans despite their subservience to the straight line.

A characteristic design in Daghestans presents, upon a field of rather light blue, a central oblong, set transversely, and flanked, at either end of the rug, by elongated octagons of old ivory, bound about with bands of red, which extend from the oblong. These three main figures are divided and sub-divided according to the Daghestan method, into multicolored geometrical shapes, the edges of all of which are trimmed with the inevitable latch-hook. Finally, the innermost figure is a diamond, filled with a lattice-work of tiny crosses, of alternate red and blue upon a field of wool white. The corners of the central field, left by the two great octagons, are taken up by triangles and stripe effects, with the hook again softening all.

Many colors serve to diversify the inner figures of the design, but they are all carefully subordinated to the tonic color. The border is made up of three main stripes, separated and bounded by a liberal number of narrower stripes in solid colors, many of them without pattern. The effect of this is to emphasize the geometrical suggestion, and yet remove the heavy, hard effect of three large stripes, one beside the other, unbroken save by the rectilinear patterns which they carry. The ground of the middle or main stripe, in the example now in mind—which, it is almost needless to say, is not the one used in the illustration—is of ivory, and that of the supporting stripes the deepest and richest of old green, of a value to balance the red of the central oblong. Upon the green is a running Greek pattern, and the main border carries in repetition, in alternate red and green, a variation of the swastika. Here it is laid in angle-wise, and is further ornamented by the addition of the latch-hook. A narrow band of light red frames the whole. Oftentimes the central ground has, in lieu of large geometrical figures, a lattice-work of diamond shapes made up of latch-hooks. Within every lozenge is a small geometrical figure, divided into harmonious colors, and with its edges further adorned with the hooks in very diminutive size. This latticed central ground is especially common in the prayer rugs. In prayer rugs of other districts—Ghiordes, for example—the field is more apt to be of plain color, unbroken save by the religious emblems at the top, bottom, and sides.

The Daghestans were probably the first of the Oriental fabrics to become popular in America. A large proportion of the rugs in use in American houses to-day, which were purchased more than twenty-five years ago, are of this variety. At that time they sold for a song, and fifteen dollars would buy a Daghestan prayer rug which cannot now be had for five times that sum. Their value is vastly enhanced by the stubbornness of the native in this part of the Caucasus. He refuses to lend himself to the making of the enormous carpets for which there is now such demand, and sticks to the small rug sizes which his forbears made for their own use. Nor will he, as a rule, consent that the character of his work shall be debauched. The result is that he cannot keep pace with the demand—a demand created solely by the ancient purity and honesty of his fabrics. Hence, the number of genuine specimens of this variety now imported is by no means in proportion to that of other rugs, and the price for the real article is commensurately high. In a lot of three or four hundred Caucasian rugs of small sizes it is not usual to find more than half a dozen thoroughly good Daghestans. Other Caucasian fabrics, resembling them in color and design, but in no wise their equals in any respect, are sold masquerading under the Daghestan name.

Genuine Daghestans are made, warp, weft and pile, of the best wool, and are tied with the Ghiordes knot. They have usually from sixteen to twenty-four threads of warp to the inch—from sixty-four to one hundred and forty-four knots to the square inch—which makes it possible to work out quite minute patterns. The warp is most often of gray wool; the ends are finished in a narrow woven selvage, outside of which the warp is thrown into a knotted fringe. The sides have a fine selvage, usually colored and made of extra threads.

Derbend.—The general features of the Daghestan are repeated, in much coarser form, in the handiwork of the Tartar and Turkoman inhabitants of the walled city of Derbend and the outlying country up and down the Caspian. This prosperous town on the sea coast is the capital of the province. It was also capital of old Albania, and in 1722 was taken by Peter the Great. The regulation rug of the Derbend variety is merely a copy of the Daghestan, but upon a heavier scale. It is of greater size, the pile is longer, the figures not so finely wrought, the colors fewer, cruder and bolder. It partakes of the character of the Kazak. Blue, white, red and yellow predominate, but the fine harmony of the Daghestan is missing. The surface has a noticeable lustre like that found in many rugs of Mosul.

The Turkoman influence has substituted in some of the Derbend rugs a goat's-hair warp for the fine wool of the Daghestans; the fringe is, therefore, darker in hue and wilder in appearance than that of the more finished product. Usually there are four rows of knots in the solid selvage at the ends, from which the fringe grows out, but not infrequently the warp and the dyed weft are woven together in a broad web after the fashion which the Turkomans learned in their wild home on the plateaus of Central Asia.

The Derbends are essentially floor rugs, and are made thicker and in larger sizes for the purpose. From an artistic standpoint they are mediocre; they are poor Daghestan and not particularly good nomad. They usually have for main design a large star or some other geometrical figure repeated three or four times transversely on a field of blue or red. The figures alternate in color, red and saffron yellow predominating if the field be blue, blue and yellow if it be red. Each is divided into other geometrical figures, in all of which the latch-hook plays an important part. The separate Kazak figures are sometimes seen. The border stripes, as in all the Caucasians, are clearly defined and their patterns pronounced.

Kabistan.—An error in a single letter—whose error or when committed it is impossible to tell—has obscured for years the origin of these admirable rugs. Kubistan would have told the story to any one who cared enough about it to study the Caucasus. The name Kabistan has become a fixture in the rug trade, and is here permitted to remain only on the ground before defined, because a substitute of the right name for the wrong would be confusing to many. In the towns of the Caucasus, the title Kabistan is unknown, save to dealers, who through executing orders for purchasers are constantly in communication with Constantinople merchants. A gentleman at whose house I visited in Batoum showed me his collection of rugs, many of them gathered twelve or fifteen years ago, when the rug-making had not become a commercial affair. Among them was a fine specimen of what we know as Kabistan. When I praised it by that name he said, "No. That's one of your American inventions. Those rugs come from Kuba, down in the southeastern part of Daghestan. They are considered about the best fabrics made in the Caucasus."

I was told later in the bazaars of Tiflis, also, that the rugs were made in the Kuba district, of which the town of Kuba is the capital. It lies on the slopes of the Baba Dagh, and almost directly over the Caucasus range northward from Shirvan.

CAUCASIAN

In point of workmanship the Kabistans equal the Daghestan proper. In texture, indeed, they are finer; in design, more diversified. In some very fine pieces the elaboration and coloring are really Persian. For hard wear under foot they are not as desirable as the Derbend. They have a wholesome plentitude of color, in the same general tone as the Daghestan, but lack in some measure the glow and brilliancy. This results from the sparing use of white to produce areas of high light, and of reds. They follow more commonly the Persian tendency to the use of dark blues in the ground, which imparts to them a sober richness. The patterns in many of these are identical with those of the Daghestans, though they have on the other hand many designs borrowed from other sources. The elongated star as a dominant figure is frequent. It is customary to find this repeated thrice, transversely of the field, in the *sedjadeh*, and a diamond shape of smaller size at each end; sometimes there are even smaller diamonds linking the main figures together. Again, and it is a standard substitute for this pattern, three large diamond figures are found, with the field space which they do not cover filled in with the ubiquitous pear pattern, diversely figured and adorned. The Kuba weavers seem to have caught a penchant for the use of this device from the Persians, once their masters and within easy reach of whom they dwell.[1] They use it in many ways; a not uncommon arrangement is to fill the entire field with it, repeated in transverse rows. Above and underneath each row runs a regular, serrate line, or rather pattern, across the body of the rug, the upward angles pointing between the pears, and the pears of the next lower row taking their places beneath the same angles. This, it will be seen, throws the pears into diagonal rows. The effect is suggestive of the pear designs in many of the fabrics of Persia, where it belongs, especially in the Saraband and Shiraz, and the alternate arrangement of the same pattern in the rugs of Khorassan.

---

[1] Even to this day a colony of fire-worshippers exists in Baku.

The stripe, for a central device as well as a border element, is popular among the makers of the Kabistans. In some cases it is clearly defined, and not merely an effect produced by the arrangement of the patterns. Sometimes the whole field of a rug is divided into perpendicular stripes of different colors. In such cases extraordinary taste and skill are displayed in maintaining harmonious tone in the entire fabric. Where, for example, the prevailing tint is a pale fawn, intensified in places to a decided brown, only two or three of all the stripes are put in red or blue for the sake of accent. Each is shaded so skilfully that sometimes the color seems almost to have vanished; then it returns to a deep value. It suggests a dyer's samples. There are sudden breakings off from pale brown into some equitable value of dull red or old rose, from which the stripe is gradually worked back to its original hue, by the most delicate shading, a trick rarely if ever employed in pure Daghestans. Each stripe carries some small decorative pattern throughout its entire length. The pear, wherever used, is more or less rectilinear, and broken in the manner peculiar to Caucasian figures. The borders in many cases have rude bird and animal shapes similar to those found in nomad rugs; and these will sometimes be found adorning the geometrical medallions thrown in upon the body of the carpet. One essentially Caucasian feature, although it is found in the Yomud weavings, on the other side of the Caspian, and in the rugs of Turkoman nomads of Laristan and Farsistan, in Persia, is the "barber pole" stripe occurring in the borders. The component diagonal stripes forming it are red and white, or blue and white, alternately, and frequently carry tiny patterns of their own. In the border stripes the Kabistans are notably rich, following generally the rectilinear Daghestan patterns.

The skill of the weavers of these rugs is conclusively shown in the close and even clipping of the pile. Only the Tekkes and Sehnas excel the Kabistans in this respect; certainly no variety of Caucasian or Turkish fabrics does, unless it be some of the particularly fine **Ghi-ordes** or **Kulah** antiques. This close trimming makes them flexible, and impairs in a measure their durability as floor coverings; but it serves to bring out with fine clearness the minutest details of the design, and adds to their beauty when employed as covers for divans or tables.

The similarity of many Kabistan rugs to the Daghestans in quality, design and color enables dealers to sell one for the other, but they may almost always be distinguished by the fact that Kabistans are overcast at the side, or if selvaged the selvage is made with the cotton weft, while the Daghestan selvage is of fine, extra, colored wool yarn; and further, that while in the Kabistans the weft and sometimes the warp is of cotton cord, like most of the Persian rugs, the Daghestan has for both warp and weft the best of wool. Herein, too, lies one element of the narrow margin of superiority of the Daghestan over its neighbor, in point of durability. Genuine rugs of either variety will wear away down to the warp and still retain their harmony of color, enhanced rather than diminished by age and service.

Very recently the Kuba weavers have taken to putting a "body finish" on the sides of their rugs. The pile is carried out to the last thread of the warp save one, and the weft, passing around this, makes a cording. The ends have the narrow cloth webbing and the warp-threads are left loose to form a fringe.

"*Tzitzi,*" *or Tchetchen.*—"Tzitzi," or "Chichi," the name given in the trade to the textiles of certain tribes and some colonies of sedentary artisans, is a corruption of Tchetchen, the tribe whose chief habitat is in the mountains north of Daghestan. The nomad tendency to individual conceit in design is apparent in many "Tzitzis." Moving from place to place, too, these rovers who make them pick up suggestions from this or that wandering company of shepherds with

whom they come in contact. These patterns, therefore, vary indef-
initely, and this very condition is made a cloak to enable unscrupulous
dealers to sell as "Tzitzi" the products of other districts. Genuine
"Tzitzi," of which the older examples are as good rugs as need be,
will be found to conform in certain points to the Caucasian notions
of ornamentation, although strangely enough a marked Persian tendency is to be noticed. The ground is frequently filled with small
patterns—rosettes, scrolls, compact geometrical tree patterns, pears,
and so forth—arranged in a manner similar to that of Kabistans and
some Kurdistans. For want of other name this may be called a grill
pattern. Usually the transverse line separating the rows in the
"Tzitzi" is straight instead of serrate, as it is in the Kabistans.

Other pieces have two or more main figures, crosses, oblongs,
stars or something of the sort, composing the central design, as in the
Daghestans, and the remainder of the ground filled in with varied
figures, disconnected and usually of the conventionalized flower
order. There is a generous allowance of border stripes, three and
sometimes four, their patterns alternating between geometrical and
floral devices. The reciprocal trefoil, to which reference is made in
connection with the rugs of Karabagh, is extremely frequent here.
The general tone of the "Tzitzis" is dark and seemly. Blue predominates as a ground color. Some few specimens are in a higher key by
reason of having pronounced border designs in bright yellow.

To acquire a correct idea of the tribes who make the "Tzitzi"
rugs discrimination must be made between nomads and nomads.
These of the Caucasus of the present day must not be confused with
the lawless Bedouins of Mesopotamia, the turbulent vagrants who
infest Kirman, or the restless Tartars who live by foray throughout
Turkestan.

The Tchetchen nomads inhabiting these northern hills move with
their flocks in quest of food and water, and the sphere of their wan-

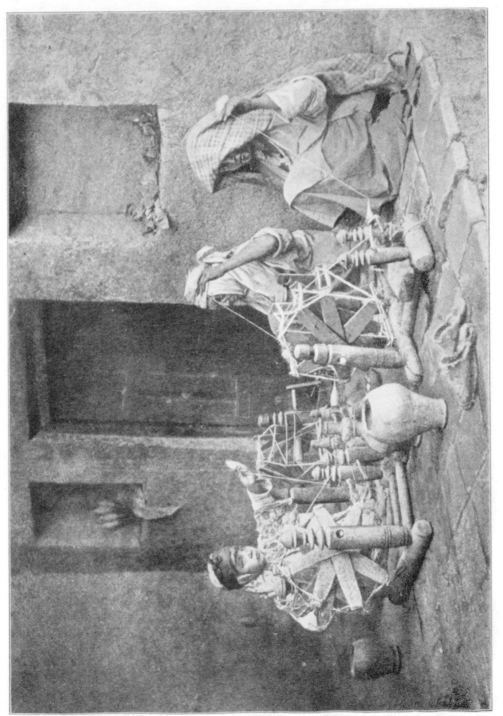

YARN WORKERS AT HOME

East Indian Factory: Stretching the Warp

derings is seldom more than a hundred square miles. **Winter finds** them in the lowlands; spring sees them starting with their sheep for the hills again. The plateau where a flock is pastured is the temporary domain of the tribe. The individual holds no land.

There have been wild wars between these shepherd tribes in the past, but the Russian government is scattering so thoroughly the seeds of civilization that it is doubtful if at the end of the next decade aught will remain here of the strange tribal life which has prevailed since the dawn of history.

Tcherkess or Circassian.—The Tcherkess rugs are few in American and European markets now, and good reason is found in the fact that the Tcherkess people, as a people, is routed, dissolved, destroyed. This sturdy, comely, and unprincipled race, whose women filled the seraglios and whose men the guards of the Turkish Sultans, and whose long, fierce struggle against Russian supremacy amazed Europe, is to-day as a race extinct. Finding it impossible to withstand the Muscovite, almost the whole people—half a million of them at least—went out in one great, wretched exodus from their native land, vanquished, heart-broken, desperate, but bound not to serve the infidels. The two hundred miles of country which they had occupied, stretching along the Caucasus and to the shores of the Black Sea, is to-day unpeopled, save for a tribe or two of mixed Circassian blood, and a handful of Russians or German immigrants huddled here and there. When in 1864–5–6 these exiles came strolling through Anatolia they were beggared, bereft of everything in the way of earthly goods and lived in predatory fashion, stealing where chance offered. They housed themselves, as do the meanest of our immigrant laborers, in huts they made of sods and clay. With part of their scant gains they bought cheap yarns and wove rugs for coverings. Little Turkish children watched with wonder the weavings of these strangers, so different from any fabrics ever seen in that part of the country before, and the Turkish mothers worried for fear the visitors should steal the toddlers, as was reported, and truthfully, to be the custom of their home-land.

In the carpets which the vagrants made there was small and rude pretence at design. Sometimes, since dyeing involved cost, they wove simply of white woollen or cotton yarn, with no sign of color and no pattern at all. Even in the most pretentious of their fabrics white areas were frequent, and the few tints used were of the most elementary kind. Rugs of the same sort filter into the Constantinople markets nowadays, and in bales of other weavings come, one or two at a time, to this country. We might know from these creations, even if history were silent on the subject, that the Circassian specialty was belligerence rather than decorative art, but in the devices themselves there is evident effort to copy, or possibly to reproduce from memory, both Caucasian and North Persian elements. Everything is positive and abrupt, an effect which is heightened by the lavish use of white.

A prayer rug of this type, which may be taken as representative, has the central field divided transversely into two parts by an attenuate form of the Mongolian cloud-band, which also, from its peculiar shape, forms the arch. Above this ground the line is black. In it, arranged in diagonal rows, are small diamond shapes. Their edges are heavily indented, which gives them a cruciform effect, and in the centre of each is a small figure of like shape, but another color. Precisely the same device is found covering the central field of Kazak *odjakliks* and elsewhere in the Caucasian and Kurdish fabrics. The colors used for it in the Tcherkess rugs are many, but all rudimentary. Whether or no these small devices are here intended for stars, shining upon the blackness of night, it is difficult to say. They give that suggestion. A like idea, but more artistically wrought out, is to be found now and then in Asia Minor prayer rugs.

At the very top of the field, and on either side of the ends of the spandrel, are heavy trees of the cypress shape, but with jagged outlines. The two lower ones are in dull red and the upper one in green. All are heavily defined in white. The middle of the foliage area is variegated by the small, parti-colored patterns. In the field, underneath, the tree principle, which in some form is found in almost all prayer rugs, is presented in the same fashion as those above. The centre tree is blue, outlined in white, and the ground-color of the field is dull red. The foliage of the tree is set off into perpendicular stripes, in which are repeated the small figures found above. Beside this, one on either side, are two smaller trees of a yellow shade, and above them two small shapes woven in red, like ladders of three rounds. The border has a heavy, flowerless, yellow vine on a ground of blue. The ends carry a well-made knot-fringe, and the sides an added selvage of cotton. The rug throughout is of wool and is excellent in point of quality. The impression it conveys is that of large feeling and inspiration, and of infinite care; but the breadth of the conception is neutralized by dearth of executive skill. The lack of manual facility and of schooling in the weaver's finer art is manifest. There is no touch of even semi-professional dexterity about it. It is the home-made product.

An *odjaklik* of the same sort, offered for sale as "Malgaran," had great triangles of black, blue, red, yellow and green upon its central field of time-stained white, so arranged as to effect the "double-end" formation. Both these and the space remaining in the field were strewn with minute patterns like those in the prayer rug, rudely woven in many colors. The inner border was a simple key pattern; the outer, or main stripe, the vine.

Among certain dealers in rugs in America the term "Malgaran" has also been used to indicate these rugs, as well as certain of the Samarkand carpets and other Central Asia products allied to them. The reason for this is plain. The Malakan or Malgaran people, another element in what Leroy-Beaulieu calls "The Babel of the Caucasus," have always been and are to-day the carriers of the region. In the early days of rug exportation from the Caucasus, when the railroad ran only as far as Tiflis, the Malakans brought the rugs there in their four-wheeled *fulgons* for shipment, and no name being then forthcoming, they went out under the distorted title of Malgarans. Their coming to the West from that section led to the belief that they were made somewhere in Central Asia, and since that time the Armenian dealers have made of "Malgaran" an omnibus name for all the odds and ends of unidentified Asiatic weaving.

TRANSCAUCASIAN FABRICS

One might suppose that, shut off from their Daghestan neighbors by so grim a barrier as the main chain of the Caucasus, the weaving peoples of the lower districts would have looked to Persia for artistic inspiration, and that their textiles would rather have followed the patterns of Kirman, Sehna or Feraghan than the severe models of the North. But it is not so; the majority of Transcaucasian rugs are more in conformity with the Daghestan theory of design than are some of the products of Daghestan itself.

They are made on the southern slope of the Caucasus and in the country included between the Kur and Aras rivers. The wool supply here leaves little to be desired, since these plateaus are famous for the quality of their sheep. The old rugs of the region generally are marked by durability and by the permanence and harmonious blending of their colors. Like the Daghestans, they were originally made with no thought that they were to be extensively sold, and were found only in small sizes. Nowadays nearly the whole output is destined for export, and rugs of all dimensions are produced. This is especially true of the Soumaks, which, under the more seductive but wholly erroneous title of "Kashmir," have attained wide popularity. They are now made as large as twelve by fifteen feet.

Karabagh.—These, in point of quantity, constitute nowadays a very considerable portion of the whole Transcaucasian output. The old carpets of Karabagh were excellent, although they never, within the memory of man, attained to the high artistic standard which has prevailed in the products of cities farther south. The finest of them were still sufficiently substantial to rank as useful rather than decorative fabrics. Competent judges declare them to have been better than the best Kazaks.

The old province of Karabagh lies to the north of the Aras river in the angle which that historic stream forms with the Kur. As an ancient dependency of Persia it acquired the Iranian mastery of color, and in the old pieces there is as fine a display of the dyer's skill as in any carpet of Kirman. The floral elements entered in, too, but most of the forms were stiff and conventional and the distribution was in the manner peculiar to the Caucasus. The rug weavers of Karabagh are divided, like those of other provinces, into two classes— the Ilats or nomads and the Takhta-Kapon (wooden door), which signifies the villagers, or people who dwell in houses. Both are Shiah Mohammedans. There are many Russian Armenians, too, in the towns. The nomad weavings have here, as elsewhere, stood out longest against the tendencies of the time, and some of them, even now, are good imitations of old-time rugs.

Since the province passed out from under Persian control, the carpets have borrowed more and more from the patterns of the North. It is to the North, now, that the people turn as the source of power, authority, learning, wealth, everything. Some of the later rugs are good copies of the Daghestans in point of design, and even of color arrangement. But as textiles they have neither the quality nor the finish of the genuine Daghestan. They have the Daghestan brightness, and more, but their comparative coarseness, and, it may be, the inferor skill of the dyers, has deprived them of all that might be termed fine effects. Where the Daghestan is brilliant, the modern Karabagh is loud, in white, blue, red and yellow. This is caused chiefly by startling masses of white, either in the grounds of the border or in the central field.

The production of Karabaghs, which can be transported from the looms to the Russian railway in two or three days, has of late been pushed forward without stint. The range of designs is almost limitless. Anything will serve. In some of them the field is mapped off into hard squares, like those of the well-known Bokhara pattern. In others there is no pretense at body pattern at all, merely the border stripes surrounding a field of solid color. Western carpets and Wilton rugs are also copied. In yet others, set devices of uncertain origin, but strangely resembling the spatter patterns seen in modern China silks, are repeated in several alternating colors, and, with little other attempt at design, make up the entire filling of the rug. The effect is blotchy, inconsistent, and anything but pleasing, especially where, as is often the case, an effort is made to retain in the borders the pure Daghestan character.

The Muscovite influence is perceptible lately, in more or less successful attempts at genre figures, such, for example, as a full-length representation of a Russian official, in gray uniform, and with a red and white bandanna protruding with most un-Oriental suggestion from the skirt pocket of his coat. This simulacrum of authority is pictured upon a black field, and set off with nondescript figures in several colors. The borders have no stripe arrangement, but consist of actual flowers, grouped about the centre-piece in a manner purely rococo.

In the borders of some of the original Karabaghs is discovered the reciprocal trefoil, as it is called by European experts, who declare it to be an essential mark of the so-called "Polish" carpets and other famous fabrics believed to be related to them.[1] This device will be noticed later in modified form in many Mosul and Persian as well as Turkoman and Beluchistan fabrics.

A point of wide difference between the Daghestan and Karabagh fabrics is the fringe. In the latter-day rugs, instead of taking the trouble to elaborate the fringe, the weaver simply withdraws the rod which holds the warp, and the looped ends are left uncut, to do duty on one end as fringe; on the other the warp and weft are woven into a web just wide enough to be turned back and sewed. The warp is white or brown wool; the weft is sometimes colored throughout. The sides in the old pieces are usually finished with a narrow selvage; in the moderns they are apt to be overcast, which saves time and labor. In the poorer grades of moderns heavy yarn is used to make up for the wretchedly coarse weaving, and dyes and workmanship are unmistakably bad. Yet these horrors are put forward for sale as "antique Daghestans."

"Soumak" or "Kashmir."—It is the shaggy ends of the colored nap-yarns, left loose at the back of these rugs, which has given them the name of "Kashmir." The dealers foster the title for the monetary value of the suggestion it embodies, and in some quarters a belief prevails that the rugs are really the product of that vale

---

[1] " The intercourse between the East and the Venetian and other Italian States in the Middle Ages infused an Oriental spirit into European work after the sixteenth century. About that time a Pole named Mersherski visited Persia and India, and on his return to Warsaw brought with him native workmen, with whom he established a manufactory of Oriental fabrics in that city. He had procured kincobs and other stuffs in India and carpets in Persia, which he used as models. In the kincobs gold and silver threads were woven with silk and cotton, and many imitations of these are still in existence. But whether he found rugs in the East with this mixture is uncertain. Of the carpets made by him, having gold and silver interwoven with silk, very few remain to our day. . . The Polish handicraftsmen seemed at first to have only copied originals, but gradually they worked details into their designs which, though tinged with Eastern ideas, are a departure from the old models, and if carefully examined these productions present a singular mixture of the old Persian character with quite a new element. . . . It is as if the Mongolians who invaded Poland in 1241 had left traces of their art, which remain as a permanent influence."—*Robinson: " Eastern Carpets."*

in northern India, whose shawls, until their manufacture was debauched and ultimately destroyed by European traders, were accounted the most perfect textiles in the world.

The true name of the so-called "Kashmir" rugs is Soumaki, derived from the old Khanate of Soumaki, lying to the west of Shirvan. This part of the Caucasus underwent rigorous political changes after the cession of its territory to Russia in 1813, and, probably for facility of administration, Soumaki as a distinct province was eliminated. The struggle of Russia to conquer the belligerent tribes of the Caucasus was a long and severe one, and reduction of the number of provincial rulers was the most effective means to the avoidance of future trouble. It is best to continue to call them by their recognized name.

The patterns of the Soumaks are mainly the geometrical forms found in all Daghestan fabrics, and for a very good reason, since the district where they are made is in the range of the mountains, and with only the ridge at its back separating it from Daghestan.

There is no difficulty in discerning the likeness between the Shirvan and Soumak rugs. In many old examples the designs and colors are practically identical; the difference, as has been stated, is in the texture. Both resemble the Daghestan in device and color distribution, though the treatment is different. By far the greater number of Soumaks carry medallions of octagon shape but somewhat elongated, transversely of the rug.

The Soumaks are woven with a flat stitch, which with the loose yarns at the back of the rug, constitutes the only ground for the fictitious title of "Kashmir." These peculiarities identify them beyond all doubt, for no other rugs resemble them in this respect.

They formerly came only in small or medium sizes, and the oldest specimens are fine, carefully woven, fast dyed, and beautiful rugs. The demand for large pieces has been met with fabrics made on the same plan, but with coarse, grayish-brown warp in place of the white wool, and with a heavy, common quality of surface yarn, loosely woven to save labor. The dyes in many of these "bargain-counter" pieces are distressingly bad, and the evil is growing as time goes on. The designs are also deteriorating. Some consolation is to be had, however, from the fact that even now something like ten or even fifteen per cent. of the Soumaks which find their way to the American market are made in close keeping with the old requirements.

The stitch may be called an over-and-over method. Sometimes each turn of the surface yarn in which the pattern is produced takes in two threads of the warp, sometimes three. The stitches lie slant-wise of the fabric, and each row reverses the direction of that employed in the preceding row, so that the grain of the surface resembles an ordinary herring-bone weave. The weft is in most cases carried across and back after every two rows of stitches. In the old carpets it was carried one way after a single row was finished, and back after the next row, making a fine, closely compacted body. In such there were ten or twelve rows of stitches to the inch perpendicular, not, of course, counting the weft threads. In the moderns, eight stitches to the inch is the average of a good grade. The coarse qualities have as low as six, the yarn being very large and heavy, and the weft is thrown across one way after every three rows.

Shirvan.—So far as numbers go, the rugs sold as Shirvans are well nigh as important a part of the Caucasian output as are the Karabaghs. In texture the average modern Shirvan is rather better than the Karabagh, but deterioration, particularly in the matter of dyes, is apparent in many of the grades.

The earlier Shirvans are not plentiful in the markets now. They are well made, and have all the old richness and stability of color. A feature of many of them is the dissonance between border and central field, in color and design. In the borders, for instance, some of them carry one broad stripe, sustained by narrow guard-stripes, and displaying in brilliant red upon a white ground, and with no trace of other colors, a combination design of the arabesque order, reinforced with conventionalized flower patterns suggesting the Ladiks, or more remotely, the Ghiordes, although more definite than either of these. All the border area presents this arrangement of red and white. In the body of the rug the ground-color is apt to be a rich and lustrous blue, almost of the peacock tinge, upon which is laid, in yellow, with the addition of some red, the diagonal lattice-work common in Daghestans; but here it is drawn in the softer, more irregular fashion of the Mosuls. Others of these antiques have the selfsame fine geometrical designs shown in the Soumaks, but knotted, of course, instead of worked in the pileless stitch. The borders sometimes depart from the Caucasian forms and, as in some old Karabaghs, show separate realistic flower devices at regular intervals. These flowers are frequently in the profile drawing, declared by some experts to be an Asia Minor characteristic, and are devoid of all the rectilinear Caucasian character.

The modern Shirvans are a multitude, and serve well the purposes of ordinary use. Their designs have not undergone the degeneration of the Karabaghs, but for the most part follow quite steadfastly the old models. The better qualities, especially those which show traces of Persian influence, are often marketed for the Tartar type of Shiraz rugs made in the Persian provinces of Fars and Lar. To forestall this substitution is sometimes difficult. The materials of the foundation offer small aid. For both warp and weft of the best Shiraz fabrics of the sort mentioned white wool is used, but in the coarse moderns black wool or even goat's-hair may be found; in the same fashion the antique Shirvans have wool foundation throughout, while the modern warp is of coarse brown or white wool, or a mixed yarn of two strands, one brown and the other white. The weft, if not

PLATE IV.   For description, see p. xxiii.

PLATE V.   LESGHIAN STRIP OF THE CAUCASUS

11.2 X 3.11

Loaned by Mr. F. B. Proctor

A considerable number of rugs proceed from the middle section of the Caucasus, in which yellow and blue prevail almost as largely as they do in the sedjadeh and prayer carpets of Kulah.   They are marketed chiefly in Tiflis and Elizabetpol, and are attributed to the Lesghian tribes, scattered all along the foot-hills of the range.   They show less of conformity to the strict letter of Caucasian design than those of the sections farther East, but like the rug here reproduced, seem to pursue in part a symbolism of their own, and in minor ornamentation lean toward the Persian teaching.   They are bright, wholesome and serviceable and in certain surroundings most desirable in point of color.

PLATE VI.   KAZAK SEDJADEH

7.2 x 5.11

Loaned by Mr. Lewis S. Bigelow

The bold character of the Kazak nomads, to which some reference has been made in the text, is quite plainly expressed in this heavy fabric.   The massing of color is infinitely strong, and it is fearless as well—witness the heavy triangular spaces of green and blue thrust against one another in the border.   How rude these people are may be seen by comparing this version of the wine-glass border with that found in the black and white reproduction of the Shirvan rug (Plate VII).

The octagons in the field, with their rough adornment of stars, as well as the larger medallion and the tarantula affair in the centre, are all recognized marks of Turkestan, whence these people long ago took their origin.   For indication of their artistic skill, as compared with that of the rovers of their parent plains, contrast the drawing of all these figures in the central part of the rug with that found in the Tekke carpet exhibited under the title Yomud (Plate XXIII), and in the small Tekke prayer rug (Plate XXI).

The nomad tendency to scatter small bits of color through a space otherwise unoccupied may be seen in its freest indulgence here.   But when considered as a savage display of strong color, perhaps no carpet in the collection excels this.   The shading of the blues and greens, a trick which these half-barbarians seem to have caught from the Kurds with whom they are in constant contact, should be noted.   The wool from which the rug is made is of the finest and its lustre is admirable.

PLATE VII. BERGAMO RUG

5.4 X 4.7

Loaned by Mr. Robert L. Stevens

This rug, one of the few specimens of the antique Bergamo, represents Asia Minor design at its best. The leaf and flower forms are unmistakable, but have been conventionalized in the manner referred to in the chapter on Design. In only two respects, so far as one is able to discover, is the Persian influence at all perceptible. There is something of Persian realism in the flowers which are stuck about the small medallions at either end of the field, in fact this same effect, so common in Asia Minor prayer rugs, is found in many fine Persian fabrics of centuries ago. The nomad element remains in the small separate flowers in the field, and suggestion of a latch-hook is had in the jagged edges of the long branches which extend from the central medallion. The rug is glorious in color, and its combination of red, blue, yellow and pink belongs to an age that is bygone in the textile art of Anatolia.

of wool, is of cotton, and four threads are sometimes put in after each row of knots, as in the genuine Kazaks and Samarkands. The most reliable way of distinguishing them is by the peculiar checked or patterned particolored selvage at the ends, referred to in the description of the Shiraz rugs. In nine out of ten of the Shiraz fabrics it will be found in some form, in the Shirvans seldom if ever. The ends of Shirvans have the cloth web woven of the warp and weft threads, extending an inch or more beyond the pile, in addition to which many have a fringe made by knotting the gathered strands of the warp after the manner of ordinary machine-made fringe. In many moderns the warp ends are simply left loose for a finishing, to save time. In some of them the sides, instead of being overcast or selvaged, have the body finish.

Very coarse Karabagh and Shirvan designs of all sorts, shipped from the neighborhood of Shemakha, ancient capital of the Khanate of Shirvan, have come to be known among Caucasian traders as Shemakinski—and the term is a synonym for bad weaving, as Kaba-Karaman is in Anatolia.

Kazak.—There is a tribe of nomad Kazaks inhabiting the hills about Nova Bayezid and Lake Goktcha in Erivan. They are an old offshoot of the great hordes whose home is in the Kirghiz steppes and whose kinsmen are scattered over the southern districts of Russia away to the banks of the Don. "Kazak" means virtually a rough-rider. It describes the whole race of these restless, roaming, troublesome people, who, in a sense, are born, live, and die in the saddle. It is the original of the name Cossack, which is familiar to all the world.

The Kazaks of the Kirghiz steppes weave rugs, but, it is conceded, chiefly for home use. Nearly all the Kazak fabrics which come to market are made—or were originally made—in the district of Transcaucasia just mentioned. This Kazak colony, which invaded the neighborhood while yet Transcaucasia was reckoned in the Persian domain, is Sunni Mohammedan in faith. For a long time its rugs were made after the models of the North, but of late have begun to show more likeness to the Karabagh type made throughout the surrounding country. This is chiefly the work, not of the Kazaks, but of Armenians, who inhabit the villages in the district, and who, having learned the weaving trade from the shepherds, proceeded to develop a type for themselves, better suited, they thought, to the requirements of the market. It leaned toward the Karabaghs. From Nova Bayezid, where most of the rugs are exchanged for other commodities, the Armenian storekeepers make large shipments from time to time. About seventy-five per cent. of these are of the old-fashioned Kazak order. The remainder are degenerate Kazaks or out and out Karabaghs.

Antique Kazak fabrics of the best sort are few now. Occasionally an old, patched, threadbare specimen comes to light to rebuke the latter-day products which bear the name. Bad dyes have made a mockery of many of the moderns. Great stains of some unstable color, usually magenta, soaked over perhaps one-third of the fabric, tell the sad story of their deterioration. Many a dealer has had these loose-dyed rugs left upon his hands.

The older ones have a remarkable softness. They are thick and heavy; the tufts or knots of the pile are longer than those of almost any old Oriental rug. The peculiar feature is that four threads of the weft are thrown across after every row of knots, as in the Samarkands. In this way the tufts forming the pile are made to overlap each other smoothly instead of standing nearly upright, as do those of most other fabrics. The only saving accomplished by thus burdening the rug with weft-threads is that of time.

The original designs are strong and characteristic to a degree— big, geometrical figures, upon fields of magnificent red or green, which half a century of wear and exposure will scarcely suffice to dim. Throughout the field are distributed detached figures—crosses, particolored diamonds, squares and circles and disproportioned representations of birds, trees, animals and human beings, all in the most archaic drawing and most primitive color. In the borders are many variations of the latch-hook feature, and a reciprocal saw-tooth pattern distinctive of some Caucasian fabrics. This same border often appears in the Persian Sarabands. Persian weavers call it the *sechandisih*—"teeth of the rat."

The Kazaks are usually finished with a stout selvage at the sides, and at the ends with a shaggy fringe, which may be omitted from one end to allow the web formed from warp and weft to be turned back and hemmed. The most common sizes are from three to six feet wide by five to eight feet long.

The whole effect, whether the rug be of great or small dimensions, is stoutness. Many of the older ones are almost square, one measurement exceeding the other sometimes by only three or four inches. Occasionally an example is found with one end finished in a knotted rope's-end fringe resembling that mentioned as belonging to the coarser rugs of the Mosul province in Turkey.

In the later products there is a tendency to imitate some of the more ornamental patterns of the Kabistans. The stripe arrangement of the field, and lumbering versions of the pear pattern are seen, but in nearly all cases there is preserved one figure thoroughly typical of the old Kazaks, a conventional form which will be recognized at once from its likeness to the tarantula, of which it is probably an actual representation, but having become a standard element in the decoration of this region, it has taken on complications and formal ornamentation which in a measure obscure the resemblance. [1] In some of the

---

[1] "On voit sous la lettre 'B' un tapis Boukhare, qui se distingue par l'éclat des couleurs et par un remarquable mélange de dessins rappelant des scorpions, des tarentules, les constants compagnons de voyage des traditions populaires. Pas de conte ou l'on ne voie jouer un rôle à la tarentule Karacoute, qui est considéré comme particulièrement venimeuse."—*N. Simakoff: "L'Art de l'Asie Centrale."*

"Boukhare" is used by Simakoff to designate the whole of Turkestan. The carpets which he here calls "tapis Boukhare" were the Yomuds. The manner in which they come to have many of the border patterns common to the Caucasians is made clear in the section on Yomud, under the general class of Turkoman fabrics.

better modern pieces this idea has been developed in the most artistic manner, two of these figures appearing in great size in the central field, upon a ground of splendid red. The borders have the heavy patterns typical of Kazaks.

MOSUL FABRICS

The diversity resultant upon mixed population is nowhere so manifest as in the rugs collected in the country about Mosul, the old city in the heart of Mesopotamia. This territory is traversed by the river Tigris. Since the beginning of history the tide of conquest has ebbed and flowed mightily here where now half ruined walls inclose a straggling and moribund town, and serve in seasons of flood to avert the encroachments of the river. A little way outside the gates of Mosul are the ruins of Nineveh, Senn and Nimrud.

Here Persians followed Scythians as conquerors, and were themselves succeeded in turn by Macedonians, Tartars, Arabs and Turkomans. Under every sway Mosul was a capital. That it has been a centre of manufacture finds proof in the one word muslin, which had its derivation here. In the population of the district are represented far more than half of all the races which go to make up the Ottoman Empire of to-day. In the city and its adjacent villages are gathered many distinct nationalities, all living in perpetual dread of the wild Kurdish and Bedouin neighbors who infest the unguarded highways or roam over the surrounding mountains, preying upon commerce and travel, and disclaiming both subjection to Osmanli and faith in Islam. The Mosul fabrics include also rugs made in the mountains of old Armenia and Erivan, and others from the south toward Syria.

The multitude of designs common to this strangely peopled region presents not only all the characteristic forms of the Caucasian class, but well nigh every device which Oriental ornamentation knows, though most of them are wrought roughly. Every corner of the East, even as far as China, has contributed some trick of texture or design to the varied fabrics of Mosul, yet most of them show affinity with the Caucasian lot. The fact that so many of the Mosul tribes are out of the reach of trade influences speaks well for the honesty of their product, and examination, in the main, bears out the inference. Wool, dyes and workmanship are well up to the average, considering always the weavers' lights, and the designs, diverse as they are, still preserve a thoroughly Eastern character. Nearly all the rugs included in the Mosul shipments are, however, more or less coarse, heavy, and suggestive in their patterns and construction of the rude life which prevails in the entire region.

Mosul Proper.—The two characteristics which, taken in conjunction, provide the first step toward identification of these fabrics are: First, the soft, flocky nature of the pile; second, a marked tendency to the use of yellow and warm, yellowish or brownish reds in the coloring. A great deal of camel's-hair and goat's-hair *filik* is used in the pile. The camel's-hair in natural color contributes a yellow tone, but aside from that, saffron seems to have taken a firm hold upon the favor of the dyers in Mosul. In the antiques, which have a glossy finish, this prevalence of yellow gives an impression, when the rugs are seen from a distance, that they have undergone some process of gilding. Blue and green are chiefly used in small areas, to brighten the figures in the border stripes; if in large areas, they are almost invariably in dark shades. In all the multiplicity of designs, the Caucasian influence is plainly visible. Some feature of it can be found in almost every rug, although the patterns are loosely wrought and, owing in a measure to the length of pile, fine definition is impossible. For example, the parallel bars—horizontal or diagonal—inclosing rows of small figures, found in the body of the Kabistans and Tzitzis, are frequent in the Mosuls, but the small patterns are usually queer reciprocal key devices, or geometrical tree forms, although sometimes the pear is found. The diagonal lattice-work of the Daghestan group has its place in the Mosuls, too. Thanks to Persian influence, the Mosul weavers are prone to do with color shading what those of Daghestan do with the oft-repeated latch-hook, in softening the contrast between one body of color and another. The latch-hook in great measure disappears in the Mosuls, although it is found in some rugs of the Turkish class farther to the westward, made by nomads who have trod this path in their migrations. The barber-pole stripe, first noticed in the Kabistans, is very common here, and the large geometrical figures used as the central design of so many Daghestans and Kabistans are often found performing the same function in Mosuls. The Persian and Kurdish influences are also apparent. The pear device is especially frequent, but in hard forms, so rectilinear in some instances that at first glance it is scarcely recognized. It is a hexagon, with a particolored square in the centre, and the elongation merely a projecting angular hook in yellow or red. The same form is found in the decorative art of India. The reciprocal trefoil border stripe, in dark red and blue as a rule, runs through a great number of Mosuls. There is found, too, the star emblem seen the world over in the decoration of synagogues, possibly an adaptation of the seal of Solomon or a copy of the Persian symbol, but held by some writers to have been originally representative of divinity.

The borders are most often three in number, and separated by heavy lines of very dark brown or blue. Geometrical or crude floral designs are used, but almost invariably one at least of the border stripes carries some well-known Caucasian pattern. Very often a three- or four-inch outside band of camel's-hair or some other yarn in the natural brown color runs around all four sides of the rug, inclosing the whole design as in a frame, and emphasizing the yellow tone which, as was said in the beginning, is a Mosul mark. The sides of the

PLATE VIII. KULAH PRAYER RUG

6.0 x 4.0

Loaned by Dr. O. Ernest Hill

While of the coarser quality of old style Kulahs, this rug contains the features which seem to have been essentially of Kulah origin, though they appear oftentimes in the Ghiordes and Ladik prayer rugs. The multiplication of peculiarly marked small stripes to cover the border tract and the serrated drawing of the prayer arch are chief among the Kulah marks. Wear and repeated washing have dimmed the areas of golden brown which in so many old rugs of this variety is the predominant color.

rug are overcast and the ends finished with a narrow, thick selvage if the warp be cotton, with a fringe if it be wool.

Turkman or Genghis.—In the sandhills along the border lines between Mosul province and Persia, roam bands of Turkomans. They are otherwise known to the Ottoman population as the "Genghis people," after Genghis Khan, in whose warlike train their forbears came westward from Central Asia. They dwell in tents and change their abode with the seasons. They are part of the mixed Turkish peoples who are scattered all through the country west of the Oxus. The title of Turkman was given by the Persians in whose service they fought during the interminable wars of the Middle Ages. It implies "a resemblance to Turks," these tribes having, from their long residence in the Iranian country, lost many of their race characteristics, both of temperament and physical appearance. They retain, however, their bold, warlike disposition and fondness for outdoor life.

In the rugs which they send to the annual fair near Mosul and to the bazaars in Tiflis, their race traits and their manner of living are plainly to be read. The fabrics are exceedingly heavy, which is natural since they are made to be spread upon the ground out of doors. The warp is a three-strand thread of goat's-hair or brown wool, and the pile about twice as long as that of the Shirvans. There are seldom fewer than forty knots to the square inch, and they are woven from fine wool which the women of the tribes spin.

The designs consist principally of the geometrical devices found in the Caucasian fabrics, but the nomad elements of crudity and simplicity and a prevalence of small, separate figures are discernible. The Persian influence sometimes crops out in the use of the vine with flowers attached. The Turkman, whose nomad impatience and poverty of artistic conception make it impossible for him to reproduce the complex designs of Persian carpets, has by crude repetition of the easier border elements made a central design of his own. He often has a series of these border patterns running side by side through the whole length of the body of the rug. The undulation, which in most Persian designs is gracefully curved, he treats in the less difficult rectilinear fashion, and his versions of the palmettes and lotus buds which the vine carries at its curved intervals are severe in drawing and immensely unlike what they are meant for. The whole effect is ambitious, and pleasing, too, perhaps because it is so badly done. He repeats the same idea in the border, using for adornment of the vine, for example, a white cross, evidently of floral derivation, upon a red octagon, instead of the more difficult rosette which belongs to the pattern in its purity. The pear is freely employed, both in the body, where it is used in alternating rows of red and blue, and in the border stripe, where it relieves other figures. Nomad authorship is shown by the detached bird and animal figures in the body of the rugs and occasionally in the border. The sides are selvaged and the ends finished with a small fringe. In this respect the Turkman follows the urbane rather than the nomad custom.

In Constantinople, as in the American market, miscellaneous bales of rugs, all measuring between three and five feet in width, and six and eight feet in length, are jobbed under the name of Genghis, or, as the bills of lading have it, "Guendje." They are made up of the odds and ends of the Shirvans, Karabaghs, Mosuls and other secondary fabrics of the Caucasian class, and usually come from Elizabetpol, the old Armeno-Persian name of which was Gandja. Of late a great manufacture of this sort of stuff has been organized by Armenian middlemen in the Baghdad district, the output of which is being marketed in this country. In addition to the rugs named some Persians, Hamadans and the like, are taken for patterns, and several low-grade mats woven on each warp.

Some Varieties of Kurdish Rugs.—More striking contrast could scarcely be imagined than that between the rough, common, mis-shapen rugs made by the Kurds in the north of Mosul and about Lake Van, and the masterly ones turned out by their kinsmen in the upland towns of Western Persia. These "Mosul Kurdish" rugs are of the same general character as the Genghis just described. In ornament the Genghis are accounted somewhat better, but the Kurdish fabrics are more closely woven, heavier, and more durable. They have, to be sure, fewer stitches to the inch, but the pile yarn—and also, indeed, the warp and weft—are much heavier. The rugs are rough and to the last degree savage in appearance. In the con-glomeration of colors a certain rude strength is manifest, but although the general effect is warm and lustrous the absence of any-thing like decorative refinement is complete. In many of them a great deal of dark brown wool in its natural state determines the color tones. Brown sheep's-wool or coarse goat's-hair thread is taken for the foundation. The sides are overcast or selvaged at the caprice or convenience of the weaver. The ends have usually the nomadic web extension, and the braids with which they are finished complete their barbaric extravagance. The ends of the warp are plaited into tight, flat strands, like the Mexican lariat, about two inches apart and knotted at the ends. In some examples several of these are worked together, and form small, compact, triangular plaited mats, from the outer point of which the braids depend. These rugs are utterly lacking in symmetry, and sometimes are so crooked that they have to be cut and sewn together again to bring them into any-thing like regular shape.

Similar to these Mosul Kurd fabrics in texture and quality are those sometimes sold under the name of Kozan, an Asia Minor vilayet to the west of Mosul. They are finished with selvage on the sides and a long fringe at the ends instead of the plaits referred to above.

X

TURKISH

THE substitute term for Turkish in the vocabulary of the rug-seller is Smyrna, or was so until the American manufactures began to bear that name. But in any event it is in essence a misnomer, since in Smyrna no rugs are made for market, nor have been, within the memory of man. Smyrna is essentially a mercantile capital. Next to Constantinople, it is the chief point of export for Oriental rugs and the products of all districts have thus come to bear its name in vulgar usage, although no fabrics are sold in the whole-sale market in Smyrna save those made in Asia Minor.

The Turkish class, though commercially very large, is small in the number of its varieties. A line drawn from Trebizond, on the Black Sea, southwesterly to the head of the Gulf of Iskanderum, in the Mediterranean, would cut off the Anatolian peninsula from the Asiatic mainland. It would have to the west of it all the territory whose rugs may properly be called Turkish. Those which alone have shadow of right to the name Smyrna are a component group of the Turkish class. They are made chiefly in the towns of the two western provinces, Aidin and Broussa, which are directly accessible from Smyrna by rail, or in their remoter quarters by caravan, and which find in that city their most convenient and, in fact, inevitable point of sale and shipment. This proximity to a commercial centre and close communication through it with the Western world has given to the rug industry of these provinces a double character not found in any other section of the Orient; has in fact in some degree robbed it of its distinctively Eastern quality, so that although many of the old-time Turkish rugs were of remarkable workmanship, fully ninety per cent. of the fabrics made there to-day are representative of nothing save the passion of the West for this form of floor covering, the aptitude of Western designers at devising new combinations of Oriental figures and of color, and the amazing, possibly unsuspected ability of the Turkish weavers to do under pressure a great amount of work in a short time.

The peninsula, so far as its rugs are concerned, is merely a workshop, and Smyrna is its counting room.[1] The great burden of the output in the Western district is, as I have said, made upon orders from outside markets. Some of these are general; some are specific; but altogether they have sufficed to wean the workman from old materials and old methods. He aims now at volume rather than excellence. Large business sagacity, to be sure, has been shown in the selection of this particular region for the enterprise. It presents facilities for shipment, and it not only produces readily and plentifully all the materials used in the construction of rugs, but numbers among its population a representation from almost every Eastern race. There is no form of weaving which may be needed in filling a busi-

---

[1] The system of dealing in the Smyrna and Constantinople markets is infinitely complex, made so, doubtless, by the Turkish dealers as a means for gaining an advantage in intricate transaction with Western buyers. Out of the accumulation of facts bearing upon this matter these will be of general interest: In wholesale dealings in Smyrna the big carpets made throughout Asia Minor are sold by the square " pick "—five square feet—while the Bergamo, Meles, and other small rugs are disposed of by the piece. Payment is made in the *medjit*—twenty Turkish piastres. In Constantinople the modern Persians, Sultanabad, Tabriz, Herez, Feraghan and the like, are sold at so many francs per square metre, and the antiques at so many Turkish pounds apiece. The Caucasian and Tartarian, excepting perhaps some of the large Bokharas and Afghanistan nomad rugs recently sent to market, are disposed of at so many francs apiece and never by the square foot.

ness order, but in this hodgepodge of peoples men and women conversant with it can be found, and the conditions of the country make it certain that their work may be had at a price which warrants a goodly margin of profit to every person through whose hands the fabric may pass before it reaches the user. In Afion-Karahissar, for example, Armenian women weave for from four to seven cents a day.

The singular conditions prevalent here present a difficult dilemma to the writer. Each weaving town has in effect two classes of fabrics. To prosecute faithfully the purpose of this book description should be given, to the end of identification, of the typical antique rugs for which some of the districts have been renowned. They have a distinctive character which the new products have not.[1] The modern fabrics made in certain towns of Asia Minor bear no relation to the antiques made in the same places, so far as likeness is concerned. These towns have in the modern fabrics almost no distinctive types at all. They produce loose, heavy rugs of conglomerate design, which recall nothing so much as young Falconbridge, who "bought his doublet in Italy, his round-hose in France, his bonnet in Germany, and his behavior everywhere."

Less, then, to emphasize this difference than to avoid inadequacy, it is necessary to make clear something of the character of each of the older carpets, specimens of which are occasionally encountered, before speaking of the coarser latter-day fabrics which are rushed out from the looms of the same towns to meet the demands of trade, and which, no matter how much their existence may discomfort the amateur, are proving themselves of vast worth and service to the house-

---

[1] All authorities upon ornament set forth that there is no original and distinctive Turkish system of ornamentation: that the custom of the Turks, as conquerors, was to command the services of artisans; that the Turkish type, so far as it may be said to exist, is a combination of Persian and Arabic. Leroy Beaulieu remarks that the Turks show in everything an imitation of the Persian genius, and it is matter of history that the Osmanli Turks, after each successful incursion upon Persian territory, sent captives of the artisan class to Constantinople to weave, carve and carry on other art industries for the beautification of Turkish palaces.

holder who has a floor to cover and a careless, hard-heeled company to tread it.

KONIEH FABRICS

Konieh province and the districts which surround it exemplify perfectly the diversity in topography, climate and population which mark the whole Anatolian peninsula. The plateaus of this section afford all the conditions required for wool growing; the valleys which traverse it are fertile in the production of dye materials.

The general methods of construction are similar throughout the entire group, but the difference between the varieties, in quality and appearance, is clear. Those which come from the north, about Kir-Shehr and the vicinity of the salt lake Tcholli, and as far as ancient Cæsarea,[1] are of sterling texture and good color and design, while the products of the south, of Nigdeh and Karaman, among the foothills of the Taurus mountains, are rough, and made in evident ignorance of any known decorative system. The designs of these are crude, and the colors, while largely vegetable, and striking in the mass, are arranged in utter disregard of theoretical harmony.

Konieh Proper.—Konieh—ancient Iconium—the name has its origin in the Greek word ἰκών (picture), on account of the legend of the locality—has never until very lately ranked with other towns of Asia Minor as a rug-producing place. Even under the old dispensation, its weavings had not the wide fame and favor accorded to those of Ghiordes, Kulah, Bergamo, or Ladik. They were made more strictly for local use than perhaps any of these. For this reason, probably, the antique specimens from the Konieh looms are more rarely met with nowadays. They are, nevertheless, of eminent merit, and though pursuing a different theory of color from the rugs of "Smyrna" towns, exhibit skill in the dyeing and a wholesome though sometimes not over-delicate taste in the adjustment of color.

[1] Kaisarieh.

Most of the antique Koniehs which have found their way over-seas are *sedjadeh*, *odjaklik*, and *yesteklik*—not, as is the case with those of the other cities named, for the greater part prayer rugs. The antique *odjaklik*, or hearth rug, of Konieh abounds in warm rich color. It is worthy of notice, too, that all the hues have a peculiar luminous quality when exposed to a slanting light such as falls upon them from the fire-place, a glow that they do not reveal when looked at point blank, in the light of common day. They are constructed with this effect in view. One excellent example had at the time of writing lain for several months in a pile of small antiques of different varieties, in a large New York rug establishment. Piece after piece had been sold from the pile, and it had frequently been replenished from new consignments, but the old Konieh, in every way one of the rarest and most desirable possessions of the lot, had always been relegated, after examination, to its old place and the more showy fabrics chosen. It was not, as a fact, of an appearance to catch at first glance the fancy of the average purchaser, yet at the time the author of this book saw it there was the best of reasons for believing that it was the only rug of its sort to be seen for sale in New York.

The feature of the *odjaklik* design, found in the majority of rugs made for the hearth, is that it has in some fashion or other the conical or pointed formation at both ends of the central field. It is as if the field were made up of two prayer rugs, joined base to base. In the piece just referred to an elongated hexagon was set in the central oblong, with its acute angles pointing toward the ends. The ground-color of the field was a singular, lustrous quality of sky blue. Just inside the border stripes and running all about the edges of the field, was a row of pinks, drawn in profile and arranged with perfect regularity. In each of the corner spaces left by the hexagon was a floral figure of some magnitude, supported by an elongated device, apparently of animal derivation, on either side, and by rectilinear flower stalks. The sides of the hexagon forming the two angles at the ends were serrated like the sides of the arch in most Kulah prayer rugs. Inside the yellow and red defining-lines of the hexagon ran a complete circumference of rosebuds arranged in the same manner as the pinks about the boundary of the oblong. These flowers were as realistic and lifelike as any found in Persian weaving. Then the entire area of the hexagon was filled with a rich growth of flowers, made up of two flowering shrubs or plants, springing from two jardinières, one at each of the terminal angles. The branches and blooms met and mingled at the middle of the space in a fashion which, though governed by the Anatolian formality of arrangement, had yet much of Persian warmth and profusion. The ground of the main border stripe was blue, of a very deep shade, in contrast with the brilliant sky blue of the centre. Upon it the waving vine was traced in red, in angles instead of curves, and with its flowers, yellow and pale blue, putting forth upon straight stalks. The narrow borders, or guard stripes, were the small, uniform, repeated stripes found in Ghiordes and Kulah, except that they were in red and white instead of black and white, and were ornamented with the barber pole device of the Caucasians, instead of the small patterns which adorn those characteristic stripes in antique Ghiordes and Kulah rugs. All around the outside was a narrow band of the pile, in the same deep red which was dominant throughout the entire fabric. Its brilliancy had seemingly been softened by age, but it still glowed with a strange sort of under light.

The ends were finished with a narrow, colored web, and reaching partly across one end—the rest had been worn away—was a selvage outside the web, formed by weaving back the threads of the warp. This had originally been the finishing of both ends of the rug and the sole bit that remained showed what long and severe wear the old piece had known. But it had still a thickness and evenness of pile far superior to that of many new fabrics. Its pile must have been originally of about the same length as the best Kir-Shehrs. The sides were finished with a narrow selvage made of extra threads of red. The technical oddity of the piece was that the weft was thrown across, two threads at once, and then another row of knots put in before it was carried back. The solidity afforded by this method was apparent.

The modern Konieh manufacture is almost wholly of the heavy carpet order. The grade names of Oushak and Ghiordes are used and the products are practically the same as theirs. The Konieh moderns are noticeable, however, for one thing, the diversity of yarns used for the warp. These are all of wool and necessarily very stout; in color they are everything, and, as if sufficient variety could not be secured otherwise, two colors are often found in one yarn.

Among the heavy Asia Minor "whole carpets" there is probably none of more worth than the Konieh variety known as Tokmak. The name itself, though really taken from a town to the west of Konieh, is in its literal meaning descriptive. Tokmak is Turkish for compact. In its primary use it means "a mallet." The materials of the Tokmak are well chosen, its patterns of a good order, and in fineness and workmanship it excels, perhaps, even the best grades of Oushak.

Kir-Shehr.—The rugs of Kir-Shehr, in the province of Angora, just over the Konieh border to the north of Lake Tcholli, lead all the Konieh fabrics in texture and color. They are renowned for brilliancy, and the excellence of the water in that section, for the solution of dyes, is proverbial throughout Turkey. The reds and greens, especially, in many of the older Kir-Shehrs are exemplary, and dyes for these colors seem to have the maximum of preservative value, since the red portions of the designs, and some of the greens and darker blues as well, protrude from the surface as if they had originally been put in with a longer yarn, for the purpose of making a raised pattern. The foundation threads, which are of wool, are usually dyed in the color prevailing in the pile, like those of the Bergamo.

In design the antiques are perhaps more elaborate than the old Koniehs, but the small moderns of the two manufactures are sold interchangeably. Geometry seems to have been overcome in the older Kir-Shehrs. Industrious attempt at Persian elaboration is apparent. There is a patent effort at unity and integrity in the design, which, particularly in its central patterns, follows closely the Arabic forms. The borders, too, are eloquent of a higher artistic aim than can be found in the Koniehs. There are fewer stripes than in most of the Persian rugs, and the main stripes carry a most pretentious form of ornamentation. Border medallions, which are seen in Persian carpets, and are plainly borrowed from Arabic forms, are found in Kir-Shehrs of old date. Rectangular border figures are relegated to the subordinate stripes.

In the modern products ambition is not so manifest, but the skilful blending of colors is still noticeable. The pile is of good length, making the rugs thick and durable. They are meant for practical use and are much to be desired. Liberal use is made of phenomenal shades of green, and brilliant harmonious effects are produced by them in conjunction with the reds already mentioned. Some of the small Kir-Shehr mats have several particolored tufts at each end, composed of all the yarns used in their piling, and formed by weaving these in clusters into the webs with which, supplemented by a fringe of the warp, the ends are finished.

In rare examples these little tufts are made of human hair, and sometimes small devices are woven with hair upon the webbing.

Kaba-Karaman.—Little need be said of these. They are simply called "Kaba" by the Smyrna traders. The word means "coarse," and describes them accurately from every standpoint. They are made by nomads in the southern province, along the ranges of the Taurus chain, toward the Zeitoun district, and furnish a good index to the tribes which make them, whose fame for roughness, cruelty and quarrelsomeness has gone over all Asia Minor. The Karamanians are migrant Turkomans, and in their weaving preserve in rude form the patterns prevalent in the Caucasian countries.

Most of the Kaba-Karamans which come to America—and they are a multitude—are small prayer rugs and *sedjadeh*. Their likeness to the Caucasian fabrics in design, heightened by the free use of bold patterns in white, enables salesmen to dispose of them for Derbend. Some of the better specimens go as Karabagh, and particularly good ones as Shirvan, and even Daghestan, to purchasers who are in a high degree credulous. Although carelessly made, they are stout, and useful for some purposes.

Yuruks.—These plain shepherds,[1] who wander with their flocks over the southern and middle ranges of Anatolia, are blood kin to the Kazaks of the Caucasus and the Kirghiz, and the Turkomans of the Mosul districts; in the fabrics they send to Smyrna the relationship is plain. The tribal name "Yuruk" means "mountaineer." It is the wild, harsh life of their mountains that they have woven into their

---

[1] "These Yuruks (called by Doctor Chandler and most of our old travellers 'Turkomans') are a pastoral, thriving, simple-minded, primitively-mannered, kind-hearted people, hospitable as far as their means allow, and always ready to shelter and serve a traveller, be he Mussulman or Christian. Though far more religious than the town-dwelling people, they are less bigoted and intolerant. Their migratory habits and their breathing the free air of the mountains during one half of the year, appear to give them the enjoyment and appreciation of freedom. Their women go unveiled even before strangers; they are very fond of their children, whether male or female, and generally have a good stock of them. . . . At the approach of winter the Yuruks come down with their flocks and their herds to the warm, sheltered plains opening on the Propontis or the Ægean, and at the approach of the burning hot summer they retire to their cool, shady mountains, where the melting snows leave sweet and abundant pasture. The most thriving men I saw this time over in Asia were among the Yuruks. Some of their *aghas*, or head men, possess immense flocks of sheep and fine herds of cattle; and it was a fine sight to see them—as we did a little later at Hadji Haivat—descending from Olympus day after day like a continuous stream. But for the Yuruks I do not know what the Turks would do for their mutton! The heads of tribes lead quite a patriarchal life—always under tents—and many of them reach a truly patriarchal age."—*Charles C. MacFarlane: "Turkey and Its Destiny."*

rugs. Most of these are dark affairs, with the heavy, ashen brown hue prevailing, brightened by titanic patterns in wonderfully rich colors. The designs seem fairly to grow out from the grim groundwork of dark sheep's-wool. They are made up of simple figures, which the artistic limitations of the weavers have forced them to repeat again and again. The corner triangles and patches at the side of the central fields not taken up by the main device are filled with stripe effects, composed frequently of the hook pattern found in the Caucasians, although the shape of it here differs somewhat from the Caucasian form.

Kazil and sometimes brown wool are used for the warp, but the fierce-looking knotted braids with which the ends are adorned are of white or gray wool, sometimes of cotton. The broad web of the middle-Asia Turkomans sometimes appears here. The sides are selvaged, but over the selvage in a few rugs is an overcasting of colored yarn, which serves at once to fortify the edge, and make it more nearly equal to the piled part of the fabric in thickness.

The Yuruk weavings have a peculiar softness, proof positive that they are made to serve the ends of personal comfort where that commodity is scarce, and not those of adornment or display of skill. Some of them lack symmetry, but as a rule they lie evenly, and, being made in the sturdiest fashion, wear like iron.

Anatolians.—Small mats are made throughout the Konieh district, and in fact all the middle and eastern part of the peninsula, and sold under the name of "Anatolians." They are seldom more than four feet in length and vary in respect of narrowness. Nothing could be more heterogeneous than are these *yesteklik*, both as to color and design. They embody every sort of device, curved and rectilinear. Those made in recognized communities of weavers follow closely the rugs of the locality, but many which come in the great consignments are merely individual conceits, the first thing that has come into the weaver's head. Their very oddity makes them attractive.

The only feature common to most of them is a soft, flocky pile. This is purely utilitarian, since originally their chief use was as pillow covers. There are in most cases strips of cloth web at the ends to facilitate making them into pillows. Clinging to the backs of many of these mats will be found seeds and specks of clean straw, showing that they have already been used, and that the collectors, seeking for everything buyable in the way of native textiles, have stripped them from the pillows and sold them for export.

The designs include everything, stripes and angular figures, Saracenic centre-pieces, heavy geometrical devices like those employed by the Yuruks, and even the neat patterns of the Caucasian fabrics. The latch-hook plays an important part, especially in the mats made by the mountaineers, who, it would seem, have brought it with them from the shores of the Caspian and the uplying country. It is of different form, however, more like that seen in Kurdish rugs of Mosul. Some of the older mats are really fine and highly prized by connoisseurs. Like the larger rugs, many of them have suffered from the use of chemical dyes, and pieces which, were their colors honest, would have considerable value, are ruined by the fading of their principal areas to dirty and unsightly stains. Poor coloring may often be detected by comparison of the ends of the pile with the part which is below the surface and has not been exposed to light and air. The under part, even in very old rugs, retains its original brightness.

There are made all about Cæsarea rugs of considerable size and enormous thickness, which in trade are called " big Anatolians." They have all the peculiarities of the large Kir-Shehrs, but the pile is much longer and thicker. In some specimens it is fully an inch and a quarter in length, and is packed upon the warp as closely as the most energetic beating with the batten can crowd it, and as the yarn is of the heaviest the fabrics are nothing less than cushions, upon which a body might fall heavily a hundred times a day without possibility of injury. There is more wool to the square inch in one of these rugs than in the very thickest of Oushak or Ghiordes carpets. Much of the material is poorly prepared. In some cases it is not thoroughly cleansed of the animal oil, and after the rug has been used for a time it flocks, like the wool on the back of a thick-coated sheep.

The designs are mostly of an archaic, rectilinear order. The colors are brilliant and their areas harshly defined. There are no half-tones. The anilines are prevalent. If, however, interminable wear is all that is required, one need seek no farther than these "big Anatolians."

In Cæsarea a large general manufacture has sprung up, both of big carpets of the Oushak type, and copies of the Persian *sedjadeh*, in both silk and wool. The latter are known in trade as Cæsarean Kirmans, Cæsarean Sehnas, etc. None of these products bears any relation to the old, spontaneous industry of the locality.

SMYRNA FABRICS

I may repeat here that the Smyrna rugs of to-day are all made for market, and are as purely commercial creations as Axminster or Wilton. The paltry rates at which weavers can be employed more than overbalance the American tariff upon imported fabrics, and there remains the indisputable fact that Americans cannot, even with better facilities and the best of Oriental designs to work from, satisfactorily imitate the Eastern products.

The genuine antiques from this region are growing lamentably scarce, but at long intervals a new rug is found, made with all the old fineness and purity of design, and colored with the old-fashioned dyes

—a very oasis in the desert. The manufacture of carpets of the Smyrna type is making its way eastward with great rapidity. It was a long stride when looms for the heavy grades were set up in Konieh, and now, since Cæsarea became a factory, Cæsarea and other towns, still farther east, have begun to contribute their quota. The great body of moderns in the Smyrna group, no matter where made, are alike in all points save comparative coarseness and some technical differences such as weight, solidity of texture, quality of wool in the pile, and the materials used for warp and weft. The names by which they are known in the trade serve merely to define grades. The designs are anything and everything, European as well as Eastern, and the dyes, in most instances, largely chemical.

The Smyrna fabrics are surely entitled to the name carpet, if size is the desideratum. They are made now to fit almost any floor. For a time the experiment was tried of making these great affairs in several sections and deftly joining them afterward. The process proved unsuccessful, as the pieces seldom matched sufficiently well to make the completed fabric seem a unit.

Ghiordes.—About fifty miles northeast of Smyrna lies the rug-making town of Ghiordes. You may see it written in nearly as many ways as there are stitches in its famous fabrics—Gördes, Gürdiz, Gierdi, Yoordis, Yurdi, Yordi, and many more. But by whatever name, it is to the native always to be revered; not so much because in the popular belief, which cannot be shaken by archæological doubts, it is the ancient Gordium, home of the Gordian knot, by severance of which, in accordance with prophecy, world-compelling Alexander became master of all Asia, but because the old Ghiordes rugs have there been woven, which to the Turk, and many people besides, are the acme of textile excellence.

From the limitless field of design and the countless possibilities of color combination, the weavers of Ghiordes, in other centuries, wrought out a type which had universal recognition as their own ; a type to the chaste perfection of which the designers, whether of East or West, have not been able beneficially to add, and from which only laziness, haste or greed has since prompted any man to take aught away. This type found its greatest prevalence in the prayer carpets, but can still be seen in floor-coverings, though they have now grown rare.[1] In the famous collections of Europe the old Ghiordes bits are placed side by side with the most prized antiques from the Persian looms.[2]

It is an interesting middle ground which these most renowned of Anatolian fabrics occupy, in the matter of design. While eschewing the Persian realism and profusion in floral patterns, the Ghiordes weavers have attained equal mastery of synchromatic arrangement. From the deep mass of solid color, sometimes rich red, canary, or pale green, but most commonly blue, which forms the arched central field of the prayer rugs, there is the most delicate alternation of colors throughout the several borders, even to the outermost band. In the ground of the main or middle border stripe, or perhaps in its chief floral pattern, will be found recurring, in subdued but still dominant value, the central blue. In the inner guard stripe, next to the central field, the blue is almost unnoticeable, giving place to red or yellow, the alternating color. In the outer one it is stronger, though not sufficiently prominent to diminish the value of the blue in the

---

[1] The largest Ghiordes antique ever known to have come to New York is eleven feet wide by fifteen feet long, and is now in the possession of Mr. George Gould. Some years ago a Smyrna dealer, observing that the old Ghiordes pieces were becoming scarce, bought every specimen obtainable. Some of them were far gone with age, but he set expert weavers at work repairing them, weaving patches in the ragged places, and refinishing the battered sides and ends. The work occupied over two years, as he had collected, all told, more than 150 pieces. When at last he offered them for sale, fabulous prices were obtained. At present the factories in Tabriz and at other places throughout the East are producing these rugs, but few of the copies have the attractiveness of the old ones, probably because the dyes are adulterated with anilines.

[2] Fine examples of old Ghiordes have lately come to be used as mats in the framing of pictures. The body of the rug is cut out, and only the border section left to do service. The effect is striking, but to the lover of fine rugs the practice will at first seem little short of desecration.

broad main stripe. Where the prevailing color is red or the pale yellow frequent in all Asia Minor prayer rugs (though most common in the Kulahs), the balance is just as skilfully maintained. To aid in this adjustment of color-balances the daintiest tints of other colors are used, pale Nile green and the paler yellow, which serve the lighting-place of white, but leave softness instead of a glare. Where particularly delicate color tone is required, cotton is sometimes used in place cf wool for the small white figures.

The patterns used in the Ghiordes border ornament are singularly adapted to this skilful distribution of color. They are chiefly floral, and so insure softness, but the flower forms, instead of presenting the broad conventional surfaces customary in the Assyrian patterns, or the severe angular indented style of the Caucasians, consist of finely broken leaves and blossoms, which assist in the production of the most minute color areas. While not harshly geometrical, they are quasi-rectilinear and so drawn as to lend themselves to regular arrangement. There are in each spray one blossom and two leaves, two blossoms and one leaf, or three blossoms. These are arranged within an imaginary square, which, repeated many times, forms the main border stripe. One corner of the square is occupied by each leaf or blossom, the remaining corner by the base of the stem and a few tiny leaves which put out from it. The fine color balance between the leaves and flowers on each branch is distinctly noticeable in all the old examples. The border stripe is virtually made up of these squares, which are so arranged that the stems of the spray point alternately inward and outward. Thus, in many pieces, the succession of stems produces the effect of undulation, without resort to the conventional vine which is the foundation of the whole Persian system. The only pronounced trace of this is in the narrow tertiary stripes which separate the borders proper. These carry a central wave line, or thin ribbon, and can be found in the majority of Ghiordes fabrics.

In some Ghiordes rugs the main border is made up of a pattern which at first glance suggests a comb. This, examination will show, is also a leaf form. There is sometimes substituted for the main border stripe, with its rich floral decoration, a series of narrow stripes, alternately very dark and very light—almost black and white. This feature, which is carried to an even greater extreme in the antique rugs of Kulah than in those of Ghiordes, lends a decided brilliancy of effect, but interferes somewhat with the fine color adjustment.

In the spandrels over the arch of the prayer rugs there is a repetition of the pear patterns or some variation of the characteristic trifoliate border design, still arranged in rows, and usually in an emphatic shade of the alternating color. The entire oblong is topped by a horizontal panel in which the principal color is even more pronounced than in the border stripe. The patterns in this panel and in a second panel nearly always put in underneath the field, may be eccentric Anatolian floral forms, but more frequently appears some phase of the old symbolism, such, for example, as the swastika.

The niche in the Ghiordes prayer rugs has a distinctive form. It is tall. The angles at the base of the arch are frequently broken ; the apex of the arch, instead of running to an acute point, is also broken very near the top, so that its angle is obtuse. In many specimens the tree of life pattern, almost omnipresent in prayer rugs, is without trunk, and consists merely of protruding floral branches, drawn after the manner of the flower designs in the borders and spandrels.

A feature peculiar to some of the best of these prayer rugs is that the fringe on the upper end, instead of being the customary finishing of the ends of the warp, is a separate affair, usually of silk, sewn fast, and reaching down each side of the rug for the space of a foot or more. The weft is sometimes cotton, and the finishing of the sides often an extra selvage of silk in pale color and of the finest weaving. So much for the antique Ghiordes. It cannot be mistaken, except for the product of the neighboring city of Kulah, and once seen at its best will scarcely be forgotten.

As for the modern Ghiordes, it marks the maximum of change in Turkish rugs, as the Feraghan does in Persia; but the Feraghan has been loyal to its antique design, while the Ghiordes has not. The modern fabric is of infinitely coarser texture and astounding color. The old vegetable tingents are little used save in the finer grades. Even when the dyes are vegetable products they are mordanted by chemical methods, and the old formulæ for preparing and fixing them seem to have been lost.

There is no special characteristic in the modern Ghiordes by which they can be distinguished from other Smyrna carpets, except that for the sake of economy a cotton thread is used, even in the best of them—Hamidiehs, Sultaniehs, Osmaniehs—for weft.[1]

The better grades are known by the greater number of knots contained in the square inch. The lowest have twenty and the highest about seventy-five. All that these big moderns retain from the old Ghiordes is the general border arrangement, and the small undulating stripe referred to in the description of the antiques. That is found, in some shape, in all the latter-day fabrics except the *fantaisie* rugs. For the rest, the fine patterns so delicately wrought in the old prayer rugs are abandoned for great and garish ones in the new carpets. "Big" colors prevail. There is no limit to them. Harsh reds, greens, terra cottas are common, and all manner of figures are used to fill the vacant space. Frequently there is a gigantic medallion in the centre, in red, green, or some other heavy color.

---

[1] In the heavy whole carpets of Asia Minor the same grade names are used by several manufacturers. A name therefore cannot indicate unerringly one and the same fabric wherever used, since the materials employed by the different makers vary in merit, and there are "shop" differences in the dyes and finishing.

The remainder of the field is filled in with all sorts of disjunct figures, a reversion, unprejudiced critics would say, to the barbarian tendency found in Kazaks, Turkomans, and the rough products of Mosul and Southern Anatolia. The pile of the great carpets varies in length from an inch downward. The Ghiordes weaver of a century ago would have laughed at these as monstrosities; to-day they are sold by the ship load. The big firms who make the *farmaish* have in Ghiordes, as in other large factory towns, expert men whose business it is to establish the scale of the patterns. They weave small sections of rugs, which are given to the rank and file to work by.

Kulah.—In former times Kulah produced rugs of much the same pattern and workmanship as those of Ghiordes, from which town it is less than fifty miles distant. So few and so fine were the points of difference that even connoisseurs often find it difficult to say positively of some of the rare examples now offered for sale in this country whether they be from the looms of one city or the other. Both have the same brightness, delicacy of pattern and fine though chaste display of color. In old Kulah prayer rugs red is oftener the prevailing color than in those of Ghiordes, and the golden brown color more frequent still—sufficiently so, in fact, to be almost characteristic. The niche or pointed arch, measuring from the base of the spandrel, is seldom so tall, and its sides are more apt to be serrated. The inner field of the rug is more frequently filled or partly filled with small figures than that of the Ghiordes, in which solid color is a rule. These figures are usually floral, of the Asia Minor character—three-leaved, and with the flowers hanging down them—and are arranged in rows like the pear and shrub patterns in the field of Tzitzis and Kabistans, but without the separating lines or bars found between the rows in those rugs.

Figures of the same sort are repeated transversely to form the main border of the Kulahs, in lieu of the large individual patterns common to the Ghiordes. The narrow alternating stripes (dark and light) referred to as appearing in the Ghiordes must really be considered a Kulah mark, from the fact that in the old Kulahs, instead of being used chiefly as a substitute for a main stripe pattern, they are employed in great number, sometimes as many as seven, or eight, or even ten, inside and outside the main border stripe. Each of these narrow stripes carries a succession of small, separate devices in place of a running pattern. The narrow stripe with undulating pattern, referred to as a characteristic of all Ghiordes, antique and modern, is rarely found in pure Kulahs, and the peculiar arrangement of the top fringe of the Ghiordes prayer rugs is absent from the Kulahs, except in rare cases where it has been supplied at the dictation of individual caprice.

The extensive manufacture of rugs for market was somewhat late to be established in Kulah, but so rapidly did it increase that the town became one of the most important rug-making places in Turkey. Certain of the makers here maintain with heroic fidelity the use of vegetable dyes, and strive to keep their products up to the old standard of merit, but for a time the general quality declined so sadly that government interference became necessary to insure its restoration. Oddly enough, much of the weaving is done by men. Carpets of the better grade are made chiefly by the Christian population. They taught the art to the Turks, who speedily abandoned it and went into the raising of rug materials. The Mohammedans now weave the low-grade carpets. For some years mohair was used with an admixture of wool, for piling what are known as Kulah mohairs. These rugs look well when new, but instead of improving with age, like most Oriental fabrics, lose their gloss, and when the mohair becomes packed, as it does with comparatively brief use, unpleasantly resemble felt. In design the modern Kulahs have nothing characteristic. The old models have been abandoned, and like well nigh all the present day

Smyrna fabrics they are made from designs furnished them by European dealers. The Kulah moderns, with woolen pile, run almost entirely to large sizes. With some few exceptions, they are inferior products; often coarser in texture even than the Ghiordes *barchanas*. The mohairs are made in all dimensions, from the single door-mat up to the whole carpet.

Demirdji.—Forty years ago Demirdji, a town of twenty thousand, was unknown to the rug trade. Its later prosperity and fame were the outgrowth of misfortune. It is commonly said that the weavers from Ghiordes journeyed to Demirdji, set up looms and taught the natives to weave. This is not the fact. In 1880, or thereabouts, Demirdji was partially destroyed by fire, and the majority of its population were left homeless, some helpless. In desperation some hundreds of them went to Ghiordes, where at that time the carpet industry was beginning to assume commercial proportions. They learned the trade, and after a short time returned home and taught it to their townsmen. Skilled dyers went there, and finding the water of a good solvent quality, opened shops. The best of wool is produced on the plateaus east of Demirdji, and to-day the carpets made there are accounted among the best in Turkey. They are more compact than the average Ghiordes, the yarn is rather better selected, and of double or sometimes of triple strand. The pile is clipped shorter than in the Ghiordes.

The rug trade in this country seems of late to have set its face most resolutely against the Demirdji rugs, maintaining that they are practically one with the Ghiordes product, and believing that the Ghiordes rugs are substituted, while the Demirdji price, about twenty per cent. above that of Ghiordes, is maintained. But as all the motives of rug sellers are not altruistic, nor all their practices wholly ingenuous, the doom of Demirdji need not yet be considered as altogether sealed. The Demirdji quality known as Hindustanieh, is a finer and perhaps better finished carpet than any of the staple products of Oushak. It is very closely trimmed, but has a large number of knots to the inch, which makes it heavier and more durable than others which have a longer pile.

Oushak.—Railroad connection with the Mediterranean seaboard has contributed to make Oushak one of the greatest rug-making towns in Asia Minor, or for that matter in the world. In the quantity of its exports, it easily outranks all other seats of rug manufacture. Growing to keep pace with the enormous demand for its products, Oushak now numbers its looms and its weavers by thousands. The city in olden time produced fine carpets of bold design and superb color, of which comparatively few examples remain. Few if any small pieces are made there. The whole working force is applied to the production of great, deep-piled carpets, which are found in hotels, in the saloons of steamships and apartments of the kind, as well as in thousands of dwellings, all the world over. There are half a dozen varieties, but they are in no wise determined by color or design, as the work at Oushak is done largely from patterns furnished by Europeans, and the colors, instead of following an established local preference, vary with particular requirements in decoration or the changing fashions of the West.

The Oushak carpets have a softness to the foot not to be anticipated from their appearance. This results from the invariable use of wool for the foundation. The colorings of the modern Oushak are similar to those of the antiques, but the old designs, which bore a strong suggestion of the Hispano-Moresque, were long ago abandoned. It is strange there has been no revival of these designs, since the old pieces are now highly prized.

Some years ago a rug dealer in Smyrna, who has an extensive trade with the United States, started a steam dyeing establishment in Oushak, to color all the wools at wholesale with chemical dyes.

While the color arrangement—wine-red ground and green border—is that common to Isaphan carpets of the Sixteenth Century, the design is of an entirely different nature from those emanating from the capital. It is far more likely a product of middle or northern Persia, for in it, though unlike in coloration, may easily be traced kinship to the row designs of Feraghan, which we know under the names of Herati and Guli Hinnai. In the alternating rosette and palmette in the border there is clear prophesy of the Herat border. There are certain textile characteristics suggestive of Sehna, as the shape also is, but, as I have said in notes upon the Marquand collection, it is impossible to make hard and fast local classification of a rug woven when Persia was in a state of such continual change, and artisans in large numbers were being transferred from place to place, taking with them their methods and designs. The work may have been done at Kashan or perchance in Resht, but that it foreshadows the Feraghan and Sehna of to-day there is little doubt.

PLATE X.   OLD KURDISH RUG

8.11 X 3.7

Property of the Author

What mastery of coloring the unschooled mountain Kurd possesses, this unusual piece of carpet goes far toward showing. Moreover, in almost every respect it illustrates the best Kurdish spirit in design and workmanship. The repetitive feature, which is in highest favor in Kurdistan, is here brought out, both in field and border. So also, is the fine skill in shading, in which these people have always excelled, but which, unfortunately, is being wholly abandoned in the newer rugs. No system of color reproduction—even one so efficient as that here employed—can bring out all that the weaver has actually accomplished with an exceedingly small schedule of color in the central field. There is a simple honeycomb pattern repeated, with a small flower figure within each cell. Only three colors are used—yellow for the ground, blue for the outlines and red for the flower, with a stitch or two of white and blue in the centre; but an alternation of sunshine and shadow, regardless of the light in which the rug lies, is effected merely by the weaver's manipulation of the yarns—the addition of a knot of blue here and there, or, on the other hand, the substitution of a knot of yellow or red, and, to complete the result, a trimming of the yellow and red yarns shorter than the blue. When the rug is looked at from a distance the yellow is hidden and the shadow of blue is intense. This throws the yellow and red in other parts into yet stronger contrast.

Something of the effect may be secured by holding the plate horizontally on a level with the eye. This will also bring out strongly the manner in which the color diversions in the border have been adjusted to coincide with the centre. This border has a more extensive range and variety of colors than almost any rug the author has ever seen. Some minute spots of faint colors have been unavoidably lost in reduction, but the color process has almost miraculously retained the effect of them.

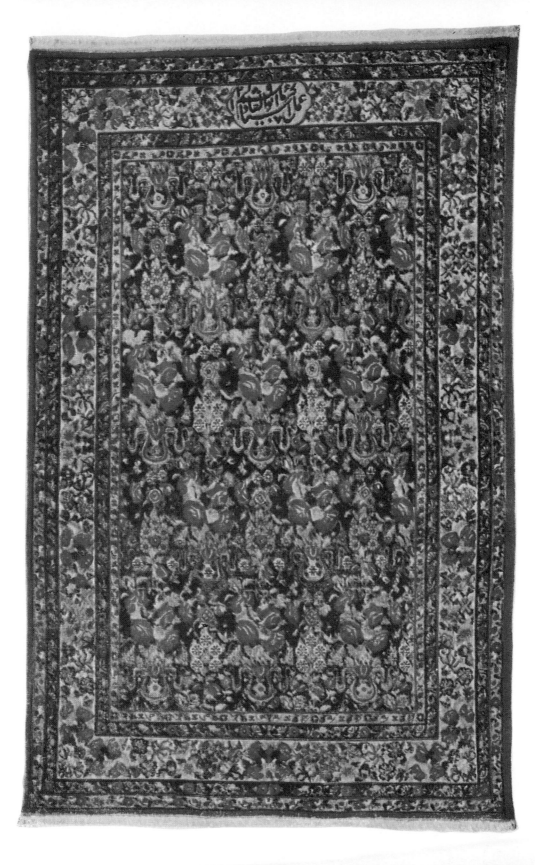

PLATE XI.   OLD KIRMAN RUG

6.10 x 4.5

Loaned by Mr. Robert L. Stevens

There is striking resemblance between this and the old South Persian Kirman published in the earlier editions.   They are alike in size and theme and even more alike in treatment.   In both the big red roses are drawn in perspective, so that even the curled petals are distinguishable.   The border stripes are the same in number, width and arrangement; the design of both rugs from first to last is simply the massing of exquisite natural flowers, a custom from which the later Kirman weavers have ingloriously departed.   The only points of real difference, however, are that the ground of the centre in the former rug is wool-white; in the present one, so far as it can be discerned through the flowers, it is blue-black, while the white ground is reserved for the border.   In the field of the other rug there were no flowers other than roses, while in this we see the pert, upright stalk of the henna, with its five staring blossoms, set alternately in white and blue; lastly and most significant, in the former fabric, the roses were contained in vases, of the antique urn type, with graceful handles; here, instead, is the cloud-band with its never failing suggestion of the over-mastering Mongol.   This weaver was Kasem; the other was Karim. Karim was the poet; Kasem, the painter.

PLATE XII. ISPAHAN CARPET, SIXTEENTH CENTURY

16.2 X 7.1

From the Marquand Collection

A beautiful survival of the great epoch in Persian history—the period of the Sufi reigns, when art and poetry were paramount in the popular life. The carpet has much of the fine quality of the Ardebil (Plate XXII).

The lotus forms and cloud band, which were introduced into Persian design from the East, are here, and they are in the Ardebil carpet, but not in the Titanic size or bold color which they bore fifty years afterwards, and which they still retain in the big carpets of modern Persia. There is also discernible in the border, in minute form, the lancet leaf, and, as dominant factors, the bold rosette and palmette, in alternation, all of which were combined to make the regulation Herati design of later times.

"That the weavers of the capital—for it seems past question that the carpets of this class were made on the palace looms of Ispahan—still worked with a masterly comprehension of ultimate general effect, is further proven by the emphases in the field of this rug. These are effected in the simplest manner, by projecting a very few of the leaf and flower forms in the centre and at the ends of the field in stronger and darker color. In the centre a perfect medallion effect is thus secured without the use of any cumbrous outline figure, and at the ends, by the aid of the palmette shape and the leaf, the accent is carried into the corners and a clever harmony established between the field and the deep green and more pronounced pattern of the border."

Fortunately for the native dyers, and probably for the entire industry, the undertaking met with no success. The water at Oushak is of such remarkable quality that much of the wool from other districts is brought there for washing, but of late much of the Oushak wool has been poorly washed.

The several denominations of Oushak rugs differ principally in texture. The ordinary Oushak, generally called Kirman, has from twenty-five to fifty knots to the square inch, and the Gulistan, and Enile or Inely, from fifty to ninety. The Gulistans are finer, in many respects, than the Eniles.

The Yapraks—the original Oushak carpets—can be singled out from the fact that they are coarsest of all, and ordinarily contain only two colors, red and blue, or red and green. The warp and weft are dyed in one of them, and the pattern, in the alternating color, is as plainly visible on the back as on the front of the carpet. The Kirmans are softer than the other varieties.

Carpets very like the best of those of Oushak are now made in Kutayah, whither master artisans were sent from Oushak to set up the looms and teach the people the required method of weaving. Kutayah does not, however, figure often as a trade name. The products of its looms are sold under the Oushak or Ghiordes classifications. Many of them are extremely good fabrics, following in the quality of foundations and some points of finish, both of ends and sides, the heavier of the Bergamo rugs. They are, of course, so much heavier than any Bergamo, and so altogether different in coloring and design, that their small textile resemblance affords not the slightest aid to identification. They affect large central fields of plain color, blue or red, or some such faint fretted diaper as is found in the grounds of Hamadan and Samarkand. The medallions and rectangular corner ornaments, as well as the borders, are generally semi-geometrical in character and small in proportion to the carpet.

Bergamo and Ladik.—Nowhere does the wealth of historic suggestion which lives in Oriental carpets assail the mind with more force than in the fabrics which, in comparatively small number, but until lately inversely good quality, come from the neighborhood of these two old towns, one lying to the north of Smyrna, the other farther to the east, on the main highway from the west coast to the Euphrates.

Bergamo, as Pergamos, was a stronghold of Christianity in its earliest periods, and site of one of the seven churches mentioned in the Apocalypse. But centuries before that they were centres of civilization. Pergamos, founded, according to tradition, by a son of Hercules, became after innumerable wars the home of royal magnificence. Its rulers discarded the barbarism of the strictly Oriental races, and espoused Hellenic art and learning. The Roman arms perpetuated its greatness. It was renowned in its time for libraries, altars, and sacred groves. It was the chief shrine of Asclepius, and all the culture of the East came to it for one purpose or another. The sculptures on its giant altar of Jupiter were famous throughout the world, and the excavations made there in recent years by German archæologists have shed more light, it is said, upon the art and architecture of Grecian antiquity than any others in the Orient.

Ladik, a corruption of Laodicea, is one of several cities, scattered through the Orient, which bore the name. It is situated some distance northwest of Konieh. This locality, too, retains relics of ancient grandeur. Fragments of superb architecture are still found, and coins of the Roman emperors are frequently turned up from the soil under which its ruins lie buried.

The towns have, of course, fallen victims to that long decadence which has made of all Asia Minor a great burial-ground of splendor, but their rugs have retained, with a tenacity that is comforting, something of high artistic character. These have been almost the only districts within the range of Smyrniote influence which have not yielded outright to the blandishments of commerce and permitted themselves to become converted wholly into sweat shops.

Their old fabrics have so many points in common that it is difficult to define the points of variance. In both the combinations of color are superb. In no other fabrics made are there to be found finer displays of red, crimson, yellow and blue. In the Bergamo *sedjadeh* the figures are notably bold, and large in proportion to the size of the fabric. This and their artistic elaboration distinguish them instantly from other Turkish carpets. There is more of the pretentious unity of design which marks the high-class Persian fabrics, and the best examples have been mistaken, even by persons well versed, for the early Saracenic masterpieces of Cordova and Morocco. The design starts from a central point, and the figures and areas balance, both in respect of color and location, and rich effects are produced by gorgeous massing as well as by a profusion of small and graceful forms. The texture is a little coarser and the pile a little longer than in the ancient Ghiordes.

In most of the points concerning which experts are critical the Ladiks are accounted the better fabrics of the two. They are glossier, and somewhat superior in material. They have more of brightness and life than the Bergamo, and are of heavier yarn and more closely woven. They show a liberal use of white and scarlet, in contrast with the madder reds which prevail in the Bergamo. Ladik rugs resemble in some respects the antique models of Ghiordes, and even more those of Kulah, particularly the prayer rugs, in which red and yellow prevail as tonic colors. The Kulah small stripes, however, are not often found in the Ladiks.

The preservation of the fine old designs has been accomplished by almost slavish copying. It is not unusual to find a Ladik prayer rug which, though forty or fifty years old, gives textile proof that it was scrupulously copied from an older fabric. It must be confessed that a deterioration has of late been manifest. At first it was shown in the omission of the smaller details of the design, and a tendency to a loose texture. Since the railroad's invasion of this part of the Peninsula the quantity of the rugs shipped out has increased vastly, while the quality has in large measure declined. Bergamo and Ladik features, though in very crude form, are now found in coarse and inferior small pieces which are offered in large numbers under the name of Bergamo, but which in color and design are unspeakably remote from the genuine antique products. The designs in these new rugs are Turanian, nomadic, heterogeneous, and the color shocking. Whether any respectable number of these are actually made in the region of Ladik and Bergamo or not it is hard to say. They certainly are a sad mockery of the name.

That the genuine products are still to be had, however, at adequate price, is beyond dispute. In a letter written from Eski-Shehr Mr. Denotovich says:

"About two hours' travel by rail south of this place is a station called Sarain. Ladik is some hours' horseback ride from the railroad at that point. I visited the neighborhood some days ago, and found a fairly good number of *namazlik, odjaklik* and even *sedjadeh,* of the old quality and design, offered for sale in the bazaars. The weavers and merchants are fully alive to the superior quality of the rugs, and demand a good price for them. The dealers inform me that the making of that class of rugs is still carried on by the inhabitants to the westward of Sarain, in the foothills of the mountains which lie between Ladik and Bergamo."

The rugs of both Bergamo and Ladik are in the smaller sizes. They run from three to six feet wide by four to eight feet long, and are inclined to be considerably wider in proportion to length than other Asia Minor rugs. The rich general color effect is heightened in both varieties by dyeing the foundation threads in the principal color of the piled design. The weft is always colored, and, closely woven upon three or four outside threads of the warp, in the khilim stitch, forms a tinted selvage at the sides, in harmony with the general tone of the rug. Warp and weft are woven into a two- or three-inch red web at the ends, usually striped with yellow or blue. Beyond this the warp forms a small loose fringe, or sometimes a narrow selvage like that of the old Koniehs, which are made nearby. In some of the older and finer examples the finishing of the ends is more elaborate, and even in the coarse and irregular modern substitutes, which retain no vestige of the artistic merit of the antiques, the web at the ends appears inwrought with its small device indicative of superstitious feeling.

Ak-Hissar.—This name means the "white citadel." As ordinarily spoken it is Axár, with a decided emphasis on the final syllable. The town lies in the mountains, less than a hundred miles northward from Smyrna. It was here, about thirty years ago, that rugs were first manufactured in any quantity from mohair. The stubbornness of the Angora goat's-hair, which had been imported to the town in 1885, made spinning it a difficult task, but a workable yarn was finally obtained by combining it with wool. The output of Ak-Hissar consisted, until lately, almost wholly of these mohairs. They are of the same general quality as those made in Kulah, and subject to the same comment. The pile packs and loses softness after a little wear. Both warp and weft are of coarse wool.

When the mohair rugs were first placed upon the market, and for some time thereafter, they commanded a higher price than almost any of the Smyrna carpets, but the quotations on them nowadays are extremely low. The little success achieved by the mohair fabrics has led the weavers of Ak-Hissar to work in wool yarns. They make carpets very similar to those of Ghiordes and Oushak.

Meles, or Carian.—In some of the seacoast towns to the south of Smyrna, and many of the scattered islands of the sea, rugs are made which bear the name Meles (probably because their primary market-place is Milassa, or Melesso), or Carian, from the ancient name of southwestern Asia Minor. They are also called Makri, from the Gulf of Makri, near which Melesso is situated. The name Makri has been applied to the general product of the coast districts of southern Asia Minor and Syria, and some of the fabrics found in these regions have the broad Turkman web at the ends, similar to that seen in the Bokharas, Afghans and Yuruks. As a rule the Meles rugs are small, and the texture is comparatively coarse. The old examples, now rare, are in rich but mellow color, abounding in a peculiar quality of red and a yellow such as marks some exceptional Ladik pieces. The colors in the moderns are largely aniline, and are almost offensive in their brilliancy and not harmoniously blended in the weaving. The red conspicuous in new Meles rugs is of a peculiar metallic quality bordering closely upon cerise, and yet retaining the solidity of a pure carmine. It generally appears in striking mass in the central field, but the smaller patterns in the border are so enlivened with it that the fabric can hardly be accused of inconsistency. The other colors, too, notably the yellows, light blues and greens, are of a commensurate value. All are garish, but after the rugs have been in use for a time, and the colors have had opportunity to fade, some of them are really attractive. The designs lack coördination in their smaller elements; they impress one as being jumbled. With more of unity the extravagant colors might seem less tawdry, but the mixture of small detached figures presents nothing to chain the attention, and so the entire character of the rug is imparted by the hues. The designs are heterogeneous, too; this is particularly apparent in the borders. In one rug the Caucasian latch-hook is prominent, while in the next the character most often repeated is the Persian pear.

TURKISH

The Ghiordes knot is used; the warp is of two- or three-strand wool, often colored at the ends in some cheap-looking shade of light blue, or perhaps a violent pink, and left to form a loose, unattractive fringe of considerable length. The weft is usually of cotton, and is worked around three or four outside threads of the warp, forming a compact selvage for the sides.

XI

PERSIAN

CANCELLING from consideration perhaps as many as half a dozen varieties of Caucasian and Asia Minor rugs, well nigh all of great refinement that remains in the Oriental carpets of the present day belongs to Persia. It is there that the Eastern carpet as an art product had its first home, and there, unless some sudden and potent saving force intervenes, will be its last. Syria, Arabia, and, in an original artistic sense, India, as producing countries, have passed from the reckoning. Turkey and Turkestan are going. It must be laid to the credit of Persia that, despite her decadence as a state and the painful decline of nearly all her industries, a strenuous effort is being made to uphold the quality of the carpets, in the face of demoralizing influences which have proved the undoing of the craft in other sections of the East. The custom of making truly fine carpets took root in Turkey, but only at somewhat isolated points. The Greek culture, warring so vigorously against Orientalism, repelled the carpet. It was only where the Persian influence gained indisputable foothold that the art survived in aught resembling elegance, and its practitioners harked back always to Persia as an exemplar. The native artistic spirit of Persia is longer-lived, as it is more spontaneous, but it is next to impossible to escape

PLATE XIII. HEREZ PRAYER RUG

6.1 x 4.8

Property of the Author

This is in the strong, heavy drawing almost universal in the Herez fabrics.
The rug is new, but the design is not of modern making. In a collection of
old pieces I have seen one or two antiques that were quite similar in figuration,
although wrought with a blue ground. The colors here are the same as are
found in the Herez and Görevan large carpets, although there they appear in
huge medallions. At first glance, the prayer-arch formation is scarcely apparent, but when seen is found to be maintained throughout the whole length
of the rug, with repeated arches in heavy blue lines, and the tree feature running through the middle. The sides of the pattern are well balanced, but the
devices, mostly floral, are very odd in character. In the border the Chinese
cloud-band is repeated, a mark suggestive of the great prevalence of Mongol
blood in the population of Azerbijan.

the conclusion that these are its latter days. The mystery of Persia, the romance of it, are being dissipated at last. The hand of the West, or to be more literal, the North, is upon it. It and its arts are going the way of all the rest of the Orient, and though some souls may cling to tradition, and strain their eyes to catch "the light's last glimmer," the inevitable has happened. Persia has become a business field. Its artisans are no longer fancy free, and even when left to their own devices are disappointing. Its idealism, its invention, its imagination, and even its manual deftness have in great measure departed. Commerce skurries along, like a man with a sack, in the path where splendor has gone by, picking up fragments. He mounts a box, now and then, to auction to the rest of the world the treasures and the gewgaws he has found.

Even so, the finest rugs come to-day, as they always have, out of Persia, but the fabrics which were once artistic marvels, as well as models, are now made, and too often poorly made, for market. It is not too much to say, however, that the standard in carpets is being upheld more sturdily than anything else that the country produces. This is due in part to the fact that until recently the rug-producing districts of Persia have been a *terra incognita* to the Western buyers, and the difficulties of inland travel are apt to remain an obstacle for some time to come. Even the Constantinople dealers have found it more to their comfort and about as much to their profit, to carry on their dealings with the Persian weavers from the easy distance of Stamboul, through agents resident in Persia. They have foregone thus all accurate knowledge of the localities where the various Persian fabrics are produced, and have contented themselves with nomenclature which is erroneous chiefly because it is long out of date. America, which has taken its knowledge at second, third or fourth hand from them, has had slender notion of the Persian classifications.

But if knowledge has gone out in scant measure, the industrial evils of the West have come into Persia in full volume, and the weavers have been only too prone to welcome them. Now—rather late in the day to be sure, but still in time to prove of infinite service —the authoritative forces of the Empire have bestirred themselves to check the spread of bad color and sham workmanship. And whatever criticism may be passed on the Persian polity in other respects, it must be credited with good intent in this. In the chapter on Dyers and Dyes I have cited the law lately issued by the Shah, prohibiting the importation of aniline colors. That it was the outcome of European suggestion need not detract from the wisdom of His Majesty in perceiving its ultimate worth to his Empire, and that he is sincere in his intention to enforce it has had ample proof. During my brief stay in the city of Tabriz there were destroyed, at public burning in the caravanserai of the custom house, over four thousand pounds of aniline dye, sufficient, had it not been intercepted by the officials, to have spoiled many a *batman*[1] of honest wool. The time was more than ripe for a positive reiteration of the royal disapproval of anilines, for a cursory journey through the bazaars of any Persian town revealed chemical dyes largely in preponderance; it was difficult, and in many places impossible, to find embroideries or fabrics of any sort which contained only the old-fashioned colors.

The carpet interests at Tabriz have been persistent in their contention for good dyes, since the only ground for criticism adverse to the Tabriz products was that the colors were not fast. The effort to maintain a high standard of excellence in the output of the Tabriz looms has been continuous, and the results good in the main, but it seems, contemplating all the conditions, to have been rightly observed, in an earlier chapter of this volume, that heretofore the real conservative force has been among the less polished tribes. Probably the most trustworthy Persian rugs, "by and large" to be had in the

---

[1] About ten pounds.

American market to-day are those made in remote parts of Eastern, Western and Southern Persia. It is in these, chiefly, that one finds the admirable characteristics both of color and weaving, which once distinguished the products of the middle district as well. This is assuming that we are speaking of the modern fabrics, and not of the half-worn but still beautiful creations of other days. It is true that European designers are maintained by the rug manufacturers at Sultanabad, and that designs made up of Oriental elements but with novel color combinations are sent from America to Tabriz to be wrought, as they are to India and Turkey, but Persian designers are still at work in the bazaars of Tabriz, and the dwellers in the mountains are weaving still the old designs, to some of which reference has been made in the chapter on Design.

The change of boundaries which Persia has gradually undergone has stripped from her some large and important rug-making districts, but the carpets from such parts, with some few exceptions, are lacking in what is recognized as distinctive Persian character. All the fabrics illustrative of Persian style and method are still made in provinces which remain under dominion of the Shah, and now and then in them is found a gleam of the old glory.

A stout profession of faith in the abiding capabilities of the Persian weaver is made by Mr. Sidney A. T. Churchill, for many years secretary of the British Legation at Teheran. He says, summing up his review of the carpet industry of Persia:

"When the difficulties of the weaver are considered; when one remembers the very little remuneration the weavers receive for their labor; when one reflects that they are utterly uneducated, living in squalor—more often in abject misery, fighting for bare existence—in a manner the most remote from inducing to art combination and high tone in color harmony, with scarcely any encouragement beyond what comes from earning a miserable means of existence; when to these troubles one adds the seizing of labor at one fell swoop by those in authority, visitation of epidemics, carrying off the weaver and bread-winner of a family or retarding her work, and the embarrassments of maternity, the wonder is, not that the carpet industry of the present day in Persia should have degenerated, but that under such misfortunes it should even exist.

"Nevertheless, I am convinced that with sufficient inducement and encouragement the Persian weaver of to-day could be got to equal the best efforts of his predecessors, if not to excel them."

Whether his sanguine view of the possibilities is warranted or not, there is abundant proof that in his description of the drawbacks which beset the weaver Mr. Churchill was well within the facts, and the conditions have, if anything, grown more severe in the years that have passed since his departure from Persia. Journeying down from Julfa, the customs port on the Aras river, where the Russian and Persian borders meet, the story of poverty and depression is to be read all too plainly. Nothing is in plenty, save tea and vermin. These are the staples at every village khan and roadside caravan-serai. In one or two towns I saw, through open gateways in the mud walls, a small loom or two, with rugs in process of making. The designs were pleasing, partaking in a measure of the characteristics of both Persia as now recognized and the Caucasian country which long ago passed from Persian control. This commingling of patterns made them resemble to some extent the weavings of Shiraz, but the colors, it was clear at a glance, left much to be desired. As we passed along the road which is the main highway between Russia and the Shah's domain, the entire country was in a state of excitement over the expected advent of the ruler, who was then on his way out from Teheran to seek treatment at the health resorts of Europe. Plans had been made for his reception all along the route, and carpets, new and indisputably bright, had been hung up to cover some part of the gray walls, the dreary monotone of mud. But for all the gaiety of the fabrics, and the laudable purpose they served, it took only half an eye to see that the dyes were aniline, of a sort to make the author of the prohibitive law shudder, had he vouchsafed them any critical attention.

In the mountain districts south, east and west of Tabriz, however, and throughout the uplands along the Turkish border, there are some fast dyes and capital workmanship, and it is noteworthy that save for some of the personally conducted carpets turned out from the looms of Tabriz, the weavings of the tribeswomen enjoy the greatest favor of any of the fabrics of Persia. The reason is plain. They are done at leisure, without any spur to haste, and altogether, much in the old fashion. The substitution of Turkoman elements, in many of the Persian loom products, for the old Persian designs, is easily understood, when it is remembered that the Persian of to-day is a transplanted Turk, that the language used over the greater part of the empire is a peculiar form of Turkish, and that the pure Persian, the Iranian, is a *rara avis* in the land whose name he wears.

In northern Persia, at least, the best carpets of tribal manufacture are woven by the Kurds, who bring them to market at Tabriz, in considerable quantities. They ask rousing prices for the goods upon arrival, but are kept upon tenter-hooks by the dealers until, weary of the atmosphere of the crowded city, after a fortnight of bootless waiting they dispose of their load for what it will readily bring, and go back to their tents in the mountains and their endless feuds.

But the low prices at which the carpets are got by the Persian or Armenian merchant do not maintain in his dealing with his customer, for with the advent of a prospective buyer from the West the figures are raised, and kept up until he either must purchase at about the price demanded in Constantinople, or go home empty-handed. It is a

familiar saying in the East that it takes two Jews to beat one Armenian, and six Armenians to beat one Persian.

It is worthy of remark that throughout Persia the medallion idea
is taking the place of the old diaper patterns. Even in such *terehs*
as the Herati, the Djushaghan and even the minute all-over designs
of Sehna, the medallion has been introduced, in one form or another.
There are medallion centres, with the ground about them filled with
the old device, but gradually the space covered in that way is being
diminished, and solid grounds substituted, for the sole purpose, apparently, of saving time and labor. Fortunately there are a few designs,
such as the Shah Abbas and the Mina Khani, which do not lend
themselves readily to that sort of treatment.

AZERBIJAN FABRICS

Important as the part has been which this northernmost province
has played in all the history of Persia, ancient and modern, and for
that matter in the history of nations which preceded Persia, little has
been heard of it as a carpet-producing field until recently. From its
geographical position Azerbijan has been a battle-ground of the
peoples on either side of it, and since fighting was suspended has
served as chief point of contact between Persia and the Northern and
Western civilization. Its population, while for the most part Turkish, is diversified by strong representation of other races. The province is a part of ancient Armenia, and relics of Armenian domination
are many. In the eastern section, and particularly in Tabriz, the
Mussulmans are Shiahs of the most fanatical type, and in one or two
instances, when the matter has come to a test in temporal affairs, the
influence of the mollahs has outweighed that of the Shah and
his ministers. Around Urumieh, in the west, are Sunni Mohammedans, Chaldeans, Armenians and Kurds of a rough and
lawless type. It is no uncommon thing, in the bazaars of Tabriz,
during the month of Muharem, to come upon a religious gathering at

noonday. Fifty or perhaps a hundred Persian merchants sit grouped about upon their outspread carpets, or perhaps upon the bales of goods, their silken robes wrapped around them and their huge lamb's-wool caps set decorously at a backward angle, listening to the voluble harangue of a mollah, who, perched on an improvised pedestal above them, lectures on the Prophet's life, and more especially on the martyrdom of the Holy Family, loyalty to whom is the vital matter of the Shiah faith.

The making of carpets in Azerbijan is as old as the province, but it was not until the vast trade sprang up in Tabriz that the Azerbijan fabrics were known as such. All the industry here has practically been developed since 1890. Prior to that Hamadan was the market-place for the carpets of all that part of Persia, and thence it arose that the rugs of Azerbijan were classified as Hamadan products. Even the Kurd weavings found their market in Hamadan. The bales were made up there, and the whole output of the region, in effect, shipped from there by long camel trains to Trebizond, and so to the West. Thirty years ago one or two New York buyers made their way to Tabriz, despite all obstacles, in the hope of securing fabulous bargains in all sorts and quantities of rugs. They found nothing at all.

Some years later, more for convenience in the conduct of money transactions than anything else, the trade of the districts to the south and east began to go to Tabriz, and the carpet industry took on new life there. To-day the output of the province is very large, not alone the rugs made in the villages, but the thoroughgoing fabrics of Tabriz itself, which, it must be confessed, are largely the result of European stimulation. There is all possible diversity in the carpets of Azerbijan. Among them are found the crudest of hill products, as well as the ornate fabrics made by boy weavers, under the supervision of the most skilful loom masters. And in both classes the work done in this hitherto unvaunted region is certainly equal, if not superior, to any carpet-making known in Persia at the present time.

Tabriz.—The type of carpet which has come to be known as of Tabriz bore at first the name of Kermanshah, generally, in Western markets. This gave rise to an erroneous belief that the carpets from which the Tabriz variety had been developed were the product of the old outpost town of Kermanshah in the mountains of Ardelan, the province which lies immediately to the south of Azerbijan, and is included in the vaguely defined territory known as Kurdistan. The model on which the Tabriz rugs were really designed is the ornamental and richly colored fabric of Kirman in southern Persia, a region which has a larger proportion of pure Persian population than any other in the realm, and which by reason of its remoteness from the tracks of travel has kept its pristine character to a considerable degree. A certain part of the district bears the name Kirmanshahan or Kirman-shah, and thence the confusion arose.

The Tabriz rugs of this order have also taken on some medallion features of the northern weavings, a characteristic which marks the so-called Sarakhs, made by the Turkoman settlers around Bijar in the Gehrous district, and in certain parts of the country around Hamadan. Upon this as a foundation idea has been wrought all the floral richness in which the old Persian artists were so fertile. The result is a carpet which for ornamental quality, opulence of color and fineness of texture fairly outdid, for a time at least, the product of Kirman itself. It is not easy to believe that any modern fabric constructed for practical use, of like material and in like method, has surpassed the fine, old, large carpets of Tabriz in craftsmanship. They are as nearly perfect as they can be made by scrupulous care in the selection of the yarn, loyal adherence to textile traditions which are accounted equivalent to gospel, mastery of color combination, elaborate taste and versatility in design, united to ability and thoroughness in the art of weaving. And yet, the true Persian loves better the mellow richness of the old Feraghan or Djushaghan, the fine-wrought harmonies of Sehna, or even the flowery profusions which still bear the names of Teheran and Ispahan.

The reason for his preference is plain. It is atmospheric. There is little of spontaneity in the Tabriz carpets. They are brilliant, showy, pictorial, beautiful; but they are suggestive of fresco. To the Iranian they sniff of lacquer. They are framed panels, splendid, to be sure, but formal. To say that they are not Oriental is a great contradiction, truly, and one that some persons will deny, but it is nevertheless true that although representing something nearly akin to perfection in every process by which the East produces its textiles, the majority of Tabriz fabrics are less Eastern than many of the rude nomad rugs.

The type of Tabriz is this: A central field, the color of ivory yellowed by age; clear and fine against it a superbly drawn, waving band of ruby red, prisoning in the corner spaces, rich, perfectly tinted blooms of the lotus, in pink upon a fawn ground, and other flowers of many colors, and shapely leaves, spreading into the shoulders of the corner areas, carried on exquisite stalks and vines of vernal green. In the middle of the broad field of ivory a medallion, traced in undulating curves of deep heliotrope. Growing out of this at either end, ornate pendants, heart-shaped, representations of the great lamps which hang in the mosques. All this shapely ornament filled with flowers and green leaves, upon an old rose ground, and wrought together with arabesques of bronze. The main border stripes grounded in deep Persian red or bright blue, with splendid floral devices, and all the intervening spaces overlaid with faint, shadow tracery of graceful leaf forms, relieved at brief intervals with other flowers. Tiny floral patterns in the borders, in deep dull red and green, upon bands of misty blue.

It sounds very like a catalogue, but it is Tabriz. And this brilliant panel, so finely toned and shaded in difficult colors, takes on an added finish and lustre from the masterly weaving. The fineness of the knots which, tied one by one, have grown into such a creation, is incredible when it is remembered that the Turkish system is used. Into a square inch of this space, oftentimes, as many as three or four hundred knots are tied. Hardness, perfect compactness, these are the final desiderata of the Tabriz rug. In this they follow the Kirman. When carpet manufacture first began to take on importance in Tabriz, Kirman weavers were brought to oversee it, and their products, made on the Kirman designs, set the pattern for others, who speedily took hold of the work. The designs gained popularity at once, but the Azerbijan weavers, whose training had been wholly in the Turkish school, persisted in the use of what has been termed the Ghiordes knot. At first the weaving was done in houses, after the primitive custom, and the carpets delivered to the merchants upon completion. The immediate favor which they found, from the fact that they took the place of the then scarce fabrics of Kirman, led to the establishment of factories, with greater or smaller numbers of looms, and the general installment of the Kirman manner of manufacture. In Kirman, as will be shown elsewhere, the best weaving had been done, time out of mind, by boys, under the direction of a loom master. This became the system in Tabriz, and every year sees addition to the number and capacity of these establishments. The carpet industry seems to grow in volume as the city's other arts and its general prosperity decline. Even now many rugs are made in the houses, on private speculation, but the tendency is altogether toward centralization, and some of the factories have as many as two hundred and fifty looms in operation.

Lads of seven or eight years sit, half a dozen or more in a row, before giant frames, tying in the knots with a swiftness and accu-

racy which are nothing short of phenomenal. The eye of the unini-
tiated will strive in vain to follow the magical twistings of those small
fingers. For the double purpose of drawing the yarns through from
the back and cutting them when once the knot is made fast, the
small weavers are equipped with a knife, the blade of which is beaten
into a hook at the point, something after the fashion of a crochet-
needle. It serves them in lieu of several extra fingers, and they man-
age it as expertly as they do their own small digits. In no land have
I seen a more intelligent lot of boys than the solemn, black-eyed
midgets who with big, black rimless wool caps on the backs of their
close-shaven polls, sit like old men and weave the superb color panels
of Tabriz.

In the factory of Mr. Hildebrand F. Stevens, whose guest I had
the good fortune to be, there was being woven, at the time of my
visit to the Azerbijan capital, a copy of the renowned mosque carpet
of Ardebil (Plate XXIII), now among the treasures of the South Kensington Museum. This famous original is perhaps without a peer in
the world ; a masterpiece of color, in the most intricate of old Persian
designs. And the master of the loom on which the reproduction was
being wrought was a lad of twelve years. Little, pale-faced, bowed
with his burden of responsibility, he spent the long summer days
walking up and down behind the eight or nine youngsters, some
smaller than himself, who in that dim and dusty place were tying in
the wondrous flower traceries over which the greatest Persian
designer, some four hundred years ago, toiled in the palace at
Kashan. I scarcely hope to see the American boy of twelve, without a day's schooling or an A, B, C to his name, who can carry on his
small shoulders a load like that, or keep that maze of colors in his
head.

In the particular sort of Tabriz carpets of which we have spok-
en, it is rarely that figures of birds, animals or human beings are

used. In this the Tabriz designs have departed from the Kirman custom, but other designs are employed which follow the model of the Saruks, the fine fabrics made in Feraghan. In such pieces, which affect a more spontaneous floral treatment, the birds and other forms will be found. In fact, the manufacture in Tabriz, at the present time, is coming to include all the old and fine designs. Many carpets are being made on the designs of the *kalin kiars*, or printed panels, sold in such quantities in Ispahan, and used so widely over Persia for hangings both on walls and ceilings. Old Asia Minor rugs are also copied, and the weavers have lately gone so far as to take the designs of Valenciennes and other European laces, which were borrowed from Persia centuries ago by the makers of fabrics in Italy, France and Spain.

A favorite device for borders in Tabriz rugs is a succession of small medallions containing inscriptions in the Persian characters. It is common to say that these writings in the "cartouches" are passages from the Koran, but it is seldom the fact. They are more frequently verses from the Persian poets.

The greatest drawback, for a time, to the success of the Tabriz fabrics was a suspicion of looseness in some of the dyes, notably the blue. I made this matter the subject of some inquiry and observation, and though the criticism on the durability of the colors seems overdone it is plain that Mr. Benjamin, former United States minister to Persia, spoke wittingly when in a passage elsewhere cited, he bewailed the lost art of making Persian blue. The dyers in the great Persian rug centres frankly admit their inability to make the old-time colors.

In Tabriz they lay the blame, and with some appearance of reason, to the water, which though brought from the outlying districts gathers a large amount of impurity in its flow, and in Tabriz is dirty as well as unhealthy. The floating particles in the water take the color and are deposited as dust upon the wool. This is, in part certainly, the cause of the obstinate blue shadows which are sometimes to be seen tingeing the white, ivory and yellow areas.[1] It is found, however, that washing the rug in cold water, sometimes for three or four days, cleanses it of this dye-dust, and leaves it clear and bright. So far as I was able to learn, the dyes now used in Tabriz, for carpet purposes, are vegetable.[2]

The warp of the Tabriz carpets is cotton, and in a few of the finer wool pieces silk is used. Formerly it was customary to dye the weft, usually with the dominant color in the carpet, and to weave with it a narrow web at the ends. This has been abandoned and the ends are now finished in white after the manner of most Persian fabrics. In fineness the Tabriz work varies between ten by ten and twenty by twenty knots.

The surface is close, and vigorous beating with steel combs makes the fabrics very compact. There is a peculiar arrangement of warp in these carpets, one set of threads lying clear forward of the other, so that when the knot is tied, albeit the Turkish method is used, every ridge visible on the back indicates a row of knots, unlike the more loosely-woven Turkish fabrics, in which two rows are visible on the back for every actual row of knots. For greater solidity, also, a heavy cotton cord, of the same weight as that used in the warp, is sometimes run straight across between the forward and rear warp-

[1] " Among the real, good old Persian carpets there are very few patterns, though coloring and borders vary considerably. A good carpet, if new, is always stiff; the ends, when doubled, should meet evenly. There must be no creases nor any signs on the wrong side of darning or ' fine drawing ' having been resorted to for taking out creases, and there must be no blue in the white cotton fringe at the ends. Carpets with much white are prized, as the white becomes primrose, a color which wears well."—*Mrs. Bishop: " Journeys in Persia and Kurdistan."*

[2] Since this book was first published, the " washing " or " doctoring " of modern Oriental rugs and carpets has become almost universal, and the solidity which was gradually developed in the Tabriz colors, strange to say, operated to the hurt of the Tabriz carpets, since they did not yield readily, as did the Kirmans, to the softening action of lime, and other caustic agents which are employed to soften color. This has diminished the activity at the Tabriz looms, but the Kirman industry has grown proportionately, and even more.

threads, and between the rows of knots. The weft itself, a lighter affair, takes in the alternate threads of warp front and back, in the regular way. This filling is a trick the Tabriz weavers have learned from their neighbors of Kurdistan.

There are other imitations of the Kirman rugs made in late years, notable among them those woven at Herek-keui, in Turkey,[1] near Ismid, on the Sea of Marmora. The industry there is the fruit of Imperial care for the people of Turkey. Silk is plentiful in the neighborhood and wool easily obtained. So great, indeed, is the plentitude of silk that even in the wool rugs of Herek-keui the central panels are often woven of it. The Sultan, like the Tabrizlis, brought Kirman weavers to instruct his subjects, and they found apt pupils. The work done here is chiefly the copying of old Persian or Ghiordes pieces, and the reversed direction of the stitches in many of the products shows the skilled rug handler that the weavers, using the back of the original for their model, have worked the new rug upside down. The field of Herek-keui is one of general imitation, and the so-called Teheran and Ispahan designs appear, though not in such plenty as those of Kirman and Ghiordes. In several towns scattered throughout Anatolia similar enterprises have been begun, since the success of the Tabriz experiment has been made manifest.

---

[1] Charles C. MacFarlane mentions this place in his book, "Turkey and Its Destiny," published in 1850. Writing of the Catholic Armenian Filatura di Seta, a silk handling concern at Broussa on the slope of Mount Olympus, he says : "About a hundred and fifty women and girls were employed here in winding off silk from the cocoons. They were all either Armenians or Greeks. Turkish females cannot and will not be thus employed. They will rather do nothing and starve—and this was what too many of them were doing at Broussa, even at this season of the year. The Greek ladies were reported to be by far the quicker and cleverer, and the Armenians the more quiet and orderly. They could earn from nine pence to eleven pence a day; and this was almost wealth, for the necessaries of life were amazingly cheap even at this short distance from the capital. An exemplary order and cleanness reigned throughout the establishment, which was under the direction of two intelligent, well-informed Italians. The silk they produced was very superior to the old Broussa's; but it was all sent to the Sultan's own manufactory at Herek-keui, on the Gulf of Nicomedia, and there either wasted or worked up at a ruinous expense, or left to accumulate in dirty, damp magazines. The wheels of this system ran somewhat off the trams; and before we left Turkey this Filatura was shut up, and the hundred and fifty females were sent back to their primal state of idleness and poverty."

HEREZ FABRICS

The carpets of Herez, which for reasons already explained were for a long time classed as a coarse grade of Hamadan fabrics, have triumphed by sheer merit over the lack of favor which such an introduction would naturally invoke. It has, in fact, been customary to class the weavings of all the villages in the Herez neighborhood as belonging to the Hamadan districts, not alone those which were plainly enough superior to the Hamadan proper but those held of less worth. It was very difficult to see clearly how the Herez pieces and the extraordinarily fine, well-woven medallion carpets known as Serapi and Görevan could come from the same looms or vicinity as the Hamadans, most of which can be distinguished anywhere by their fretted grounds and their broad outside bands of what is made to look like camel's-hair. A very brief inquiry into the matter, near at hand, made the error plain.

The Herez rug district, so called, lies in Azerbijan, a little journey to the eastward of Tabriz, on the road which leads by Ardebil to Astara, the Russian outpost, and other ports on the Caspian sea. It is wholly dissociate from Hamadan and all its works, for between the two lies a long stretch of Kurdish country, where rugs of an altogether different sort are made. Its relation with Tabriz is scarcely greater, although it has taken some notions from the Tabrizli weavers and the product of the district, perforce, goes to the capital to be sold.

The story of the Herez weaving industry is interesting, and the different localities are so related to one another in it that it is hard to make the customary division, but as now produced, the rugs of the district may be set down as Herez proper, Görevan, Serapi and Bakhshis. It will be necessary to begin with the inferior variety.

Bakhshis.—The first day's stage on the route eastward from Tabriz brings the traveler to the mud-walled village of Bakhshis.

The name of this settlement, where the weaving is quite in evidence as an occupation, has strangely enough never become prominent among the rug-sellers of America, though its rugs long ago acquired a standing among the Persian dealers, and its patterns were recognized among weavers throughout Iran.   This attracted the notice of the Sultanabad firm, which was first to promote in an extensive way the weaving industry of the town.   That was almost twenty years ago.   An Armenian had been the leading spirit in the management of the business there, and made advances to the weavers in the usual way, securing the carpets as soon as they were finished.   Famine, which is too often recurrent in Persia, brought about complications, for in their distress the weavers spent the money entrusted to them for food instead of wool.   Another manager took up the task, and for a time the rugs of Bakhshis were among the best of the Persian whole-carpet output.   A dealer began selling them in Constantinople under the name of Herez.   Then when they fell off in quality it became necessary to find some other title for the native products of Herez, which retained their sterling character.   The name of a neighboring village was chosen, and from that time Bakhshis was lost sight of in the Western market.   The deteriorated carpets continued to be known as Herez, and it was thus that they obtained classification as a coarser grade of Hamadan, especially as at that time Hamadan was the point of shipment.   The Bakhshis of to-day, which no dealer will call Bakhshis, is loose, full of colors which besides being of inferior quality are ill-combined.   The designs, while of the standard sort, such as Herati, Sardar, Shah Abbas and the like, are wrought with such haste that they are far from perfect. The medallions, when used, are apt not to be in the centre of the carpets, the borders are clumsily woven and without corner-pieces. The whole thing is eloquent of hurry.

Görevan.—When it became necessary for trade's sake to change

A NOMAD STUDIO

KURDISH GIRLS AT THE LOOM

the name of the Herez rugs, they were entered upon invoices of shippers in Tabriz as Görevan, the name of a small village in the Herez district—a village which had no status at all as a producer of rugs. The name quickly took root and was utilized to the full by dealers in Constantinople and Tiflis, for at that time, as has been said, European and American buyers had scarcely found the way to the market in Tabriz.

At first the carpets sold under this name were the old-fashioned Herez products, which follow a type in design and color almost as closely as do the Tekke and Bokhariot products of Turkestan. The Herez idea, which has lately regained all the favor it lost by reason of the Bakhshis carpets' masquerading under its name, has for its essential the medallion, but this medallion, as well as the boundaries defining the corner spaces, is in rectilinears and not with the curves which figure in the designs of Tabriz. The corners are set off by serrate lines, somewhat like the arches in the Kulah prayer rugs. The smaller figure in the centre is plain, solid and unpretentious. The color scheme is almost unvarying, and the dyes are all of a peculiar tone which distinguishes the genuine Herez at once from other fabrics. The ground-color, outside the small central figure and enclosed by the serrated lines across the corners, is an extraordinary blue, which while bright is soft and of a peculiarly pleasing quality. The corner areas are of a reddish brown, sometimes with small figures to break the expanse. The borders in the better examples are in entire harmony with the rest of the design. The main stripe is very broad, buff-gray in the ground color, and with pattern large and clearly defined. The Herez rugs have somewhat of the Sarakhs in design, but the colors are softer and the weave not so heavy. At first sight they impress one as being too pronounced, but they are remarkably wholesome, and in dining-rooms, libraries, or any apartment where the woodwork and decoration are plain, and the furniture sub stantial, are among the most desirable of the large carpets. They are made chiefly by women weavers, who work only in their leisure. This, without doubt, explains the thoroughness of the workmanship.

Rugs of this type had become scarce at the time of my journey into the Orient and commanded a very high price, whether singly or in quantity.

This was mainly due, of course, to the sudden accession of popularity, and beyond that to the state of practical famine that existed throughout the Shah's dominion, for the Herez weavers who have escaped from the control of the big contracting firms lacked money to carry on their work. That by sterling quality these rugs have regained good standing in spite of all disadvantages is an encouraging sign of the survival of native ability. It goes far to establish, too, the main point for which I am bound to contend, that a just and adequate price and ready sale can be found for honest rugs, honestly dyed and in native design.

After the institution of the name Görevan, Tabriz dealers began sending designs into the Herez district to be woven by the women there. This resulted in a new type of rugs, bearing the name which had now come to be associated with the Herez. It was a medallion, but of the Tabriz and Kirman drawing—reminiscent of the sixteenth and seventeenth century art carpets. The ground about it, however, was in solid cream color or ivory white, and the border of a heavy but very ornate character. The thing aimed at was perfection in weaving, solidity and pronunciation. The result proved the experiment a wise one. The rugs, while for the most part not of carpet size, had all the Herez and Bijar firmness coupled with the Tabriz fineness. In thickness they were something between the two. In workmanship they left nothing to be desired. Their quality and finish commanded a high price and their brilliancy made them impossible in plain rooms. Gradually, after their introduction, the name of Görevan came to be applied almost exclusively to these rugs, and Herez resumed its rightful place in the catalogue.

Serapi.—Encouraged by the success of the new Görevans the Herez weavers went a step further and took from the Tabrizlis some designs which, while preserving the medallion forms added floral elements in the ground. These partook in a small measure of the ornamentation found in the Tabriz rugs, but in color scheme and general device followed the *tereh* Lemsa of the Sultan-abad factories—known in market as the "Extra Modern Persian." In quality they were almost if not quite as admirable as the high-class Görevans. These rugs were named for the village of Sirab, and American dealers have converted the Persian form into Serapi.

The graceful medallion shape in the Serapi field, commonly in old ivory or a camel's-hair shade, is usually defined in some other light color or combined with some other area of pale tint, to further the general purpose, which is to make the whole fabric light and bright and afford clear ground for the display of the elaborate vine and floral designs, drawn in a half impressionistic fashion and in colors strong but dull. All this light in the central part of the carpet is balanced by generous use of similar values in the borders. The Serapi is in nearly all respects a praiseworthy and desirable thing. Despite some points of resemblance the elaborate details which strike one in the Tabriz carpets are lacking here, and in the color scheme there is no similarity. In the borders and sometimes even in the field of Serapi, inscriptions are found, either inclosed in Arabic medallions or on the plain ground. The method of weaving employed in all the varieties is practically the same. The warp is cotton, as in most Persian carpets, but the knot is Turkish. All three varieties are apt to be broad in proportion to their length, instead of following the long Persian shapes. In this section at the present time few runners are found.

Kara Dagh.—Among the mountains in the northern part of Azerbijan province, and to the east of the highroad leading south from Julfa, are shepherd tribes of the most bigoted Shiah sect, who weave rugs somewhat similar to those made by their neighbors in Karabagh on the north side of the Aras. The designs, which are bold, have more of Persian character than the Karabagh, and resemble in some points those of the Kurdish rugs. The colors are rather more diversified than those of the Karabagh and differently distributed. The flowers, which are employed in imitation of the old Persian designs, are put in broadcast, which, it may be well to repeat, is the mark of the nomad. It seems to be a cardinal principle with the weavers of the Kara Dagh (Black Mountains), as it is with the Tchetchens, never to leave an expanse of ground-color vacant.

It is noteworthy that the Kara Dagh weavings are not often seen in market, but that they have maintained their quality well. The reason is not far to seek. The Karabagh weavers are within two days of the Russian railroad. They have the great market of Tiflis at their doors, and with that incentive, as shown in the Caucasian countries, sacrificed everything to a rage for increased production. The Kara Dagh people, on the other hand, took their carpets to Tabriz, where they were brought into competition with the Kurd fabrics and other excellent products of the western uplands. The comparison discouraged them and they practically withdrew from the field and continued to make carpets in the old way, merely for home use. Even among these mountaineers the aniline colors have gained a substantial foothold, though not to the extent noticeable in some other localities.

Weft and warp of the Kara Daghs are wool. The weft, if not dyed, is usually in the natural brown color, and is woven into a selvage at the sides. At one end the foundations are made into a selvage and turned over, at the other is a selvage and fringe.

PERSIAN

EASTERN KURDISTAN FABRICS

In some respects the carpets made in Eastern—or what is popularly called Persian—Kurdistan, are the best that come to market. The Kurds in their fastnesses have kept more aloof from the demoralization of towns than any of the other races found in Persia, and have been slower to take up with the meretricious tricks which other weaving folk have learned with such lamentable thoroughness. Their rugs have always been accounted representative of what is good in texture and color, and since they are woven principally in the tents, away from town influences, the quality has been fairly well preserved. Another element which goes far toward maintaining it is that Kurdistan has an unfailing supply of wool which is not surpassed anywhere, unless it be in Kirman and certain parts of Turkestan. The greater part of the yarn, moreover, is spun by hand and with infinite care, and the result is apparent in most of the rugs which the Kurds bring to town for sale.

The aniline invasion has made headway among them, and that is not surprising in view of the fact that throughout the wilds of Kurdistan the dye-shops are as rare as Eiffel towers. The Kurdish weavers are their own dyers, and the ease with which chemical dyes can be mixed is tempting. Nevertheless, after examining many hundreds of rugs, in the bazaars and on the looms, I am of opinion that the Kurds have clung to the old colors more tenaciously than any other of the weaving peoples. If the old processes are to be saved, they must, it would seem, be sought among the Kurds. In the dye-shops in the towns, certainly, they cannot be learned. Take, for example, the single matter of Persian blue, the essential color in all high-class Persian carpets. It is confessedly lost. I put to the most competent dyer I could find many questions concerning his variegated business. He expounded and explained and brought samples of his dye stuffs and his mordants, but at the close admitted that while he could make dozens of desirable blues the old color was beyond him, and he didn't know anybody who had any more idea of producing it than he had. The average Persian will lie, on principle, but the proof that this dyer was telling the truth was that the best blue that he had to show was a dead and uninspiring color when contrasted with a ragged scrap of an antique Herati rug, which I had found kicking about the bazaar in Tiflis.

Two days later, looking over a mixed lot of runners collected during the preceding six months by a Persian merchant, I saw a Kurdish pair, comparatively new, but in one of the best old Persian designs, and grounded in that same indescribable dark, deep and yet almost translucent blue, which had forced such a frank confession from the dyer. Under a voluminous turban, somewhere in the mountains of Kurdistan, the ancient secret of color lurks. A decade hence, in all likelihood, it will have gone the way of all the good things which once made the Persians the most enviable people in the world.

In the rugs of the Kurdistan region there is wide variety. Within its confines are made not only the finest, thinnest and most delicate fabrics in Persia, but also a profusion of the heavy, board-like and unfoldable carpets before spoken of as "Lulé." There are all the intermediate grades and a diversity of designs. Most of the spontaneous product of the region is in the shapes used for component parts of the *triclinium*, and the long runners or *kinari* predominate. *Sedjadeh* are few.

Sehna.—In the single matter of fineness of texture these rugs, named for the city of Sehna, situated in the mountains near the Turkish border, have few equals. They are of a peculiar character and not apparently close kin to any other floor covering, even of Persia. They are fully equal to the Tabriz in quality, perhaps better, but in design, texture and color theory are of an altogether different order. Barring the deterioration which has come to all the Eastern weavings they have remained virtually unchanged, which is singular when the location of the city is borne in mind. On every hand Sehna is surrounded by rug-producing districts, each with its special type and all furnishing fabrics as different as possible from the Sehnas, but from none of these do the Sehna weavers seem inclined to borrow.

In design these rugs run to small patterns and diaper arrangement, principally the pear or the fish pattern, woven with infinite fineness and with a skilful toning produced not by shading or grading, but by minute variations in color. The pear, and other small patterns, with the arrangement of stalks with which some of them are combined in the body of the rug, as well as the fine border devices, are all wrought by painstaking and artistic method into a harmony which makes the whole fabric at once rich and restful as it is fine of texture. In most of the Sehnas the diaper of small patterns covers the entire field, but in many a diamond-shaped centre-piece appears. This is covered with a close array of the small figures, while the surrounding space, except the corners, is in solid colors or in some fine diaper pattern different from that of the centre either in the character of the device, or the tint of the ground-color, or both, just sufficiently to make the demarcation distinguishable. In any case the evenness and harmony are preserved. For ground-color wool white prevails, although blue, red, or the ivory tint is sometimes used. The borders are divided into well-adjusted stripes, the middle one very wide in proportion to the others, and carrying a form of the Herati border design. They are all in fine consonance with the general character of the fabric, red and yellow predominating in the larger border devices. A few Sehna rugs have the pear pattern wrought upon a large scale, perhaps half a dozen pears covering the whole field, but even in these the device is treated with the characteristic minuteness and the soft effect is retained.

The maximum size of the old Sehnas is about five feet wide by eight feet long, but owing to the constantly growing demands for larger rugs they are now made in other sizes. Except in rare instances the modern fabric is inferior to the antique. The material is coarser and the colors not so soft, so fast or so delicately blended.

Sometimes the Sehnas are confused, through the general similarity of tone and pattern, with other varieties, notably the Feraghans, but they may be distinguished by the weave. The maximum in the Feraghans, even in the antiques, is about one hundred and sixty knots to the square inch. The true Sehna has far more than that. It has, in fact, no equal in this respect save the Kirman, Tabriz, Saruk and a few very old Turkestan rugs.

The warp is of cotton, linen or silk. So tightly are the knots in some of the old Sehnas put in that a slight puckering is visible on the back—an appearance suggestive of crêpe. The effort at compactness often results in a curling up of the fabric at the sides. This, and a growing decadence in the quality of the colors, are the chief faults in the modern Sehnas. The pile in the best pieces is more closely trimmed than any other rug, save the finest old Tekke or so-called Bokhara. Imitations of the Sehna are now included in the general manufacture of Tabriz.

Kurdistan Proper.—The geographical position of Persian Kurdistan has had a remarkable influence in fixing the character of the rugs produced by its tribes. They are different in almost every respect from those made by the Kurdish tribes just over the border, in the hill ranges of Mosul and Van. In these provinces, as has been said in the note on the Mosul fabrics, the products are of the nomadic order, loose of texture and rough in appearance. The Persian Kurds, on the contrary, have learned and continue to practice a more finished form of craft. Propinquity to the cities of Azerbijan, Ardelan and Luristan has made them familiar with the carpets produced by the skilled artisans of those districts, and the points of resemblance between the rugs are many. The influence of Kermanshah, where for a long time the finest of weaving was done, has had much to do with uplifting the character of the weaving throughout the entire district. The ideals thus established seem to have lingered among the Kurds. They have even outlived the glories of Kermanshah itself. In place of the long pile common among the Mosul Kurds, their relatives of Persian Kurdistan trim many of their fabrics almost to the closeness of a pure Persian carpet. They show a great diversity in design, and a particular leaning to repetitive patterns, arranged usually in rows so as to form a diaper. In some parts of Kurdistan, to the north, the weavers have caught the Karabagh and Kabistan idea, and have taken up with large geometrical forms for the central fields, and compromised by filling in the remaining space with the small patterns peculiar to Persia. Another concession to the Caucasian idea is their choice of method. The fabrics are tied with the Ghiordes knot. That with this it is difficult to effect the minute alternations of color distinctive of the finer Persian carpets is, without doubt, the reason that these Kurds have fallen back, when weaving rugs for market, on Caucasian designs for filling in the central space. Where the Sehna or Saraband influence predominates, the entire field of the rug is well covered with small figures, closely crowded in regular rows, vertically and horizontally. Popular patterns for this purpose are flowering shrubs, probably a modification of the widely distributed tree pattern. To most of these the limitations of stitch have imparted erectness and symmetry which only frequent diversifications of color soften and save from being mechanical. A typical form of this device has an upright stalk, with a cluster at its roots. The first output of branches, ascending, is quite broad, heavily leaved, and flowered at the ends. Then come four other and longer branches, two on either side, bearing lumpy clusters at the ends.

One similar but smaller cross branch is above these, with clustered ends, and a clump of foliage at the junction with the trunk; then the heavily leaved crest, and above that one flower as a top tuft, red bodied, perhaps, with a border of bright blue. All the branches stand out at right angles with the stem, and so far has the figure taken on geometrical character, that to any but an imaginative person, study is required to discover that the design in all of its varied forms is arboreal. In the Turkish rugs and some Caucasians this same device, in even more geometrical drawing, may be found playing the part of border. To produce a precise stripe effect in the rows of these patterns, diagonally, the colors in the different parts of the figure—pale blue, brown, old gold, black, olive, and several shades of red—are alternated in every second figure. On the ground of dark blue or perhaps red, this effect is striking, and the number of these figures, crowded into the field, makes it seem ornate and flowery. The main border often carries the same pattern.

Frequently, however, there is in the body of the rug a central design of some established medallion shape, covered with small figures, while the space about it, if dark blue, is filled with repetition of the pear, in dark red. If the ground-color be red the pear figure is in blue. Occasionally the central design consists of several large, lozenge-shaped figures, minutely decorated with smaller patterns. In the border, which carries a rich array of red and blue, relieved with bright yellow in small dashes, are small, variegated block and key patterns carried through the length of the stripe. The wider stripes are varied with daisies, wrought with much accuracy. The borders show concessions to both the influences by which the makers are surrounded.

The Kurdistans are finished on one end with a small fringe, and the sides are overcast with worsted yarn, usually some shade of brown. The general effect and finish must be relied upon to distinguish them, as their patterns are too widely used in other rugs, both Persian and Turkish, to be at all characteristic. One mark which is almost invariably found in Kurd rugs is a single line in colored wools, embroidered on the webbing across one or both ends. The warp should be wool. The "Irans"—as certain of the Persian nomad products are called—are often mistaken for Kurdistans, but in almost every case may be recognized by their cotton warp, and usually by a difference in the knot used.

Kurdistan rugs are very often found in which a coarse, heavy, two-strand wool yarn is passed straight across, between front and back weft-threads, after every row of knots, as filling. In such, one of the regular weft-threads is omitted. The weft is the smallest of dyed single-strand yarns, just sufficient to hold the filling and knots in place. The result is amazing firmness and durability. The Bijars illustrate this method of filling.

Kermanshah.—Amid the mountains which stand sentinel against the Turk, all along the western border, is the outpost town of Kermanshah. It has long been a foremost town of the province of Ardelan, and the chief fortress of the West. Any intelligent Persian will tell you that it got the name of Kermanshah from the fact that one of the governors who was sent to administer its affairs, so long ago that tradition fails to fix the time, came from the southern province of Kirman. However this may be, Kermanshah, with its famous bazaars, its extensive garrison and its busy population, was a place of moment, and, thanks to the carpet-making carried on in the palace under the governor's patronage, its weavings became famous throughout all northern Persia. It has been customary, until very lately, among the rug dealers of the West and Constantinople as well, to attribute the Kirman rugs to Kermanshah. The fabrics here, however, while more pretentious in some ways than those of the surrounding Kurd country, are no longer to be classed with the weavings of Kirman.

The days of the palace are ended. The population of the town has dwindled from forty or fifty thousand to one-fifth the number. There is still a garrison of some strength as Persian garrisons go, which is saying little. The fortress and the walls are in ruins, the once crowded caravanserais are empty. The carpet industry, as a matter of fact, is no longer carried on to any extent in the town.

The rugs which come to the Persian markets with the name of Kermanshah are chiefly made in the surrounding mountains, but the weavers hold in some measure to the traditions of the olden time. This is evident not only in the designs but the shape of the fabrics. The *sedjadeh* are still in vogue, which cannot be said of the other districts in that part of Persia, most of which produce only runners and the large, long centre-pieces.

In design, the best of the Kermanshahs affect the floral treatment. The texture is looser than in many of the rugs in Persian Kurdistan. The pear is used in design, but in the coarser rugs it is woven after the manner of the Mosuls. In many ways, indeed, the influence of the Turkish models is made manifest in the common grade, but in the better pieces much of Persian quality is displayed. The pear pattern in these, for example, has quite the Iranian character. Instead of being drawn as it is in the Saraband and Shiraz, it appears with a shape and degree of elaboration suggestive of the Khorassan and Kirman designs. A singular arrangement of the pattern, too, is frequently seen in the Kermanshahs. Instead of being placed in rows, unattended by any other element, the pears are trained on undulating vines, which run diagonally across the field, and each figure is surrounded by some floral conceit. This design is also found in Kirman rugs and lately has been adopted, as everything has, by the factory weavers of Tabriz. The colors in some of these floral designs are rich and unusually good, and considerable skill is shown in the shading, which in most districts has been abandoned.

There are also found in abundance the standard Persian and Kurdish *terehs*. The knot of the Kermanshah is Turkish, the warp sometimes cotton, another survival of the palace teaching. The sides are overcast with dark brown wool like most of the Kurd rugs, and the finishing of the ends conforms to the custom of the group.

Sarakhs or Bijar.—These are the true " Lulés." They take their name from the old fortified city on the Tajend, in the angle where Persia and Afghanistan come to the borders of Turkestan, and where now the Russian bear rests preparatory to swallowing both. They are of what may be termed native production, to distinguish them from factory products of the cities. Their makers are Turkish tribesmen who came under Genghis and Tamur from the districts around old Sarakhs and settled in the neighborhood of Bijar, in the Gehrous district of Kurdistan. The name Sarakhs is not known in Persia in connection with these carpets. Some of the older pieces which are preserved in collections were apparently the work of skilled artisans, and the graceful Arabi-Persian curves were used in defining the great central medallions which constitute the Sarakhs design. The ornamentation was limited, since in the old carpets even more than in the new, the characteristics were simplicity and power. The medallions found in the best Görevans are imitations of the oldest and finest Sarakhs. The modern fabrics preserve the general design, the strong color-massing, and for the most part the colors also; but they have yielded to the seduction of the straight line.

The hues are few and elementary. Blending seems to be an almost unknown art to these people, but the plain grounds are dexterously shaded. In the staple carpets recently turned out at some weaving centres, effort has been made to imitate this peculiarity, but the intent is so apparent and the deftness of the Sarakhs weavers so plainly lacking, that the charm of the thing is lost, and the variation set down as *rayah*, one of the cardinal sins in the eyes of the master weaver of to-day.

Red predominates in the Sarakhs, but the primary blues, greens, yellows and even black and white are used in brave plenty. The common design is a central piece in a medallion frame, surrounded by a field of plain color. The corners are set off sometimes in curves, but oftener in rectangular triangles, a decadent substitute for the masterly scrolls which beautified the old examples. The grounds of the border, field and centre-piece, if not in any of the camel's-hair shades, are usually in the wonderful Sarakhs red or some bright blue, upon which are boldly displayed vari colored rectilinear flowers or unequal figures of some sort. The pear shape, crudely drawn, is often met with, and the daisy of our own fields is truthfully if rudely shown.

Nothing could be more indescribably gay than the modern Sarakhs carpet of purely nomad manufacture. The fear which haunts the school-trained colorist, of clashing with accepted theory, does not hamper these hill folk. Contrast, not complement, is their creed. They have been accustomed to see the greenest of trees against the bluest of skies, the most flamboyant of reds and yellows side by side in the sunset. This model they know no valid reason for not following, with such fidelity as their scant skill in dyeing makes possible. The result is a marvel of consistency in high key. These rugs have a particular place in furnishing. Western industry and invention probably could not have designed them or an equivalent for them, and if it could, would not have dared. Every color is a climax, and their crudity gives a breadth and massing which are most available to complete and set off apartments where the wood, walls and furniture are dark, and the general effect is coarse and heavy. Their design has been followed, and elaborated, in many of the great Anatolian carpets.

There is in some of them, too, a brightness other than that of tingent. The weavers have drawn, from some source, a reckless tendency to ornament their works by the inweaving of birds, animals and men. Their production does not seem to be along the Chinese or Persian lines, however. The figures are more European, but it is the pictorial art of the child rather than of the ancient. The men and cows, the hens, horses and sheep are of the selfsame order as those which the American school boy draws upon his slate, but there is abundant evidence of close observation, of a humor far keener and broader than the power of expression which bodies it forth. It is the humor of the unskilled caricaturist. The man with the three-cornered head who stalks in the field of the nomad Sarakhs, has a body shaped like a city block, viewed from the avenue side, but the rainbow of gaudy horizontal stripes which makes his whole torso gay, is doubtless a memorial to some tribal dandy, or a message of fellow feeling to the lurid youth of the Occident.

In lieu of the medallion design there often appear scroll-like or shield devices, with some conventional floral bits interspersed. These are distributed sparsely upon a field of richest blue or red. The colors are dark and indescribably rich, the small scrolls, for example, being laid in deep leaf-green, true madder red, and a peculiar blue several shades lighter than the ground, and so lustrous that it seems to be woven in silk. In this same blue the main border ground is often laid. This border is broad, and usually carries a graceful design of the Herati order. Sometimes where the field is of dark blue, the border ground is a correspondingly deep red, and the figures in light shades, with pronounced effects in yellow and old ivory, which give brightness to the whole expanse. These also appear in the central field.

Warp, weft and pile of the Sarakhs are of wool, and the material with which the best of them are piled is as fine as in many of the costly Persian carpets. As in the Kazaks, one end is often finished with a fringe, while at the other the warp is turned, twisted and woven back upon itself with the weft, to form a broad, heavy selvage. The sides are overcast. The knot is Ghiordes.

Koultuk.—There are made in the many small villages of the district lying between Gehrous and Zenjan, partly in the province of Ardelan and partly in the northwest corner of Irak Ajemi, a multitude of small runners of various sorts, including even some of the Herez type. They are worked on a cotton warp and with woollen weft and in other respects follow the Kurd models. They are heavy, but not of the "Lulé" weight. The knot is Turkish. One end has a plain selvage; the other a selvage and loose ends. The new dyes are used in most of these and the coloring of course is not of the best. A dealer in Zenjan, on the road from Tabriz to Teheran, began collecting these pieces, adding to them such as came to hand of the Kara Dagh and other weavings, and marketing the whole as Koultuk or Zenjan. The extreme diversity noticeable in these shipments forbade their taking rank as a distinct class. Constantinople rug men, reassorting the bales, cast each piece into the lot which it resembled most closely, and abandoned, so far as American invoices were concerned, both Koultuk and Zenjan; so neither of the names has ever found a prominent place among the shop titles employed in this country. The "variety" is in reality merely a hodgepodge of the same sort as the so-called "Guendje," in which are comprised the odds and ends of all the Caucasian and Mosul weavings.

Souj-Bulak.—Another variety of rugs offered in considerable numbers in Persian markets comes from the neighborhood of Souj-Bulak, the old Kurdish capital on the border, some distance to the south of Tabriz and Lake Urumieh. The population of the district is overwhelmingly Kurd, and the rugs are in all the essentials Kurdish, with slight local variations. The yarns are doubled, which makes

PLATE XIV. OLD FERAGHAN SEDJADEH

6.8 x 4

Property of the Author

An excellent example of eighteenth and nineteenth century work in the Feraghan district. The Herati, or "fish" pattern in very compact form, with the corner spaces distinctly set out and a species of Herat border. In the narrower stripes will be observed the pear pattern, something after the manner of the older Khorassans. The broad border has the characteristic light green ground, which appears in most of the better and older rugs of the pure Feraghan weave. This green wears down quickly and leaves the other colors in relief. The pile yarns are trimmed closely in the beginning, and long wear has brought them very near to the foundations, but the design is still clear and the general color effect is of almost a heliotrope quality.

the fabrics very compact. The wool is of the best and the pile soft and pleasant to the touch, but by reason of the close texture it stands straight instead of flattening like that of the Kazaks. All the patterns are Kurdish and the colors are dark—chiefly red, blue and brown. While strong and serviceable, the Souj-Bulak rugs are far from maintaining the standard of the first-class Kurd products.

Two rows at the back of the rug indicate the single Ghiordes knot and the number of these to the inch measuring vertically is greater than when measured on the weft. The average is 7-8 by 10-11. The finishings are of the Kurdish character.

FERAGHAN FABRICS

Mainly for the purpose of condensation and in order to bring the matter into easier focus, I have chosen to consider the Feraghan rug district as comprising practically all the central province of Irak Ajemi, extending from the eastern slope of the Bakhtiyaris to the great salt deserts or "Death Valleys" of Persia on the east, and from the Caspian Sea southward to the grim left shoulder of the Kuh Banan. The adjustment is somewhat arbitrary, and considered from a geographical standpoint would be erroneous, for the Feraghan district is clearly defined by the maps and does not include the localities where some of the rugs here classified as of the Feraghan group are manufactured. There will be imparted to the Feraghan by this arrangement a great diversity, but in reality not greater than the small territory enjoys, since the actual Feraghan industry has become wholly commercial, and under direction of European managers the weavers of the province now turn out copies of almost every known fabric as well as the original variety which made it famous.

But aside from this, viewed as a whole its fabrics show, under the present classification, more nearly than those of any other section, all the features of design and color common to Persian carpets, whether recent or traditional, though in all save one variety they are lacking in the peculiar ornamental character which abides in the Kirman and Tabriz. In examples which will be noted, it is plain that some of the group have to a certain extent been made in imitation of the medallion rugs. Where they have been the expression solely of the Persian genius they preserve more of apparent spontaneity ; there is more of nature in them, more likeness to the carpeting of blossoms upon which, in imagination if not in fact, the Persian treads his whole life through.

There is close resemblance between some of these carpets of Feraghan and the fine fabrics of Sehna, which, as has already been said, are, in spite of proximity to the Turkish towns of Bijar, Hamadan and Tabriz, fairly loyal to Iranian tenets and fashion in art. The difference between the several products of this comprehensive group lies mainly in the designs adopted and the quality of material used.

As floor coverings they are of about equal value. Exception, however, must be made to the common grades of Feraghan proper. This variety marks in Persia, as the low class Ghiordes does in Turkey, the maximum of deterioration from an artistic standpoint. With quantity alone in view and with an ancient reputation to trade upon, quality, for which its name was for centuries honored, seems to have been lost sight of for a time.

Feraghan Proper.—The saving clause in whatever may be said of modern Feraghan rugs must be that until lately they have retained the typical patterns and colors, but it requires some imagination to form from some of the Feraghans of to-day an idea of what their prototypes were. More wholesome, well wrought and altogether likeable floor coverings than the old-time Feraghans it would be hard to find. To the Persian they are the acme of carpeting. The Herati design, which has been held almost a distinctive mark of the Feraghan, has been, on the whole, quite steadfastly adhered to in one form or another—possibly because familiarity enables the weavers to produce it quickly. In the better examples it is repeated upon a ground usually blue, with rich but modest variations of color. The borders, well balanced in width against the body of the rug, are wrought after the common plan of alternating rosettes and palmettes upon a waving vine. The borders have more white and pale tints, and more pronounced blues and red than the body. The ground of the main stripe is often laid in some shade of green. The very old pieces leave no room for doubt that this diaper and the same general character have long been distinctive of Feraghan carpets.

The other design most often found in old and finely wrought Feraghans, is the Guli Hinnai, or Flower of the Henna, to which reference has already been made in the chapter on Design. It is more ornate than the Herati, and when well woven and in the antique coloring makes a much richer and more effective carpet.

Within the past year or two the Sultanabad firm, which is paramount in Feraghan, and some weavers in other sections, have begun reproducing this design in some excellent rugs, though chiefly in small sizes. For some time hitherto the Guli Hinnai had been much used in large, slipshod form, in coarse carpets.

Many modern Feraghans, borrowing from all sources whatever will fill space, have a huge medallion in the central field, which, with the small corner spaces, has usually an ivory or white ground. The medallion is broken by three more or less geometrical diamond-shaped devices, two in blue, supporting a central and larger one in red. All of the central field not taken up by these labor-savers is filled with the recognized small Herat pattern on a blue ground. This design for Feraghan has been largely adopted by the manufacturers of Persian carpets in America as well as in the factory towns of Persia and Turkey. Its borders sometimes preserve vaguely the old conventional Herat or Persian ideas, but more often the main stripe is made up of separate flower devices. Running patterns are retained in the small border stripes. Some of the latter Feraghans have wandered so far from their traditional designs as to use, for the central medallion, geometrical shapes somewhat like those of the Caucasians, or the singular medallion with plain ground so common in the Hamadans.

The true Feraghans are worked in the Sehna knot. The weft is of cotton, which in the moderns has deteriorated commensurately with the rest of the fabrics. Their pile is of wool. Instead of from ninety to one hundred and fifty knots to the square inch, moderns sometimes run as low as thirty.

Sultanabad.—In its practical phase the whole enormous rug industry of the province of Feraghan itself and much of that of the surrounding territory centres in Sultanabad. It is the carpet headquarters of the European firm which controls so large a part of the weaving business of this section of Persia. Aside from the old designs and the modifications of them to which reference has been made above, the Sultanabad carpets are the conceits of European and American designers, working, in a way, on the old Persian models, but changing the colors and supplying such additions as seem likely to meet capricious demands. The regulation grades are heavy carpets of the same sizes as those made in Ghiordes and Oushak, but rather superior to those in quality. In the American markets the Sultanabads are often called " Savalans," after the range of mountains which towers to the north of the district. In the wholesale trade they are classed as " Extra Modern Persians." The designs of this order are known to the weavers as *tereh* Lemsa. The groundwork is usually of a pale yellowish cast, and the patterns, vines, flowers and the like, are boldly drawn, in stable shades of red, blue and green. The general effect is brilliant and the carpets have on the whole given satisfaction. Harsh criticism has been passed on the Sultanabad enterprise, in various quarters, on the ground that it had urged the weavers to hasty work and by confining them strictly to the designs placed in their hands had substituted European ideas for the "spontaneous originality" which in times past has been the greatest charm of all Oriental art. On the other hand it may be, and is, contended that the Persian populace, having little or no means to prosecute the work of carpet-making, would have been forced to forget its craft entirely if some competent agency had not intervened to supply the necessary materials and support. In this measure, at least, concerns of this sort have been conservative forces and the employment which they have afforded has without question kept life in the body of many a poverty-stricken Persian who otherwise would long ago have surrendered in the struggle for the wretched bread of the country.

Saraband.—It has been commonly believed that the name Saraband, as applied to floor coverings, had some connection with the Saraband dance. In a way it has. The Saraband rugs are made in the district of Sarawan, lying immediately to the south of Feraghan. It is easy to understand how the Mediterranean dealers, familiar with the graceful terpsichorean function known as Saraband, interpreted the Persian Sarawan into something that was sure to strike gratefully upon Western ears.

In the Sarawan district the *tereh* Mir, so called from the village where it is said to have originated, is the almost universal design, and outside influences have not availed to wean the weavers from it. Artisans in other localities have copied the Mir Saraband, changing the borders or coloration to suit their fancy. Even the Herez peasants have taken to making large *kali* in this design, but after their own textile methods.

The pure Saraband rugs are probably as clearly defined and adhere as closely to type as any class of carpets in Persia. Almost without exception the field is filled with the pear pattern.

In its arrangement in the Saraband alternate rows will in most instances be found to have the stems turned in opposite directions, which adds more than might be believed to the balanced effect of the design. The colors are quiet but rich. The deepest Persian red and blue are used for ground-colors, one almost invariably appearing in the border when the other is used for the field. Sometimes the main ground is white or ivory color. In such cases the pear pattern appears in red or blue.

A feature of the Saraband, which adds much to its attractiveness and decorum, is the multiplication of the border stripes. These are all narrow, but of different widths, and sometimes there are as many as a dozen of them. The undulating vine is always present, but in very small form, and little rectilinear flowers are thrown in in place of the recognized lotus forms. The narrowness of these border stripes could scarcely be defended if the design in the body of the rug were other than what it is. If it were pretentious and coördinate the multiplicity of small stripes would be beneath it in dignity, and the imposing Herat or Persian borders would be in order. But the adaptation of the border value to the small pear shapes which make up the filling shows these Sarawan weavers to possess a sense of balance and harmony which could scarcely be improved.

The adoption of geometrical elements into the borders is only one of the several evidences in the Saraband of influence other than Persian. Another is what has been called the reciprocal trefoil, referred to as a feature of the " Polish " carpets and having a place in certain Caucasian fabrics. It is found in a vast number of Sarabands, and the reciprocal saw tooth is perhaps even more common.

The genuine Mir Sarabands are tied in the Sehna knot. It is not unusual to find the date of manufacture worked in them.

There is common in the Levantine marts, and frequently found in rug stores in this country, a fabric known to the Turkish dealers as Selvile. It is nothing more or less than a coarser form of Saraband, made by the mountaineers and copied by the weavers in other sections. It is tied with the Ghiordes knot, and is of about the quality of the upper middle class Shirvan, which in some of the border patterns it much resembles. It presents the pear pattern in large, loose form, and the field is overweighted by the number and solidity of its border stripes. It has a two-thread overcasting at the sides, made with the colored weft. The narrow web at the ends is of the same color. On one end there is a rather long knotted fringe of the warp which is of fine, grayish wool. On the other end the loop of the warp through which the rod has passed is allowed to twist and left for finishing. Rugs of this description are sold in this country under whatever name happens to be most convenient at the time.

Hamadan.—In the shadows of Mount Elwund, in and around the city of Hamadan (ancient Ecbatana, burial-place of Esther and Mordecai), a great rug industry is carried on. Most of the fabrics made here have, until lately, followed an established theory in design, and to a large extent in color as well. Shortly before the year 1900, so great was the success of the Hamadan weavings, looms were set up in many nearby neighborhoods where before no rug-making was done. In these the designs of other parts were well imitated, and the object was to substitute regular "factory" output for the old production which was wholly characteristic of Hamadan. Cause for this may be found in the decline in popularity which the typical rugs of the district have suffered. There is little difficulty in distinguishing the Hamadan carpet from all other weavings, unless it be from others made in imitation of them at the time when their vogue was greatest.

A considerable quantity of filik, as well as camel's-hair in the natural color, is used in the pile. The prevailing colors are red, blue and yellow, all in strong values, which gain a lustre from the materials. The real camel's-hair antique examples are very rare now, and

vast prices are demanded for them. The moderns, while rougher, and harsher in color than the older rugs, are honest and service-able fabrics.

They have generally a plain color, in most cases ivory-white or some shade of camel's-hair, for the groundwork of the central field ; if not this, then a fret diaper in camel's-hair shade upon a back-ground of ivory-white or cream color. There is a medallion of some pretension in the middle, and the corner spaces are set off to accord with it. These divisions are very positive, but the outlines are shapely. The flower patterns with which the inclosed areas are adorned, are laid in a rather light blue and striking shades of red. Around the outside of the rug is the *tevehr*, or broad band of natural camel's-hair, of a tint like that used in the body, or of wool dyed in some pale ivory or primrose tint. Sometimes a stripe of rich red is thrown in just inside this band, fetching up against the border stripes, which are adorned with rectilinear forms of the vine and flower pattern.

There are also some peculiarly compact diaper patterns used in the Hamadans, which are seldom found in any other fabrics. The most common of these is known as *Ina Dar*—or the "Mirror" de-sign. It is complex and leaves little if any of the ground space visi-ble. The essential outline of the design is at first glance indistinct. It is involved with the accessories in such a way as to obscure it. The colors, dull red, blue and yellow, are so intermingled as to give the whole design a dull pinkish tinge, which comports well with the plain band of camel's-hair with which it is enclosed at the sides and ends. The general color effects of the typical Hamadans are shown in Plate XVI of the illustrations.

Among the principal tributaries of the Hamadan market is the Kara-Geuz field, lying to the east. It has long been a weaving section and the workmanship is fairly well up to the Hamadan stan-dards, solid and substantial. In order to supply a demand made upon the Tabriz, Tiflis and Constantinople dealers, runners from twenty-five to thirty-five feet long are now made in the Kara-Geuz. They are in all sorts of designs, and in some of them the anilines are rampant.

The old Kara-Geuz runners resembled in many respects certain rugs of Kurdistan. They have been sold in America under the name of Iran, a never-failing retreat for the vendor who is in doubt about the precise origin of a Persian rug. The warp and weft in most cases are of cotton and the sides are overcast. The texture constitutes the chief difference between them and the Kurdistans.

On the road leading south from Hamadan is a group of villages, chief of which are Oustri-Nan and Burujird, where some sterling rugs are woven for the Hamadan trade. They are compactly made; the ground of the border is white, with some conventional device remotely derived from the pear set at short intervals transversely of the border, and with the apex of the cone pointing inward. The Saraband pattern is used for the field, and but for the borders and texture the rugs might be taken for Saraband. They have cotton warp and weft, the latter dyed. They are overcast with colored wool. There is a solid finish at one end and a fringe at the other. The knot is Turkish and the average from seventy-five to ninety to the square inch.

A new and important branch of the Hamadan system is Bibik-abad, where the industry has recently been begun upon a considerable scale. The designs are diverse, the texture somewhat looser than that of the Kara-Geuz rugs and the colors, up to the time of the Shah's edict, not all that could be wished for.

Teheran–Ispahan–Saruk.—Nothing could illustrate better the way market-places throughout the Orient give their names to commodities brought to them for sale, than the survival of these names in rug nomenclature. Just how long a time has elapsed since carpets in any number were made in either the present or former capital of Persia, it would be difficult to determine, but there is scarcely a rug shop of note which has not Teheran and Ispahan rugs to offer to the customer. In the Tabriz bazaars the dealer has no idea what is meant by Teheran and Ispahan. And yet the types, as represented in America, are fairly well defined. After careful inquiry, and examination of rugs sold in Persia, I believe that all the fabrics called Teheran and Ispahan are the products of the village of Saruk in the Feraghan district, and, for the rest, vagrant pieces which come from the looms of Kirman, by the way of Bushire or the Indian ports, to England. In Kirman, longer, perhaps, than in any other place in Persia, the ability to weave well the pure floral and realistic designs has endured. A similar form of craftsmanship still exists in Saruk; the old designs of this order are also copied faithfully in the great factories of Tabriz.

In these " Teheran " and " Ispahan " fabrics the national genius for rich realistic floral decoration maintains very clear expression. There is in them a profusion that makes them known instantly. The freedom with which the designers have gone abroad in the whole realm of nature in quest of forms has resulted in a prodigality of ornamentation which only halts short of redundancy. All the forms and hues of trees and plant life, birds, animals, fishes, clouds, arabesques, thus broad is the field in which the designer of these carpets counts it his privilege to gather materials. With such a range it is plainly impossible to suggest anything nearly approaching a common design. It is the very richness and multiformity which are typical.

There can be little doubt that many of the designs seen to-day were devised in another century, and that they have been copied with slight variation, generation after generation. The best of them reflect an artistic spontaneity which does not abide in the atmosphere of Persia or any other part of the Orient in our time. It is likely that such designs of this class as impress us as being meagre and inept have undergone the greater changes and express more truthfully the present tendency.

In most of the "Ispahan" rugs there are to be found, prominent among the forms upon the dark red or blue field, the clearly marked cones of the cypress tree. Its peculiar dull green, in such perfect complement to the value of the red which is usually dominant, lends a sombre suggestion, a note somewhat funereal in the midst of all the vernal brightness. It is strikingly demonstrative of the artistic melancholy which pervades the Persian mind. This cypress, indirectly an emblem of mourning, but really conveying, as all trees do, the idea of perfect and renewed life, distinguishes the great carpets made for use in the mosques and the grave carpets, once so much used in Persia. Additional evidence of their character is afforded, especially in those of Ispahan, so called, by the presence of a willow with solemnly trailing branches—a combination recognized by Persian weavers under the name of *Tereh Asshur.* The cypress and willow, carved upon headstones in the old graveyards of our own land, may perhaps be a survival of this design. The prayer rugs of this variety often have the willow in the centre, and a succession of cypresses along the sides of the field, with two of them so inclined as to meet at the top, forming the prayer arch.

Some of the "Teheran" rugs show a more formal tendency in design and while retaining the local richness of color have their fields covered with small pear patterns of the elongated forms found in Persian and Indian shawls. Sometimes the effect is made diagonal, when the small patterns are used, by alternating the colors.

In the borders the old pattern of vines carrying rosettes at regular intervals, is common; so in the "Ispahans" is the Herat border. In many "Teherans" the realistic flowers take on a formal decorative character, and the spaces between them are occupied by the long medallion forms known as "cartouches." In rugs of the highest class these cartouches often contain, after the Moorish fashion as preserved in the decoration of the Alhambra, verses from the national poets, appropriate to the designs, or—though religious scruples make this rare—passages from the Koran.

The designs here described have recently been made in the factory towns in very large, almost whole-carpet sizes—another indication of the change which has come over the weaving art of the East. Rugs are now looked upon as carpetings—and little more. But these big, new pieces have retained the old patterns and coloring, and to a remarkable degree the fineness of stitch. There was for some time a scarcity of rugs of this order which showed any sign of age. As manufacture for Eastern markets progressed, Constantinople became well supplied with the profuse floral pieces, and now their importation is very great.

A word further should be said concerning the village of Saruk and its weaving. It is situated in the Feraghan district proper, but its rug-makers for a long time refused to come under the protection of the European firms. They produced only a limited number of pieces in a year, pieces of a fineness to put Tabriz to the blush. Nearly all these were taken to Teheran and immediately bought up by wealthy Persians, who paid for them a far higher price than they would command if offered for sale in the open market. The interesting feature of it is that these same Persian magnates, who might reasonably be expected to stickle for carpets dyed with vegetable tingents, never demur at the loose colors which until lately have marked the Saruks. This contradiction seems to be universal throughout the kingdom. I visited the home of a Persian merchant, and upon arrival, was ushered into a reception room where we had tea Persian fashion, that is, sitting on the floor. In the apartment there were spread half a dozen or more *sedjadeh* pieces—the floral panels of Kirman. From all of them the color had faded. In some only misty shadows remained of the designs, ghosts of what—and not so very long ago—had been riotous masses of color. The master of the house, with Persian quickness, saw that his carpets had attracted notice. "I know what you are thinking," he said. "You are thinking it is strange that a Persian who can afford anything else should content himself with carpets dyed with anilines. The truth is, I like them. The softer the tone of the carpet, the less aware you are of the colors in it, the more restful it is. These loose dyes fade quickly under the sun, and then you have—that. It is beautiful."

And so the fine, flower-strewn rugs of Saruk, with their questionable dyestuffs, are sold for three prices, before the warp of them is stretched upon the loom.

"*Jooshaghan*," *or Djushaghan.*—Among the best carpets in Persia are the soft-toned but hard-woven fabrics which are called Jooshaghan. The name is another of those which are brought in for every emergency. The genuine carpets of this variety have not been largely sold in America, since the district where they are made is within easier reach of the Persian Gulf ports than the markets of the North. The fabrics are therefore better known in England than here.

The Djushaghan or Dshushekan district is some distance south of Feraghan. Its weavers, like those of Feraghan, have shown a decided loyalty to the local design, which, when in its purity and well woven and colored, is one of the most pleasing to be found in Persia. In general effect it resembles the Saraband, but the design has not the definition which is afforded by even the most delicate rendition of the pear pattern. It has something of likeness to the " Mirror" pattern found in the Hamadans in point of color, and also in the fact that the main features do not obtrude themselves upon notice. The foundation of it is Arabic, and the outline, like so many of the Arabic traceries, is continuous, passing on from one figure to another. The principal element is a cross, the ends of which, instead of being square, are angular, and the lines forming this angle intersect each other, and are carried along to form points of adjoining crosses. This, it will be seen, leaves an eight-pointed star space between every four crosses. This space is filled with the subordinate elements of the design, and the centre and arms of the cross itself are likewise adorned with conventional floral figures—four-petaled flowers and a diagonal arrangement of leaves. The border ground is of much lighter red than the body of the carpet, and the patterns are small floral shapes in dull colors, relieving a geometrical key shape similar in conception to the X-shape in the Shiraz rugs. The entire fabric is usually in a soft tone of red.

The warp is wool, and there is a hard, thin, narrow web at the end. The sides are overcast, and the knot is Turkish. There are from nine to twelve knots to the inch measuring horizontally and eight to eleven perpendicularly.

KIRMANIEH FABRICS

All the rugs sent from the southern part of Persia between the Shat-el-Arab and the Persian Gulf on the west, and the plains of Seistan and Beluchistan on the east, may be classed as Kirmanieh fabrics. They are made chiefly by the nomadic Karmanian tribes, some of them descendants of the old Parsees, though the Turkoman elements contribute largely to the product of the district, and their fabrics are thorough counterparts of some of those still found in the Caucasus. The excellent carpets made by the people of the villages throughout Laristan are included under the head of Kirmanieh.

The honesty of these weavings has hitherto brought them great popularity, and though signs of demoralization are visible, remoteness from the avenues of commerce and travel makes it seem likely that some time will elapse before they can come wholly under the influence which has utterly changed so many classes of Eastern carpets. An

E.iglish firm, however, has established an agency at Bushire on the Gulf coast and another at Bassorah, for the collection of carpets from this territory. Their collectors journey to up-country towns, hire a khan or building of some sort, and send out word into the surrounding hamlets and countryside that they are there to buy. The heads of weaving families bring in their whole year's product in response to this notice, and thus a thoroughgoing market system will ultimately be built up. The rugs can be got to Bender Abbas or Bushire, and thence shipped to England or Constantinople.

The materials used in the best of the Kirmanieh fabrics—the Kirman proper and the high-class Shiraz—are taken from the flocks which herd on the shores of the salt lake Niris.

Kirman.—American rug dealers have never had very intimate acquaintance with the rugs of Kirman, capital of the southernmost Persian province. In the early days of rug importation to this country Kirman, like other and even less remote parts of Persia, was little known. The European travelers who had visited it were few. Those entering Persia from the south disembark at Bender Abbas or Bushire, go to Shiraz and thence directly North, to Ispahan, leaving Yezd, Kirman and the desert far on their right. Kirman's communication is chiefly with the East. Even to-day it stands out of the beaten path of travel, and the cities of the North, which count Shiraz as neighbor, though not a very near one, still look upon Kirman as far away.

This explains, in a measure, the confusion which has always existed in regard to the character of the Kirman carpets, which hitherto have come in limited numbers to this country, though in London they have enjoyed renown. In the section devoted to Kurd rugs reference has been made to the current belief that Kermanshah, in the mountains of Kurdistan, was the birthplace of these very interesting fabrics. This error, which only existed outside the confines of Persia, has been dispelled. After the Tabriz rugs, modeled after the later fabrics of Kirman, had fairly choked the markets, the Kirman exports began to appear in comparative plenty in Stamboul.

The carpet industry in Kirman is old, and has been, if Reclus is to be believed, more tenacious of life than some of the arts which throve there in other times. He says; "Since the visit of Marco Polo Kirman has lost its manufacture of arms, but its embroideries and carpets are always high prized." The endurance of textile industry here, when other arts have failed, is due, no doubt, to the plenitude of unequalled wool. The descriptions given of the manner in which carpet weaving is carried on in Kirman show that it was done studiously, and freedom from contact with the rest of the world served to perpetuate local methods and characteristic designs.

In the book of Sir F. J. Goldsmid, upon "Eastern Persia," published in 1876, is to be found the clearest utterance regarding the carpets of Kirman, an utterance formulated on the notes of eye witnesses of the manufacture. It says: "The curiosities of Kirman are the carpet and shawl manufactures. The former, once the most celebrated in the East, have much diminished in number since the siege, from which date all the calamities of Kirman. In the governor's factory alone are the finer qualities produced. The white wool of the Kirman sheep, added perhaps to some quality of the water, gives a brilliancy to the coloring, unattainable elsewhere. In patterns the carpets are distinguishable from those of the North and West by this purity of color, and a greater boldness and originality of design, due probably to a slighter infusion of Arab prejudice on the subject of the representation of living forms. Not only flowers and trees, but birds, beasts, landscapes and even human figures are found in Kirman carpets. The Wakil-ul-Mulk gave me two in return for a pair of breech-loading pistols of greater value that I presented him with, and I purchased a still finer one in the bazaar."

PERSIAN

This is supplemented by the report of Major Oliver B. St. John, embodied as part of the same volume. His description of the way in which the Kirman weaving is done would serve almost equally well as a picture of the work in the Tabriz factories.

He says : " From the shawl manufactory we went some little distance to that of the no less celebrated carpets. These are manufactured in a way reminding one strongly of the Gobelin tapestry made at present, or rather, before the war, in Paris. The looms are arranged perpendicularly, and the workers sit behind the loom, but in this case, unlike the Gobelins, they have the right side of the carpet towards them. The manufacture of carpets differs from that of shawls in this particular, that each carpet has a painted pattern, designed and drawn out by the master of the manufactory, which is pinned to the centre of the carpet, and which the workers can consult if necessary, from time to time. Advantage, however, is rarely taken of this facility of reference, for the boy who sits nearest the pattern reads out in a monotonous voice any information required concerning it. The carpets are made entirely of cotton, woven by the fingers into the upright web. Their manufacture is tedious and costly in the extreme, but they are beautifully soft and durable. The work is constantly hammered close together by a wooden hammer every few stitches. The man whose manufactory we visited was said to be without a rival in Persia either in the designing of beautiful rugs, or in skill in making them. We saw a beautiful carpet that he was making for a shrine at Meshhed, which was to cost five thousand tomans, or two hundred pounds, being eleven yards long by about two and a half broad ; than which nothing could have been more beautiful. The boys and men do not look so unhealthy as those in the shawl shops."

The designs of Kirman, to this day, are of the floral order, but in the recent carpets—those which have been taken as models for the Tabriz rugs—the medallion idea is paramount. The panels are not so hard or so heavy as those of Tabriz in appearance ; the flowers are treated with a light and natural touch and with that appearance of relief found scarcely anywhere else, save in very old carpets of the neighboring province of Khorassan.   But in the older Kirman pieces —the sort which one seldom sees nowadays, there is evidence of greater freedom, of individual conceit.   An indisputable example of this was found in a loan exhibition in the Library of Pratt Institute in Brooklyn, N. Y.   Its origin was proven by an inscription woven in a cartouche in its border, " Amli Kirman, made at Kirman," and then, " Karim," doubtless the name of the weaver.   It was an old rug and the registration of its date, which was also included in the inscription, brought to light another interesting fact, that Karim, the weaver, was not of the ordinary type of Mohammedan Persians, but a descendant of the ancient Persis or Zoroastrian fire worshippers, who had refuge in the city of Kirman.   That city and Yezd are known to be now the only places in Persia where any considerable colonies remain of the Zoroastrians, who in modern Persian are called Zerdusht.   Record of date in Eastern carpets is usually made by the reckoning of the Hegira, now inching along into its fourteenth century.   This rug of Kirman bore date of 2918.   The solution was obvious, since this is the thirtieth century of the Zoroastrian era.   Rough computation showed that the rug was in the neighborhood of a hundred years old. The pile had been so worn away that it was difficult to determine the knot used.   So Karim, the weaver, had years ago been gathered to his fathers, but this old rug, perhaps the meanest of his handiworks, was one to do him credit.   It amuses one to wonder what would have been the thoughts and impressions of Karim if he could have seen it hanging there with the trader's tag upon it, and the strange, " Ferenghi "-looking people staring at it and looking up its number in the catalogue.   It was listed, by the way, as an India Kashmir.   And there is yet another story, for much of the export of Kirman is across

PLATE XV.   OLD SIRAB

6.10 x 5.4

Loaned by Mr. Arthur H. Scribner

The inspiration of the makers of big Herez carpets, and even of the fine woven modern Serapis, woven sometimes on the looms of Tabriz and sometimes on those of Sultanabad, is found in such rugs as this, rare pieces enough since the eastern villages of Azerbijan became a carpet factory, feeding the great Tabriz market with their wares.   In the strong, serrated medallion and in the peculiar drawing of all the odd floral elements, in the red of the medallion and the lighter blue of the big ribands at sides and corners, is declared the local genius of the Herez district, but this rug, fine as cloth in texture, and as pliable, yet strong, was made decades before the so-called Herez, or Görevan or Serapi "whole carpets" were heard of in the West.   Its centre is a very sapphire in coloring and all the shades of camel's-hair that are known to the loom-worker lie within its borders.   There are shadings which at first look like soiled streaks, but they are only capricious changes in the color of the wool.

PLATE XVI.   LARISTAN RUG

15.0 x 5.6

From the Marquand Collection

As fine a display of the old blue of Southwestern Persia as one will ever see.   This type of rug is ordinarily classed as of Shiraz, but the finishings of this piece warrant placing it, more accurately, among the products of Laristan. Its unity of design is as admirable as its color, the only deviation from the re- gular repetition of the pear pattern being few—only such as are really required by superstitious belief.

PLATE XVII. SEHNA KHILIM

6.4 x 5.2

Property of the Author

The Sehna product is by far the finest of any known in the khilim stitch, and has all the appearance of completeness which marks the piled fabrics of Sehna, which, indeed, the khilims follow rather closely in design and color. The pattern is the close form of the Herati, for the centre, and Sehna has developed it to a greater measure of perfection than any other weaving district except Feraghan, where, as will be seen, by Plate XIX, it is used with almost equal perfection. In border, the fine khilims do not usually employ the Herati stripes which are found in nearly all the piled rugs. This really is a fine artistic touch, since the small vine and flower design here used is much more appropriate in a fabric of such extreme lightness as the khilim. In the matter of weight, this piece itself is little more than a shawl, and the threads with which the pattern is woven are quite as fine as many of those used in the making of lace. It is the habit of the East to wash the khilims as one washes a garment, and even where the dyes are vegetable and thoroughly fast, this process and the subsequent drying in the sun makes very strong colors take on a soothing softness. Nothing could be more delicate than the rose-pink of this covering, which by the aid of the blue is converted in its general effect to something very like violet.

PLATE XVIII. OLD PERSIAN SILK PRAYER RUG

5.5 x 3.8

From the Marquand Collection

Singularly enough, this rug is identical in design with that which occupied this same place in the earlier editions of this book, save for small differences in the floral array and coloring, which two centuries' difference in their ages would quite justify. The other—and younger—rug was made in Shiraz, as the parti-colored over-casting, the figured webs and the tassels at the corners told plainly. Whence this far older fabric comes it is quite impossible to say, since the finishings have all been worn away. The similarity in design would, as the reader is aware, not be conclusive. But it is plain, since this piece is so very much older than the other, that it was parent to the other. Whether this rug itself was the first woven in this design, or is itself a copy, is a thing no man can know. "At any rate the god whom the first designer worshipped must have been a generous deity, for throughout it tells a story of plenty and gladness. The idea of actual growth and continued blessing is especially emphasized by the jardinière, which is the central feature of the design, and from which spring in great prodigality practically all the flowers that Persia knows. There is certainly no floral form to be found in any Iranian carpet design, old or new, that does not smile at us from this rug. The rose, the hare-bell, the henna, the poppy and all the rest, even down to the little blue forget-me-not, all are here, crowded as closely as the weaver could crowd them and keep the balance of the design, and that he has done perfectly."

flame. It was as if he had laden them with all the fire his old Iranian ancestors worshipped. Such was the true rug of Kirman.

For all that, it is only due to the spirit of technical accuracy to add that the old weaver had used a two-strand cotton warp and woollen weft of a single strand; that the sides of the fabric were overcast, and the ends finished with only a narrow web and the white tips of the warp, which, across half of one end, were plaited into little ropes. Karim put in about a hundred and twenty knots of Kirman wool to every square inch of his rug. May his soul dwell forever in the smile of Ormuzd.

Shiraz.—Here in Farsistan is one of the most Persian towns in Persia, for here during a dozen centuries the ancient Parsa had its capital. Shiraz, home of wine, roses and nightingales, birth-place and tomb of Hafiz, smiles to-day in the very shadow of older Persepolis, "the courts where Jamshyd gloried and drank deep."

While Shiraz remained the centre of government, the palace manufacture of carpets to be given by the Persian lords to potentates of other countries was conducted upon a splendid scale, and the work produced was the finest of which the Persian genius was capable. The few specimens of the old handiwork which remain show traces of northern influence, but their workmanship and color handling do not suffer by comparison with the most artistic creations of old Kirman and the later capitals of Persia. The untutored elements have, however, so far prevailed in the rug-weaving of late years that the fabrics, while thoroughly good floor-coverings and attractive to a degree, show none of the several phases of artistic advancement which have distinguished the weavings of places farther north, or, in days gone by, of Shiraz itself. The distribution over a wide expanse of country of the people who make the Shiraz rugs, and their exposure to differ-ent decorative influences on all sides have resulted in a wide variation of design; but in most of these the same clear, clean drawing is manifest, and the colors—blue tones seeming to predominate—are bright and strong, and have the merit, even now, of being largely vegetable.

Numberless Shiraz carpets are found with the central field covered with pear patterns. They may be distinguished from the pure Sarabands without difficulty, since the Shiraz treatment is on a rather larger scale and more rectilinear than that found elsewhere, excepting in a few Kabestans and some of the carpets of Mosul. The whole field, again, may be filled with a succession of narrow perpendicular or diagonal stripes, in plain colors, or adorned with figures, animals, and trees. In yet other examples appear the rectilinear central figures of the Caucasians, with hard, clean-cut decoration like that of Daghestan and Shemakha. But in such case the ground surrounding the central figure invariably carries rich, bold flowers, or the pear or tree figures.

The borders are almost always of generous width, and richly ornamented. Some of the flower patterns are quite large and gay, but still conventional. The waving vine is poorly, but almost invariably illustrated in the narrow stripes by a typical pattern, consisting of two full, oval-shaped flowers, in alternate red and blue. Another favorite small stripe is made of X-shaped figures, with diamonds in the spaces between them. The Shiraz displays unusual features of finish. At the ends of some rugs, for example, between the pile and the narrow cloth web, the weaver makes a heavy but very narrow selvage, by weaving together in a coarse check pattern, in the Sumak stitch, red, white and blue yarn, in thick strands of each color. Something resembling this is found in certain of the Turkoman rugs and in many Kurdistans, where it takes the form of stripes of colored yarn embroidered across the narrow web at the ends. The sides of the Shiraz are usually overcast, sometimes in one color, sometimes two or three. Additional lengths of all the yarns used in the piling are occasionally laid along the sides and bound in by the overcasting. This does the double service of strengthening the edges and making them as thick as the piled part. In some rugs an ornamental use is also made of this binding. At intervals of from twelve to fourteen inches, loops of these added strands are left outside the overcasting, and then cut so as to form a series of particolored tufts along both sides of the rug. The effect is very odd. The foundation threads are of wool, fine and white, or in coarse, colored grades, according to the rug's quality. Shiraz carpets are made as large as nine by twelve, but such sizes are rare. The small pieces include many saddle covers, in the making of which the nomads of Farsistan excel.

Most singular, perhaps, among the Shiraz fabrics which reach America are certain rugs having a field of plain color, and for borders successive three- or four-inch stripes of several colors, all without vestige of a design. They are about four and one-half by seven feet, and have on an average eighteen or twenty knots to the square inch. The paucity of stitches does not indicate flimsiness of texture, as might be imagined, for after each row of knots there are six or eight threads of dyed weft, causing the pile, which is long, to lie flat. The wool is extremely fine and soft. These are nothing more than "comforters," made to be used as coverings, but the genius of trade has converted them into carpets. They have the Shiraz peculiarities of finish, the checked colored selvage at the ends, and tufts of yarn adorning the overcasting at the sides.

It will be well to recall here the fact that Shirvans, of the Caucasian fabrics, are frequently offered as Shiraz. The true Shiraz rugs may be known almost invariably by the small checked selvage at the ends. They are worked in the Ghiordes knot, which makes the task of distinguishing them from some Caucasians a difficult one where the patterns are alike.

Niris.—These rugs are made by the hillmen in the uplands

around the salt lake Niris, in Laristan. A city of similar name is near by. The fabrics show many marks of relationship with the modern Shiraz, especially the checked selvage at the ends, and though usually rougher than the Shiraz, excel them in some respects as floor-coverings. They are never as closely woven as the finest of Shiraz products, but on the whole are stronger and more durable. The wool of the sheep grown hereabouts is unsurpassed. The best of it is used by the Niris weavers for piling their rugs. Both warp and weft are of stout, well made woollen yarn.

Madder red is the prevailing color. The designs vary, though not to so great an extent as in the Shiraz. In some Niris rugs there is a well wrought centre-piece, surrounded by a wide space in plain color, and corners elaborately woven. In some an all-over design is employed for the field, showing a pronounced stripe effect, one perpendicular row of odd geometrical figures alternating with a row of stiff floral forms. The borders are quite elaborately woven. In these, as in the Shiraz, the barber-pole stripe of the Caucasians occurs, but in both cases shows several strong, contrasting colors instead of simple alternation of red and white, as found in the Caucasian forms. The Niris are also worked in the Ghiordes knot.

These rugs are one of several varieties which have long been grouped together by English rug men under the name of Laristan. The peculiar geometrical figures mentioned as occurring in the field are souvenirs of the Mongols, who overran these parts, and whose posterity still remain in force in some localities. Some of the designs are clearly Tartarian, and the fabrics seem more like some product of Turkestan than of southern Persia.

Mecca.—One of the pet delusions of rug purchasers, which has for years been industriously fostered by the trade, is that there exists, for commerce, such a thing as a " Mecca " rug, and that it can be bought with all its sanctity upon it, in shops in this country.

"Mecca," as a name for a rug, tells nothing positive concerning the locality of manufacture, and usually nothing but untruth in any regard. "But," a New York dealer said, "you must have something which you can tell them is a Mecca."

There journey to the holy city of the Moslems, each year, more than half a million Mussulmans, bound upon pilgrimage. They come from all parts of the vast territories of which Abdul Hamid II. is spiritual, if not temporal, ruler; from Morocco and the Barbary coasts, from the South, from India, from Persia and Afghanistan, an endless procession moves to display its faith at the Kaaba. Through Constantinople, by boat from Batoum, one hundred thousand of these devotees pass from the Trans-Caucasus, Turkestan and the north of Persia alone. All of this multitude bring offerings proportionate to their store, to be laid upon the shrine. Jewels, shawls, scarfs, armour, furs, perfumes—everything of value is accepted, and the accumulation creates an admirable stock in trade for the mercenary mollahs, whose happy function it is to fix the rates of sacrifice. This consecrated gentry drives a thriving trade in textiles, jewelry, and bric-à-brac, and the carpet export from Mecca is enormous, and heterogeneous in proportion.[1]

---

[1] All the rugs and other commodities carried by these pilgrims upon their journey are not in the nature of religious sacrifices. The Prophet left them this thoughtful paragraph in his message : "It shall be no crime in you if ye shall seek an increase from your Lord by trading during the pilgrimage." The Prophet's understanding of his people, past, present, and to come, was intimate and acute. That it was based upon experience and practical test rather than pure inspiration, is strongly suggested by the first set of tenets which he established, and which later were much modified to meet the requirements of the Mussulman case. Among them are these :

1. Do unto another as thou wouldst that he should do unto thee.

2. Deal not unjustly with others, and thou shalt not be dealt with unjustly. If there be any difficulty of paying a debt, let the creditor wait until it be easier for him to do it ; but if one remit in alms it will be better for him.

3. O merchants, falsehood and deception are apt to prevail in traffic. He who sells a defective thing, concealing its defects, will provoke the anger of God and the curses of the angels.

4. Take not advantage of the necessities of another to buy things at a sacrifice ; rather relieve his indigence.

There are commandments here which, conscientiously kept, would alter the whole complexion of the Eastern rug trade, were that trade in the hands of Moslems, which it is not.

As a rule, the rugs purchased from the mollahs, who bring them down to Jiddah—since no infidel foot is permitted to enter the confines of the Holy City—are of good quality, for a faithful Moslem would scarcely offer an unworthy gift to his Deity; but they are of every sort that the Orient sun shines upon. The greater number are Shiraz. To such an extent have these been wont to predominate that a certain order of Shiraz *sedjadeh* of a blue cast, and about five feet wide by seven feet long, came to be known in the trade as "Mecca" rugs.

This was the doing of the English dealers, who, having received shipments direct from Jiddah, had noticed the predominance of the Shiraz type, and so called that type Mecca. The maintenance among American rug sellers of the belief that these are really Mecca rugs is primarily due to the fact that until fifteen years ago only a very few buyers for American houses had ever gone to Constantinople to secure carpets. The rest, instead, had bought from the importing firms in London, and taken their terminology with the goods.

Nearly all the carpets left by the pilgrims, and thousands with which no pilgrim has ever had aught to do, are sent from Jiddah up through the Suez Canal to Cairo, to be sold to tourists. Others are carried to England, and an infinitely small number to Constantinople. Of late years, so great has grown the business of the Mecca priests, thrifty captains of sailing vessels and tramp steamers plying in the Persian Gulf pick up at small prices what rugs they can in seaport towns, and as they come out through the Red Sea on the way westward, drop them at Jiddah, and sometimes turn a pretty penny thereby. This, doubtless, accounts for the prevalence of the Shiraz type.

One thing is certain, that since the great majority of American merchants do not go to Cairo, but to Stamboul and Smyrna for their rugs, the actual number of Mecca relics of the textile sort which find their way to this country is almost wholly confined to the private purchases made by American idlers about the Delta of the Nile. So greedily are the rugs picked up there, that consignments are sent from Smyrna and Constantinople to be peddled in Cairo as sacred things from Mecca or furnishings from Egyptian palaces.

KHORASSAN FABRICS

Sterling carpets, some of which possess much artistic merit, come from this far eastern province of Persia, which even now extends from the borders of Irak Ajemi, in Central Persia, to Afghanistan, and from the Turkoman boundaries of Asiatic Russia, southward to the province of Kirman. Most of the western portion of Khorassan is desert, in the scattered oases of which only small villages are found. The greater part of the weaving is done in the hill country, along the northern and eastern borders. Fragments of many races populate the province—Iranians, Arabs, Turkomans, Kurds, and what not— and the fabrics therefore are of many sorts. The Iranian element is for the most part sedentary, and has assimilated many of the Arabs and Kurds. The Tartar tribes are wanderers, as they have ever been. The Afghans and Baluches who roam in numbers along the eastern and southeastern confines are robbers to the manner born, and prone to violence.

The best varieties of Khorassan fabrics show something of the same opulence in design which is found in old Ispahan and Teheran carpets, though with more of the treatment of the Kirman rug previously described. The works of the nomad classes are devoid of fineness, but like those of similar tribes in the Caucasus and Asia Minor are rich in bold effects, and durable beyond belief. In Khorassan both the upright and horizontal looms are used, also both methods of knotting.

Khorassan Proper.—The realism which marks certain carpets of the Feraghan group is fairly outdone in many of the proper Khoras sans. There is, perhaps, not so much of poetic feeling apparent, but the floral designs are more interesting for the reason that passably successful effort is made to portray them in perspective. In drawing and coloring the floral masses with which the grounds are covered in some of the more pretentious Khorassans suggest European treatment. The largest and most difficult forms are undertaken, not only without much concession to Oriental decorative convention, but with evident intent to depict them as growing out of the ground. As compared with the flowers in the Teheran and Ispahan rugs, these are as exotics to the exuberant growths of the field. In brilliancy of color and general treatment they resemble somewhat the Kirmans; but even where the central medallion is used the "painted panel" appearance of the Tabriz fabrics is absent.

In some rugs lavish use is made of animal figures, birds and humans. They are all most brilliant in coloring and are drawn with much skill though in rather bad proportion. They are not represented in motion, as is customary in the Teheran and Ispahan fabrics, but in the most photographic and everlasting of poses. A favorite device in these creations is the Persian heraldic emblem, a lion, sword in hand, with the great sun rising at his back. The geographical location of Khorassan and its history go far toward explaining the prevalence of many of the features in design. That part of the province in which the rug-making is almost wholly carried on lies in the main track of travel between Teheran and the East. Its cities have been for centuries the religious centres of Mohammedan Persia, although they have been taken and occupied at intervals by Mongol invaders. Nishapur, most important of these during the Middle Ages, and under one dynasty the capital, was the home of Omar Khayyam and other learned men whose writings have survived to our era and found translation into other languages. Thus, in close touch, with China, and yet a home of Persian culture, and withal famous for the industrial skill of its people, this one city alone must have had much to do with the establishment of the high type which prevails in the best of the Khorassan carpets even now.

It would seem, however, that for a long time the superlative carpets of Khorassan had been made farther to the south. Bellew in his book, "From the Indus to the Tigris," says:

"Birjand, the modern capital of the district of Ghayn, or Cayn, an open town of about two thousand houses, . . . is the centre of a considerable trade with Kandahar and Herat on the one side, and Kirman, Yezd and Teheran on the other. It is also the seat of the carpet manufacture for which this district has been celebrated from of old. These carpets are called *kalin*, and are of very superior workmanship, and of beautiful designs, in which the colors are blended with wonderful harmony, and incomparable good effect. The best kinds fetch very high prices, and are all bespoke by agents for nobles and the chiefs of the country. The colors are of such delicate shades, and the patterns are so elaborate and tasteful, and the nap is so exquisitely smooth and soft, that the carpets are only fit for use in the divans of Oriental houses, where shoes are left without the threshold. The best kinds are manufactured in the villages around, and those turned out from the looms of Duroshkt Nozad enjoy a pre-eminent reputation for excellence. . . .

"Sihdih, as the name implies, is a collection of three villages on the plain to which they give their name. Only one of these is now inhabited, the other two being in ruins. Very superior carpets are manufactured here, and they seem to fetch also very superior prices, to judge from those asked of us for some specimens we had selected. . . .

"Ghayn exports its silks mostly to Kirman raw, but a good deal is consumed at home in the manufacture of some inferior fabrics for the local markets. The carpets known by the name of this town are not made here, but in the villages of the southern division of this district."

The genuine Khorassan is not, however, confined to large, showy designs. All of the more minute patterns in vogue among the artisans of the other districts of Persia are made use of by the people of the eastern province. The pear, the fish pattern, and the conventionalized floral devices recognized as belonging to the Persian decoration are frequent. In their use of the pear, the Khorassan weavers have devised a complex pattern of their own, which, though it has been adopted into other families, is looked upon as the property of the inventor. Two small pears in light color rest their narrow ends, or tops, upon a larger one, at right angles, so as to form a cross, the arms of which lie diagonally to the field of the carpet, and the repetition of the pattern makes of the small, light-colored pears a pronounced diagonal stripe throughout the entire area. The large, dark red pears are so arranged that their stripe is broken at regular intervals. At these points of fracture two of the large pears are placed side by side and a new stripe is begun. The smaller pear figures are jewelled with tiny patterns in bright color. A recurring perpendicular stripe is made by yet other and longer pear shapes, placed vertically between the cross patterns. The blue of the ground, showing between these groups, itself forms a horizontal stripe, and the effect of the whole is rich and striking.

Sometimes the medallion is used, always covered with a skilfully arranged design in small figures. A pronounced waving vine is usually found in the main stripe of the border, drawn in white on a ground of dark red. Frequently, as a substitute for the rosettes, palmettes, and lotus buds common in Herati design, the pear groups are used. The narrow borders repeat the undulating effect, some-times in two vines on a blue field, or in some mixed pattern on a lighter ground. Where the body is filled with the great, rich flower designs before mentioned the border usually presents a consistently large pattern composed of the established Assyrian elements.

The knots of the old Khorassans are closely woven. The compactness which this insures makes the rug lie firmly, even on a highly polished floor, a virtue which looser fabrics have not. In length of pile the Khorassans vary, but in almost all lengths, even in some of the more closely trimmed examples, there is a peculiar appearance of surface, similar to that of rugs which have undergone wear, and in which the corrosive effect of certain dyes has begun to be apparent. It is most evident in pieces which have large patterns, and in which it is not necessary to bring out minute points of color. This uneven clipping adds to the softness given by the fine wool with which the rugs are napped. It gives to a carpet which has from a hundred and twenty-five to a hundred and fifty knots to the square inch, and in its foundations is excessively solid, the appearance of being fleece to the foot. This same peculiarity occurs in some varieties of antique India rugs.

Through ignorance, probably, vendors often sell old Feraghans for the fine-patterned Khorassan. The Khorassan dyes have hitherto been to a laudable extent vegetable. Lately a new line of products has been brought to this country, woven in the Feraghan pattern, but upon a red ground instead of blue, as is the custom in the real Feraghans. The foundations are cotton, but the weaving is compact and careful, better, in fact, than most of the modern proper Feraghans. The pile is not finished like the Feraghans, but is trimmed unevenly, after the Khorassan fashion. The dyes in these new fabrics leave much to be desired.

Meshhed.—This, the capital of Khorassan, was once almost wholly a city of worship; it holds the shrines of Imam Riza and Caliph Haroun al Raschid. It lies in the eastern part of the province, and for centuries has been the objective point of Mussulman pilgrimages from all over Asia, particularly by the Persians and others of the Shiite sect whose saints are entombed there. Thousands whose scant worldly store did not warrant them in making the journey to Mecca have contented themselves and no doubt demonstrated their fidelity satisfactorily, by accomplishing the devotional trip to Meshhed.[1] It is really the most central place in Asia, a veritable hub, from which great highways, like the spokes of a wheel, run out in all directions. More or less weaving, some of it of the highest merit, has always been done in and about the city. Many rugs were brought, too, by the pilgrims as offerings, and a vast trade in textiles sprang up. Little by little Meshhed lost its religious tone. Its situation made it a perfect emporium, a natural commercial centre. Its wonderful road system, by which it can be directly reached from any part of Asia, has been utilized more and more every year by caravans, until now it is one of the greatest marts in all the East.

The rugs vended here are among the best that the Khorassan district knows. Traditionally they are rich and lustrous beyond measure. All the opulence of color and perfection of floral and animal design that distinguishes the pure Khorassan is found in the rugs which bear the name of the Shiite Mecca. The chief features of the antiques are preserved, but the more modern fabrics, while they hold high rank even among the Persian loom works, have sacrificed much of artistic finish to strength and durability, and are now almost as substantial as the Herati or even the Kurdistan Sarakhs. They present as patterns the great cone or pear shapes, in larger form perhaps than any other rug. In the border these take the long form

---

[1] How great a multitude of rugs came into the possession of the mollahs is indicated by the statement of Dr. Bellew. He describes the vast graveyard at Meshhed to which, from all parts of Persia people brought the bones of their kinsfolk to be buried. "Prior to the famine," he says, "these interments amounted to forty thousand annually. After the great national disaster poverty caused a widespread neglect of the custom, and the number fell to something like twelve thousand. It has never returned to its former maximum since Meshhed, of late years, has taken on the character of a commercial centre."

common to India and Kashmir; they are placed transversely and often alternated with the crossed arrangements described as a feature of the proper Khorassans. The designs in the most pretentious examples include also the animal forms, set in luminous colors upon the brightest of grounds. The pile is not trimmed in the uneven manner of the other Khorassans, but presents the smooth, compact surface common in the Herat, to which they are nearly related. In finish of ends and sides they follow the Khorassans. They are worked in the Ghiordes knot.

Herat.—The state of facts which has seemed to warrant the classification of the Mosul fabrics with the Caucasian finds exact duplication here, in the case of the carpets named for Herat, the City of a Hundred Gardens, which, from its strategic importance, has become famed world-wide as the "Key of India." Though now outside of the geographical confines of the Persian realm, it bears intimate historical relation to Persia, and its carpets are allied in design and coloring to the Persian family of textiles, rather than to those of the Turkoman districts on the north, or the Mongolian on the east. The fish pattern, which has been referred to as prevailing in Feraghan rugs, is in its purity known among experts as the Herat pattern. It seems tolerably clear that it originated neither in Herat nor in the Feraghan district, but was primarily a gift, in which two at least of the older civilizations contributed each its part. However that may be, the design, as a diaper for the body of the rug, and the accompaniment recognized as the Herat border are preserved in their integrity in the modern Herat fabrics. The Herat border has been utilized, with more or less modification, in half the rug-making sections of the Orient. In many of the finest pieces in the European collections it is used to enclose a central design of the purest Persian, the distinctive Persian character being maintained, as one authority points out, by the employment of dark red for the ground-color of the central field, and a corresponding value of green for the ground of the border, a combination which seems to have enjoyed the highest favor among the Persian masters.

The majority of Herat rugs adhere religiously to the old design, and whatever their dimensions are in every essential point, materials, dyeing and weaving, unsurpassed by any which come out of the East. Aside from the recognized Herat pattern, almost the only other device used is the pear shape, repeated throughout the field after the manner of the Sarabands, save that the Saraband has the hook turned in opposite directions in the alternate rows, while in the Herati it is drawn uniformly. This seems to be employed only in the finest of the modern examples, and the elongated, gracefully curved shape of the patterns gives indication of the close relation which, by reason both of trade and conquest, has for centuries existed between India and the Afghan capital. When used for the field the pattern is often upon a ground of cream yellow or some other light shade, though the usual ground color is blue. In the border which accompanies it, in these instances, the weavers retain the typical Herat forms. Although the fish patterns used in Feraghan and Herati are essentially identical, the latter is woven in the Ghiordes knot, the former in the Sehna.

It is a common belief that the Herat rugs are woven in Khorassan. The ground for this is without doubt the thoroughly Persian character of the fabrics, the knot being the only point of variance. In this connection it is important to know that the Herati do not speak of their country as Afghanistan, but always as Khorassan, a usage dating back to the time when the Persian sway was less circumscribed than it is to-day.

There is a coarse form of Herat carpet which is offered under the name of Aiyin, or Kayin.

XII

TURKOMAN

FROM the Caspian Sea to the Chinese frontier, and from the Sea of Aral to Afghanistan and Persia, stretches an immense territory, comprising thousands on thousands of square miles, and inhabited by numberless rug-making tribes.

In the deserts and sand-hills of Turkestan, both east and west of the Oxus, and among the foot-hills of the Hissar and Turkestan Mountains, the rough, quarrelsome Turkomans, most of them under Russian rule now, make rugs which follow quite closely a general type, and which have attained a high degree of popularity as strong, well made, and serviceable. Some of them, too, are models of fineness and solidity. The wool used in them is of good quality. The lower grades of wool are made into heavy cloaks, tent-coverings and thick felts, all of which play a large part in the wild, outdoor life led by the Central Asian hordes.

In considering these Turkoman weavings we encounter again the misunderstanding which has arisen in the case of so many rugs. The great majority of the Turkoman fabrics are accredited to Bokhara, and by that name are widely known in Europe and America. The plan adopted in this volume — of letting the accredited rug names stand for what they have stood for hitherto, instead of inviting the reader to learn a new distribution — is particularly harassing here, for what are called Bokharas in America are not Bokharas, and no one in Asia, save the most case-hardened rug vendor, understands what an American means by "Bokhara" rugs. On the way up the Black Sea I talked rugs to a Frenchman who for years had been "expediting" all sorts of Eastern carpets — Persian, Caucasian, Turkoman and even bales from farther east.

"Do you have any Tekkes in America?" he asked.

I told him I had heard the name applied to khilims, and to some coarse nomad weavings out of eastern Anatolia.

"Oh, no!" he said. "That is not the Tekke. You must see the real Tekke of Turkestan. When we arrive in Russia I will show you some, but they are not for sale. All the veritable Tekkes are in private hands, and no one will part with them, for they have become very rare. Once in a while one is offered for sale, but the price is very, very high."

When we reached Batoum I saw the Tekke — the "veritable Tekke." If it were displayed in a Broadway window, the rug merchants would declare it the finest Bokhara they ever saw.

Before the Trans-Caspian railroad was built, the wild tribesmen of all that part of Turkestan, it seems, always took their rugs to Bokhara for sale. When they reached Tiflis or Constantinople, which latter they did years ago by caravan to Trebizond, the rugs bore the name of the Turkoman capital from which they had been "expedited."

That name has become fastened on them, and will not be changed. Tekke rugs, or their unworthy successors, will continue to be sold as Bokharas. But what is even more perplexing, under the circumstances, is that the carpets which are made in Bokhara itself, and far to the south and east of its confines, are the coarse, Brobdignagian forms of the Turkoman design which we know sometimes as Afghans and sometimes as Khivas. For the rest, the Samarkands and the Chinese weavings have been included in this group, not because they resemble the others in any respect (for they are essentially Mongol) but solely upon geographical grounds.

"Bokhara" or Tekke.—In the whole range of Eastern fabrics there is probably no pattern which so conclusively identifies a textile as does the hard-and-fast division into squares and oblongs and the unvarying octagonal device which are the features of the so-called Bokhara. These rugs, which are now found in almost tiresome plenty, are made by the Tekke-Turkomans who inhabit the plains to the west of the Oxus, and who, until the Russians whipped them into something like civilized procedure, found their chief delight in stealing their fellow-men of all other races whenever opportunity offered, and, having tortured them for diversion, selling them into slavery.

The Russian artist and traveller, Simakoff, who has been spoken of elsewhere, told in the all too meagre letter-press of his splendid book something of these Turkoman weavings. Each family or clan, he said, had its carpet design, as one has a sign manual. Nothing that could be offered could ever tempt them to weave any other.[1] Several of the characteristic tribal designs he reproduced in his very interesting work. The particular conceit which in the West has come to be considered most thoroughly typical of Bokhara is one which when once seen cannot be forgotten. No matter in what minor details it may vary, one feature will proclaim it instantly. The lines of demarcation in the pattern are heavy and hard, and as true

---

[1] "Types des dessins les plus fréquents dans les tapis des Tourkmènes. Ils se distinguent par la finesse et le caractère serré du tissu, la solidité des couleurs, et l'harmonie reposante des nuances. Ces dessins sont composés de figures fantastiques, formées de lignes droites, que ne rappellent ni des fleurs, ni des oiseaux, ni d'autres animaux. Les figures rappellant des oiseaux que l'on voit sur un fond d'octogones, dans le tapis 'a' ne se rencontrent qu'à l'état d'exception. Il en est de ces dessins comme de ceux sur les tapis étroits ci-dessus mentionnés [the narrow strips used for friezes around the tent walls]; chaque famille Tourkmène a son dessin propre, qu'elle travaille et varie, mais à aucun prix elle ne voudrait en exécuter un autre."—"*L'Art de l'Asie Centrale,*" par *N. Simakoff.*

as those of a checker-board. The arrangement of the devices on these oblongs is also characteristic. A single figure does not lie within a single oblong, but on the intersection of the lines. Each quarter of it is in one corner of each four adjoining oblongs. The centre, usually filled with a diamond shape, marks the actual point of intersection. The pattern itself is an elongated octagon, divided in four parts by the lines referred to above. Inside of it lies a similar shape, the diagonally opposite quarters of which are colored alike, and in contrast with the alternating quarters. For example, one and three will be of red and brown, two and four of white and black. In the outer part these colors are reversed, which gives balance to the pattern. The ground of the rug and its dominant color throughout is red — kermes, madder, or glowing scarlet. The other colors are brown, black, blue, white and sometimes a shade of orange. All these are, however, thoroughly subordinated to the dominant reds. Some conventional diamond-shaped figure occupies the spaces between the octagons.

In some of the smaller pieces there is a complex border, the stripe effect of which is multiplied by many narrow lines of contrasting color, arranged after the fashion of the Chinese fret, between the broader stripes, which carry a definite pattern contrasting with the bold body of the carpet. The red-and-black effect is maintained, but lightness and brightness are imparted by the addition of small areas of orange and diminutive fillings of pale blue and white, and sometimes, though rarely, of green. This border, which has much of the East Indian about it, is wider at the ends than at the side, and of a more broken design, usually suggesting some form of the tree of life.

A feature of many Bokharas, shared by kindred fabrics, is the web, sometimes ten or twelve inches deep on the ends. It is a Turkish device, and has travelled with the race. In color it is similar to the pile in most antiques; and through it, in most of the pieces, run narrow stripes, single or double, at intervals of two, three or four inches. They are blue or black and white. Instead of this there is sometimes a plain piled surface, running out clear to the small selvage and carelessly twisted fringe which finish the ends. In the small moderns the web is white. The rugs come in all sizes, though it is only within the last few years that they have reached real carpet dimensions.

The prayer rugs differ entirely from the *sedjadeh*. Barring the borders, there is little to indicate that they are of the same variety; but in each the type is strictly adhered to. The bold reds of the carpets are usually missing from the prayer rug, which, when of fine, antique quality, is soft, sedate, but indescribably rich. The customary color tone is mahogany, relieved with the wonderful deep copper bronze tint found in some few of the Beluchistans; and the skilful, artistic use of the lighter shades gives to the variations of the design a lustre little short of marvellous. There is a multiplied tree pattern in the border, the high lights of which are in thin lines of pure white. The conformation of the arch and niche would be too heavy and severe if the coloring did not soften them so completely. The field design is of the same order as the borders, presenting in more elaborate but still rectilinear form the tree motive. Across the field, midway, runs a broad horizontal band, which, aided by a perpendicular, divides the whole area into four quite distinct parts, in each of which the tree appears. What the significance of this division may be it is hard to say. So plain in some points of the prayer rugs is the likeness to the Beluchistans that it is not wholly unreasonable to believe that the quartering, even though the fabric be Mohammedan, harks back in some way to the quadruplicate division which maintains throughout all the Vedic worship writings of India.

It is worthy of note that the Bokharas are wider in proportion to length than most other prayer rugs, always excepting the old style Bergamo. The only light color used in them, aside from the white and yellow and the orange values, is pale blue, in which the minute floral patterns are sometimes laid. The pile, which is woven in the Sehna knot, is trimmed very close in the old pieces, and the surface is fine and velvety. Very rarely a pure Bokhara is found with a field of blue instead of red. These are greatly prized. What are frequently sold in America as "Bilooz," or "blue Bokharas," are Beluchistan rugs, made in a blue tone instead of the reds and bronzes which prevail in most of their class.

Many of the multitude of Turkoman designs of which Simakoff speaks could be seen up to a few years ago in Tiflis, whither the Turkestan bales were sent for redistribution; but since the extension of the railway to Bokhara and Samarkand the Turkoman tribes can intrust their weavings to the freight agents at any point on the railway, with the knowledge that they will go straight through to the Constantinople dealers. The result is that in Tiflis, where ten or a dozen years ago good Tekke carpets could be had, there is now an utter dearth of them, and small fragments of the old rugs are deftly sewn together to make a piece as large, perhaps, as a prayer rug. For these patchwork affairs astounding prices are asked.

It is impossible for any one to fix the right names and places of manufacture for the manifold weavings of Turkestan, unless, indeed, it be a native intimately acquainted with all the strolling companies scattered over that well-nigh boundless waste.

They differ in detail, but the fundamental parts of the design, as well as the general scheme of color, vary little. It is well to take what we know as Bokharas as a point to reckon from. There are designs which approach this very nearly, and there are others which, while following the color scheme and general arrangement, have eliminated many of the features. What some American dealers have chosen to call Khiva-Bokhara, for example, are identical with the Bokharas in knot, color and finish, and so nearly resemble them in pattern that at first glance they are easily mistaken for the Bokhara pieces. There are points of difference: first, the Khiva-Bokharas are inferior to the Bokharas in fineness. Superlative Bokharas have as many as two hundred knots or even more to the square inch, and a good specimen has a hundred and twenty. The best of the Khiva-Bokharas has not more than a hundred. Second, scrutiny reveals that the hard division into squares or oblong spaces which is the feature of the Bokharas is omitted from the other class or classes.

In yet other pieces which have departed even more widely from what we have adopted as a standard design, animal figures are used to diversify the quarterings of the octagon, instead of the geometrical and quasi-floral shapes. This, there is little doubt, denotes that the rugs were woven by tribes making their home in the more westerly part of the plain. They have caught, though in a degree diminished by distance, the fashion of the Caucasus, so frequently illustrated in the Kabistan and Kazak rugs. They have adhered, however, rather strictly to the Bokhara traditions, and the rugs are a happy and convenient medium between those formal fabrics and the less conventional weavings of the Yomuds.

The "Bokhara pattern" has found greater popularity in America than any other of all the Turkoman lot. It is repeated and repeated in rugs great and small, which are sent to this country by thousands annually. In the majority of them, lately, the colors are bad. Effort to make antiques of some pieces by washing has reduced them from glowing reds to the palest of pinks. The market weavers have abandoned, apparently, the other designs, and yet the finest specimen of Tekke weaving I saw presented an altogether different pattern—one which was based upon the diamond shape, after the style of the Yomuds, and not on the square and octagon. These were the carpets of which my fellow-voyager had spoken. They had an incredible number of knots to the inch, a surface fine as velvet, and while thin and flexible, almost, as paper, were strong, and in their design and texture perfect.

Dealers offer to sell what are known as "Royal Bokharas." If there were any "Royal Bokhara," it would be the kind I have just mentioned, and they are made no more—and probably never will be.

Yomud.— There is one variety of the Turkoman weavings which carries upon its face indisputable proof of its origin. Its designs tell where it was woven.

Away at the western end of Turkestan, scattered over plains, along the shores of the Caspian and in the foot-hills of the mountain chain which has for a time stopped, nominally, the southward march of the Russian, dwells the great Yomud horde of Turkomans. There are, perhaps, no rugs which from an ethnological standpoint are more interesting than theirs. They are satisfying, not more by reason of their warm color, admirable weaving and neat, cleanly defined patterns than because in every minutest particular they are what one observing the geographical position of the Yomud territory must expect them to be. Following religiously, on one hand, the color, textile traditions and general theory of the Tekke folk, with whom they are by race, customs and political affinity allied, the Yomud weavers have yet reached out across the Caspian to their near neighbors of Daghestan, Derbend, Kuba and the Shirvan district, and borrowed for the borders of their rugs and the adornment of the pure Turkoman figures all the elements and decorative tricks which distinguish the fabrics of these parts. With a skill of which they might scarcely be suspected, they have perfected in these praiseworthy carpets an adaptation, or better, an amalgamation of patterns, in ideal accord with the outline of the process as given in the chapter on Design.

The task has been simplified by the fact that the decorative quantities with which they have had to deal, on both sides, are purely rectilinear; nevertheless a great obstacle lay in the way, in the matter of coloration. To so temper the uncompromising blood-reds of the Bokharas on the one hand, and the bright yellows and blues of the Caucasians on the other, that there should be peace and harmony in the finished carpet, was a labor for masters. It has been accomplished in masterly manner. To judge by the side borders alone, one might reasonably say, looking at some of the Yomud rugs, that they had come from the Shirvan or Daghestan looms. And yet the end borders and the body of the rugs are Turkoman. In some cases the colors follow the red schedule of the Tekkes; in others that is mellowed almost to an old rose, to meet and harmonize with the alien hues of the Caucasus. They retain the striped red web and the long fringe of goat's-hair; they retain in general the Tekke division, but it is in the drawing of the Caucasus. The latch-hook is everywhere. In many cases there is a broad white or wool-colored stripe at the outer edge of the web on the ends, and in it, oftentimes, a small outline border pattern, embroidered in red yarn. Occasionally the fringe, instead of being left loose all the way across the end of the rug, is twisted at irregular intervals of from three to eight inches into stout ropes like those of the Kazaks. Between these the warp-threads of goat's-hair lie loose.

In the majority of Yomuds the pattern is an array of diamond shapes, distributed upon the field in the Turkoman order, but equipped inside and out with the latch-hook. In the borders, too, Caucasian hand-marks are apparent. There is the stiff form of the swaying vine. Where it crosses from one side to the other it is heavy with latch-hooks. Where it lies parallel with the sides it is nothing but the barber-pole stripe found in nearly all the Transcaucasian fabrics, and in so many Kabistans. Even in the rugs in which it may be held to have originated, this stripe does not play a more important part than in the Yomuds. It furnishes both broad and narrow elements for the sides and in the end borders; it figures as trunk in the tree patterns, the branches of which are composed of a form of latch-hook.

There is one feature which seems to be wholly the property of the Yomuds. It is a coarse side selvage of two ribs, which, instead of being wholly red, has alternate squares of red and blue, red and brown, or two shades of red, in each rib, so that a sort of checker-board effect is secured. Even when the rugs are piled out to the last thread of warp (body finish,) this is preserved in the pile. The nearest approach to anything of the sort, in any other rug, is the selvage of red, white and blue at the ends of the Shiraz, but that is worked in the Soumak stitch, while the selvage of the Yomuds is in the khilim or tapestry stitch. The piling of the Yomuds may be either in the Sehna or Ghiordes knot.

One division of these Turkoman carpets, which avoids on the one hand close adherence to the Bokhara device, and on the other the latch-hook style of the Yomuds, is called Beshir. In the matter of web and fringe it follows the example of the rest of the group, but the web is more generously adorned with stripes than in any of the other varieties. The patterns manifest somewhat more of the Arab character, but the manner of arranging them upon the field is still that of Bokhara. A feature of the border is the "reciprocal saw-tooth," the *sechan disih* of the Persians.

Afghanistan-Bokhara.—Another interesting although perplexing feature of the confusion in which these rugs of Middle Asia have become involved is that what we have been wont to purchase as Afghan carpets are really the product of Bokhara, though they are, naturally enough, made also by the dwellers in northern Afghanistan, on the slopes of the Hindu Kush and all along the Bokhara border.

They are great, coarse carpets with the Bokhara octagon device much enlarged, and without the dividing-lines which make the field of the finer fabrics look like a decorated checker-board. Though on a greater scale, they are more after the order of the Khivas, and have been commonly sold under that name. All of boldness, all of wild force, that is read or imagined of the dwellers in these stern uplands, finds record and expression in the Afghan carpets. They are fierce and full of character. The spirit of the mountains and gorges is in them. The gloom of wind-swept highlands is over them. They are of a dark, savage red, or rather of two reds — one with an ugly suggestion of blood in it, the other darker and more sombre, dulled by the admixture of indigo almost to brown.

The patterns, great and grim and impressionistic, are thrown in with much freedom and energy. Dashes of white, positive to a degree, but minute in such a desert of grimness, only emphasize the rude grandeur of the fabrics. The border is crude, but in it is recorded the finer spirit of the people. Whatever there is in them of leaning toward civilization and the politer arts has its expression here. Outside of this, formed by the ends of the goat's-hair warp, is a long, straying, ashen-brown fringe, suggesting the beard of the Cossack. Some pieces — the minority — are wrought out in lighter shades, but the ratio between the values is still justly maintained. The web takes on a brighter tone and better finish as the colors of the pile grow brighter; the fringe is a lighter gray. The consistency of it shows a certain artistic impulse strong in the nature of the people. Other examples manifest a leaning to orange and bits of light blue. In some the squares are resumed, some of them being laid in orange, others in rich green. The borders grow in complexity, and flower patterns creep in; but at the brightest they are in harsh contrast with the flower-strewn carpets of the Persian or the brilliant panels of the Caucasian.

BOY WEAVERS OF TABRIZ

A Rug Market in Iran

TURKOMAN

The Afghans are sometimes made of goat's-hair and sometimes of wool. The warp is of brown wool or the coarser hair of the
goat. Spinning these filaments is a difficult task. When wet they
curl so tightly that they cannot be spun at all; therefore the hair is
not always washed, but after the shearing is carefully combed. There
sometimes remains in a warp made of this thread a strong odor
which it is quite difficult to remove.

The nomad products of Afghanistan itself show a diversity which
quite entitles them to a separate classification, after setting apart the
Herat carpets, which have been placed with the Khorassan group of
Persia, and most of which are to-day really made in Persia. Perhaps
the most singular, as they are the rarest, of these "independent" Afghan fabrics are made by the Turkoman tribes dwelling in the defiles
of the Barkhut Mountains, the gateway through which is the renowned
Pass of Herat. Their rugs are a positive announcement of their
position on the map, for they have borrowed the design, fish pattern
and all, from the Herati, but have wrought it out in the colors of
their kinsmen and neighbors on the north. The relationship, the
strong general likeness of the fabrics in color and theory of contrast,
and finally that they are both worked in the Sehna knot while the
Herati use the Ghiordes, would perforce lead to placing these rugs
in the same class as the Tekkes. This version of the Herat pattern
is wholly rectilinear. The leaves which inclose the rosette are like
bent spear-heads, and the flowers and stalks are stiff to the last
degree. Aside from the blood-red of the ground and the dark brown
or blue which is used to outline the patterns, there is small show of
any color in the body of the rug. In the borders there is more life.
The pattern here, usually a great, indented octagon, combined with
some form of the tree, is adorned with several bright colors, orange,
light blue and the like. Its lines are plainly copied from the old
Beluchistans.

These weavers seem to have caught from the Herati, too, the notion of magnitude. The carpets are meant for *chef-d'œuvres*, and are pretentious affairs. Some of them are twenty feet or more in length. Until the manufacture of whole carpet sizes in the Bokharas was begun,— after the railway had opened the wilds of Turkestan to commerce,— these Afghan fabrics were far and away the largest of all the Turkoman carpets. They have the broad web at the ends. Some of them have coarse goat's-hair for warp, and the pile contains sufficient of the soft goat's-fleece to give them a lustre like to that of the finest of the Tekke fabrics.

Throughout the southern ranges of Afghan hills, down as far as Kandahar, rugs similar to these are woven, all copying in some measure from the Persianized patterns of Herat and Khorassan, but adhering to the stiff, rectilinear treatment found in Turkestan and Beluchistan carpets. Many of them have the Beluchistan coloring instead of the Bokhara red. All these are without doubt the fabrics referred to by Mr. Robinson in his " Eastern Carpets" thus : "The weavers of these particular carpets are not able to give the floral patterns they use their true forms ; and the explanation of their inability to do so probably lies in the fact that they are a Turanian people, settled among Aryan neighbors, by whom they have not yet been completely Aryanized."

Beluchistan.— The rugs of Beluchistan, ever since rugs began to be an article of commerce, have been brought laboriously across the rugged reaches of Afghanistan to find market in the Turkoman cities. They are of many types. Some of them are of no type, embodying features from more than one form of decoration. They have not escaped the general decadence. The modern Beluchistans have fallen about as far from the high standard established by the old ones as any rugs which find their way out of the East to-day. It is not surprising, for the production is enormous, and even the coarsest and poorest of these are stable and full of "wear." This modern stuff from Beluchistan is nearly all made on one model, with some small diversity in color and less in design. The old rugs were in many forms, and although the colors differed according to the influence under which each piece or collection of pieces was wrought, there was always a depth and luminous quality in the dyes, a lustre in the wool, which, with certain textile peculiarities which never seemed to be omitted, made them easy of recognition. That they should have maintained any fidelity at all to pristine design is singular when the geographical location and history of the country are considered. On one side they have the Kirman province, where the old Iranian creed and textile methods are still preserved; on the northwest is Khorassan, with its rich floral fabrics, bright in color and full of realism; to the north is Afghanistan, whose principal carpets, from the earliest times to the present day, have retained the most perfect Persian character, and have, as a matter of fact, been sold as Persians; on the east, India, where Persian models have for at least three hundred years been followed with scrupulous fidelity.

This little four-cornered country has been constantly traversed through all the centuries by Greek, Arabic, Persian and Mongol invaders of India, and by the great caravan trade which long before the Christian era was carried on between India and the Mediterranean coast. Still the Beluchistan fabrics have preserved a system of design and coloring which bears little resemblance to any other of the East. There is found now and then among the Yuruks of Asia Minor a rug which in general tone, patterns and principal colors forcibly suggests the Beluchistans.

Ethnologists are at a loss to determine the derivation of the Beluchees and Brahoes, who inhabit Beluchistan, having long ago wrested it from the Hindus. They are generally believed to have come from Syria or Arabia, but in the turbulent course of time the stock has been replenished by wandering tribes of Kurds, and even large bodies of Grecian adventurers are known to have settled there and ingrafted themselves permanently upon the population. It is significant that the Beluchistan weavers use the Sehna knot. Aside from this there is small trace of Persian influence in their weaving.

The predominating influence in Beluchistan for several hundred years has been Turkoman. The chronicles of invasion show it, and there are corroborative marks which still abide in the textiles. Occasionally a piece is found which while borrowing something from the Chinese, with whom the Beluchees have always had caravan communication, follows in a general way the Tekke arrangement and also the Turkestan theory in coloring, while preserving in its finishing the Beluchistan marks.

All the Beluchistan rugs are heavy in tone. Where the principal figures are laid in madder or deep blues, they have a richness not surpassed. The greater number of them, in the American market at least, are of a brown cast. The range of colors is narrow. Few bright ornamental figures appear, though orange and some light shades of red are sparingly used. The rug in such cases takes on a brown key, and the design, which invariably has a certain ruggedness about it, is drawn simply, in lighter shades of the same. Brightness and accent are sometimes secured by working the outlines of the patterns in orange or a yellowish white. Most of the figures are big hexagons, octagons,— all sorts of loose geometrical devices,— ornamented inside and out with broad lines and keys in parallel arrangement, which emphasizes the rectilinear effect. The field in many Beluchistans is divided into two or three parts by transverse stripes of the same character. Sometimes, in the old rugs, these figures are woven in floral form, suggesting garlands. The derivation of the treatment is not clear.

PLATE XIX.   MINA KHANI SARANDAZ

16.1 x 4.1

Loaned by Mr. Robert L. Stevens

The Mina Khani design is one of the simplest, but most effective that has ever come out of the East. Although copied into the rugs of Khorassan and Turkestan, after their own methods, it belongs distinctly to the Kurds and they alone have been able to avoid giving a hard mechanical appearance to it. This is undoubtedly due to their independence and skill in the use of color, and also to the fact that the Kurdish colors, particularly the blues and yellows, are of a splendid quality, which lends to this design its strength. This particular piece is woven by the ruder class of people, as the lapses from accuracy and even from general regularity, especially in the handling of the vines, proves. The filling of the side spaces in the field with small nondescript items instead of perfecting the vine arrangement, shows this very clearly. The piece has undergone hard wear, but is still thick and incredibly heavy. These reds are always beautifully softened by age, which increases their effectiveness in such a color combination as this. It will be seen that the weaver has indulged in the prevailing Kurdish trick of leaving bands of color, for no less than three distinct shades of blue are here; but it is altogether intentional, and the charm of the carpet is much enhanced by it.

PLATE XX. SHIRAZ RUG

10.4 x 4.10

Loaned by Mr. Reginald H. Bulley

This piece, though made for practical use, is fully up to the best traditions of Shiraz weaving. The three principal colors, rose, ivory and blue, are equal to those found in any part of Persia, even of old time. It is woven of the Niris wool, extremely soft and glossy, but the body of the fabric, thanks to stout foundations, is most substantial. All the characteristic finishings of Shiraz are here.

PLATE XXI. TEKKE PRAYER RUG

5.4 x 4

Loaned by Mr. Ralph O. Smith

The octagonal device of the Turkoman weaving is familiar to almost every-
one, so common, in fact, that it is reproduced in numberless machine-made fabrics, the regularity of the pattern lending itself particularly well to mechanical
repetition.   Equally prevalent in Turkestan is this design for the prayer carpets.   With some small variation as to coloring and border ornamentation it is
used by nearly all the weavers of the Turkoman steppes.   The piece here shown
has a band of lighter color in the ground at one end of the field, a quite unusual
manifestation among the Tekke weavers, though frequent enough in the rugs of
Kurdistan and parts of Caucasia.

one in the centre, and rectilinear floral forms appear about it. In the borders the fret is further utilized in various shapes and colors, or there are decorative symbols of animal origin but floral form, which alone bear the mark of Persian treatment. Yellow predominates in the borders, giving the fabric a warm tone.

In many of the rugs of Samarkand the fretted field and its medallions have been abandoned for an attempt at floral display, but the rich, almost lurid coloring remains; the reds and yellows, and in a smaller degree the blues, in which these flowery fields are wrought, are superb. But amid the profusion there always creeps in some feature reminiscent of the old pattern. In most cases it is the largest of the flower forms, which stand out so straight, so heavy, so prominent, so octagonal, that they utterly obscure the accompanying patterns, and, stripped, before the mind's eye, of all the stems and leaves which surround them, are naught but the old figures after all.

It is to be noted, in connection with this Mohammedan floral development in the rugs of Samarkand, that upon the taking of Baghdad and other Western cities the Mongol ruler took back with him to his capital the greatest artists and artisans, in the hope of instilling a new art impulse into his people. The elaboration noticeable even in the present day in many of the Samarkand carpets must be considered a remote result of that effort.

The borders of the Samarkands carry two main stripes, of medium width. One usually presents the undulating vine in more or less angular form; the other, a lotus pattern, three flowers on a stem, which calls to mind the similar formation in the old Ghiordes border. All around the outside of the rug is usually a narrow band of some solid color. In nearly all the Samarkands four threads of the weft, which is of cotton or brown wool, are carried across after every row of knots, as in the Kazaks. The warp is usually of cotton. The knot is Sehna. The ends are finished with a narrow web

PLATE XXII.   YOMUD TURKOMAN
10.2 x 7
Property of the Author

While this rug, by reason of the old rose tint of its ground color in certain lights, must be classed as a Yomud, there is a certain paucity of coloration in the border, to wit, an absence of yellows and blues and other shades prevalent in the Caucasus, which makes it likely that it was woven among the Akhal or Salor Turkomans, or some tribe a little remote from the Caspian coasts. The central design, however, with its tendency to an ornate and picturesque diamond device instead of one bounded only by the hard octagon of the Bokhara, so-called, shows that the carpet is not a product of any of the eastern Turkoman provinces. It is a sterling rug and the extreme accuracy with which the patterns are wrought predicates at once the fineness of texture—which it has—and skill on the part of the weaver. There is a suggestion of vine and flower in the latch-hook and tarantula arrangement of the border stripes.

The pile is quite long and compact. The ends have a web
that of the Bokharas, extending sometimes ten or twelve inches bey
the pile. This, figured in colors or worked in a minute diaper
tern, makes a most artistic finish.

Although in point of propinquity these carpets might natur
enough be counted among the India fabrics, the rug dealers and
makers of the peninsula do not so consider them. Even the wool
Beluchistan is not, as a rule, taken for the modern India carpets, s
most of it is of a dark hue, and experiments have failed to mak
take on the light colors required in the India designs. Bleach
which has been industriously tried, serves only to impair its qua
Perhaps this has had much to do with the long preservation of
tinctive character in the Beluchistans, a character which makes tl
easy of identification, even among a multitude of other fabrics.
weavers have made of necessity a virtue which has redounded gre
to their credit and to their advantage as well. They have util
the dark natural hues of the wool, and attained additional de
lustre and softness from a free admixture of goat's-fleece, whic
produced in plenty in their mountains.

Samarkand.—The rugs named for the city which was the ca
of the conqueror Tamur, and which is now his burial-place, ar
numberless characteristics eloquent of Mongol influence. Most
them show only the smallest trace of Persian or Caucasian fc
The central field, to begin with, is usually covered over with the i
cate Chinese fret, laid in some shade of red or blue on a groun
some other value, or red on blue, or vice versa; sometimes it is
pale tint of fawn brown on a background of yellowish white. I
tributed in this area are medallions, one, two, three, four or five
seldom more,—in which sometimes appear Chinese devices, such
the dragon, fish or pheasant, and sometimes flowers. These me
lions are round or polygonal. Occasionally there is a single la

241

and loose warp-ends. Sometimes the broad Turkoman web is employed.

Armenian dealers often apply to the Samarkand rugs the name of "Malgaran," mentioned heretofore as a common substitute title for Tcherkess and Mingreli. The confusion arises partly from the tenacious belief that Mingreli is a corruption of Mongolian.

Yarkand and Kashgar.— Little is heard in American markets of the rugs of Yarkand and Kashgar. They are exported from Asia through Peking, and a few examples have found their way to Constantinople with other consignments, and have been picked up by American buyers there. Of late there has been a considerable influx of these fabrics to American markets. The Yarkand district is somewhat out of the way of the Persian influence. The city is a hundred miles or more east of Kashgar. It is well aloof in a southeasterly direction from both Bokhara and Samarkand, being eight hundred miles from one and six hundred miles from the other. After the shaking off of Chinese rule and the establishment of an East Turkestan empire, with capital at Kashgar, Yarkand became an important trade centre, but on the death of Yakub Beg in 1877, Kashgar was again taken by the Chinese, and Yarkand reverted to the old sovereignty. Cut off by such a stretch of wild upland country from the trade centres of the West, and with the Great Pamir and other vast mountain ranges towering between it and the markets of India, Yarkand for a long time escaped the demoralization which had attacked most of the rug-making districts. Mr. Robinson found its fabrics many years ago at Srinagar in Kashmir, along with some of the weavings of Thibet. He described the old examples as being made with silky wool, taken probably from the yak. "The quality of these rugs," he adds, "is admirable, and the colors harmonious, the designs having a Tartar character in the geometrical figures, circles, medallions and octagons, alternately blue, red, green and yellow—the green of an emerald hue, obtained by dyeing strongly with Persian berry over indigo."

It is plain that either the quality of these carpets has declined amazingly, or that those which Mr. Robinson saw were show-pieces and far superior to the average, for the consignments which have come to America during recent years have presented but little that was attractive. Consistency is their chief merit. Interest in them is based principally on their oddity. They are nothing if not Chinese. They show no trace of the Western influence noticeable in the Samarkands, no indication of effort at floral diapers. The fretted grounds are most frequent. The circles and octagons, with their Chinese emblems, are a multitude. Dragons and fishes and variations of the fret are everywhere. In some pieces the medallions, instead of being large and few in number, are small, contain a wonderful diversity of figures, and are distributed, more or less regularly, all over the field. A favorite form is the combination of four dragons, so arranged that they form a swastika. The entire filling in some examples is made up of realistic animals.

The border space is small in proportion to the size of the rug. There are usually three stripes, a broad middle stripe, with a guard stripe on either side, but the guard stripes are not figured alike, as is customary in Persian or Turkish rugs where the borders are similarly distributed. In most cases there is some form of the Chinese-Greek border, most frequently of two meanders, so intertraced as to form swastikas at intervals, and so shaded as to present the material effect of relief. The narrower stripes are adorned with some fret forms or Chinese floral conceits.

The colors are garish, and, though in some cases brilliant, are not warm nor attractive. Pale terra-cotta, tending to pink, is common. Some rugs are made up of grayish white and yellows; others present only white with two shades of blue, suggesting delft. The greens

PLATE XXIII. THE ARDEBIL MOSQUE CARPET

32.0 x 16.0

Considering that the actual size of the Ardebil carpet, which is now in the South Kensington Museum, is sixteen feet in width by thirty-two feet in length, the enormously reduced representation here offered preserves quite well the essential features.   Beyond question the Persian masterpiece of the sixteenth century, made for the tomb of Sheikh Ismael, is to-day the most famous piece of weaving in the world.   The fabulous fineness of its workmanship, and the accuracy of its design, may be proven by selecting at random any flower upon either side of the field; examination will discover its companion-piece in the same relative position on the opposite side.   A monograph on this carpet was published by Edward Stebbing in London in 1893, in folio, with hand-painted plates, which showed its splendid color effects.

and yellows are of the lemon order. There is some vermilion and orange in the figures.

As to texture: the material is coarse wool, the pile about the medium length of that in the Demirdji carpets; the warp is of four-strand cotton; the weft is thrown across four threads at a time, as in the Samarkands; the sides have a selvage built upon two threads of the warp, and the ends are finished with the loose warp threads.

XIII

KHILIMS

THE hard, smooth coverings known as khilims (double-faced) are exported in large quantities from different parts of the East, and are of such thoroughly Oriental character as to entitle them to a prominent place in consideration; but their scope in the matter of execution is so limited, they follow type so closely, that there is no call, and indeed no latitude, for exhaustive discussion of them. In many respects there are no carpets made in the East which are more attractive than genuinely good khilims. There they have been employed as floor-coverings from the very earliest times; in America they are used for portières and covers. The artistic skill shown in them consists in the novel adjustment of colors. So deft are the Eastern weavers in this that two rugs of the selfsame design, but with colors differently distributed, look utterly unlike, and will pass for altogether dissimilar conceits. The hues are broad and in some degree crude. The treatment is wholly rectilinear, but harmony and softness of effect are secured in most of the khilims by projecting a series of rectangular extensions from one body of color upon that adjoining, as in Daghestan, Soumak and other Caucasian piled rugs.

This peculiar but most effective edging does not interfere in the least with the design. It is as complete as though its outlines were smooth and direct instead of being broken by such numberless serrations and indentations. Indeed, when it is considered how confusing these irregularities are, the skill of the designer and weaver seem magnified fourfold. To one unfamiliar with the fabrics the serration and diversification seem paramount. It is only when viewed from a distance, where the unity of the design may be seen and the softening effect of these notched edges understood, that the comprehensive beauty of the khilims is apparent. This singular factor, which rather engrosses attention at first, is only the skilful means to an end; but it accomplishes its mission so well that it seems to be the ruling motive of the fabric, and it creates in the khilims some subtle force of fascination which precludes their ever becoming wearisome. And to heighten even further the efficacy of the square-notched edges, the weaver puts in at the end of each of the reciprocal projections a tiny patch or line of some third color, often woven into ornamental shapes. At first inspection this escapes the eye; it is only when one wonders how these uncomplementary colors can join in such a restful ensemble that this fine device is discovered. The small patterns are usually outlined all about, in the same fashion and with the same purpose. It is doubtful if such an array of startling colors, in such large areas, could be combined in any other way without palling. The necessity for some such trick as this, in working out the khilim design and color scheme, suggests itself at once. In the first place, they are smooth-surface carpets, and so devoid of all the softening effects which naturally come from the use of pile. The yarn of which they are woven is twisted so that it is harder and more linen-like than any wool yarns used in the pile carpets, and makes, where entirely different colors are brought close to one another, the most severe line of demarcation. The method, or stitch, is calculated to emphasize this harshness.

It is probable, from the general character of the stuffs, that the khilims present more nearly the primitive fashion of weaving — working out with weft-threads of different colors, by passing them around the warp, the patterns which in most Eastern fabrics are produced by knotting.[1]

Sellers of rugs rarely go to the pains of distinguishing between the several varieties of khilims, and indeed it may be difficult to do so, save in the case of the Sehnas, which differ radically from all the rest. In everything except the difference of method they are exact reproductions of the Sehna piled rugs, and can be identified by the description given of the Sehnas under the head of Persian Fabrics. The designs and colors are the same, and in point of fineness they as far excel the other khilims as the Sehna piled products do the rugs of Karabagh or Shirvan.

Aside from them, nearly all the khilims offered for sale in America are comprised in four classes — Kurdish, Shirvan, Merv, and Tekke or Karamanian. The Karamanian and sometimes the Kurdish are made in two sections and sewed together afterward. The discrepancy between the two sides, where parts of the pattern are supposed to unite at the seam, is greater or less, but rather adds to the interest in the fabric than detracts from it. The Kurdish khilims are made all through Kurdistan, but those from the Persian side of the border show more of finish. The Karamanians are mostly woven by Yuruks and Turkomans in the Sanjak of Tekke in old Cappadocia, along the plateaus of the Taurus. The population is mixed, but Turkomans predominate. Some khilims which bear the name Karamanian are also woven by Christian women in the towns.

The Kurdish and Karamanian khilims differ chiefly in point of

---

[1] " As velvet probably originated in Central Asia, and certainly felt, I think it very likely that there also the Turkish tribes first developed the art of sewing tufts of wool on the strings of the warp of the carpets they had learned to make from the Persians, and that the manufacture of these piled carpets was thus introduced by the Saracens into Europe from Turkestan through Persia. The Turks were driven to the invention by the greater coldness of their climate."—*Birdwood: " Industrial Arts of India."*

coarseness. The Kurdish are finer. There are noticeable in both, and also, in a lesser measure, in the Sehnas, small open spaces at the edges of some figures, where one figure ends on a certain warp-thread, and the adjoining one begins on the next. The uniting stitches of a third color referred to above are omitted, and the multitude of open spaces thus left makes the design seem like a loose insertion. In the heavy pieces known as *kis khilims*, or winter spreads, these gaps are less frequent, the aim being to make the fabric as compact as possible.

The patterns are chiefly the geometrical ones of Turkestan and the Caucasus, but though some of the Persian and Arabic ornamental forms appear, all are worked out in a manner peculiar to themselves. Many seemingly intentional irregularities are found. Where, for example, some figure is to be repeated several times in white, it is woven once or twice in cotton, while all the rest are in wool ; or where two or more small variegated patterns balance each other, and seem at first to be alike, examination shows that the weaver, evidently out of sheer caprice, has made some curious difference between them.

The border stripes are not, as a rule, the same all the way around the fabric, as is customary in most of the piled rugs. The stripe patterns across the ends are different from those along the sides, like those of most Turkoman carpets, and the rotation of colors is by no means regular. There is much latitude for the exercise of individual whim in the khilims, and the weavers avail themselves of it to the full.

In the Merv fabric the number of open spaces is reduced to a minimum. Instead of making the patterns rectangular, and ending on the perpendicular line of the warp, where a gap must be left or the additional labor of joining be incurred, the defining lines of the figure run diagonally, the projections are more pointed, the gap in the web is avoided, and the carpet gains greatly in compactness.

In design these Merv khilims, some of which are of great size, are not so startling as the Kurdish and Karamanian. The garish colors are few; the white is more sparingly applied. The field is usually divided transversely into three or four parts, by ornate line patterns. The designs strongly suggest the Beluchistan rugs in this regard. The high lights, as in the Beluchistans, are found in the border — white lines, serrated, very pronounced, running sometimes the entire length of the fabric, with small geometrical devices worked in the angles.

The methods of weaving are much alike in all the khilims thus far named. The work is done with shuttles, on which the weft-threads are wound. By passing them the colors are carried in and out across the warp, making an even, corded surface, the "grain" of which is the warp itself. Whole figures of the pattern are woven separately. It is this that causes the open spaces between them. The Shirvan khilims follow in general the Daghestan idea of design.

The Persians have a khilim known as *doru*, woven in simple stripes all the way across the field. It is made in manner similar to that of the Kurdish and Karamanian. In Turkestan there is made what is known as the Bokhara khilim, which is an altogether different thing. A web is woven in the deep Bokhara red color; upon this is embroidered with thread and needle the characteristic Bokhara design. In Shirvan the same thing is done; all through Turkey, in fact, are made these djijims, following the rug patterns in vogue in their respective localities. They resemble the khilims but little, and should properly be classed with the Baghdad portières. Among the Kurds and Karamanians, but rarely among the Persians or the people of Merv, the khilims are woven in the form of prayer rugs. The niche in the Karamanian and Kurdish prayer khilims is patterned after the Ghiordes.

KHILIMS

Khilims have of late been extensively made in Servia, Bosnia and other parts of Turkey in Europe.

In many parts of the Orient a fabric called *tzoul* or *tzul* is made of coarse wool or goat's-hair and in the khilim stitch, but with no effort at design, except in some cases stripes of the several natural shades of the hair. It is strong, durable and sometimes water-proof. It is the burlaps, the tent-canvas, the horse-blanket, the grain-sack, the travelling-bag — in short, the universal handy wrapping material of the East. It is also used as a filling on floors, and the gay-colored rugs are placed upon it, gaining in brightness by contrast with its dull shades. Among the Karamanians in eastern Anatolia it is customary to work some lively designs upon these tzouls with the needle.

XIV

INDIA

WITH the barely possible exception of two or three varieties, the Indian carpets sold to-day are wholly modern
creations. The antique fabrics, many of which were
admirable, are no longer to be had and scarcely to be seen, least of all
in American markets. Such of the genuine old-time examples as remained after the English exploitation of Indian arts and industries
were obtained by English and European collectors, and have disappeared from view. The East India Company, owner of most of the
good ones, sold them, and so eagerly were they taken up that even
the British museums were in the end unable to secure such specimens
as would have been desirable. The industrial development of India
under English rule dissipated the old methods so rapidly that within
twenty-five years after the first public exhibition of these fabrics in
London, in 1851, the carpet product had become entirely altered in
character.

There are preserved in the museum at Jeypore a number of the
old India carpets found at the time of the British occupation. All
give proof of Persian derivation. The story of carpet-making in
India, and in truth of all Indian arts, dates practically from the
supremacy of Akbar in the sixteenth century. There is small doubt

that by reason of previous invasion the Persian manufacture and use of carpets had already become to some extent popular among the vanquished people. It was one of the wise accomplishments of Akbar to crystallize the custom, establish it as an industry, elevate it as an art. Following the system which has prevailed in the great cities of Persia, he set up looms in the palace, and installed weavers there. How thoroughly the Khorassan and Persian-Afghan influence dominated Indian art from that time forward is shown by the antique carpets of Lahore, one of which Mr. Vincent Robinson has reproduced in his " Eastern Carpets." The central field is almost identical with that of the Herat fabrics heretofore described. The border presents a long, straight, graceful cone pattern, in a most ornamental shade of light blue, approaching turquoise, and so ornate in its workmanship that it seems to belong to a shawl design rather than to a carpet border.

The example set by the Emperor was followed almost universally throughout India, not alone in the weaving, but in all the arts. Rulers of provinces and districts and even the village dignitaries maintained an extensive patronage. With such support weaving took on a sumptuary character, as it had in Persia. With these royal examples to inspire them, the weavers wrought ambitiously in their less pretentious pieces. The village and caste systems did much to foster effort and to perpetuate high standard. By the first of these each community was established as a unit, under control, generally, of one man whose function it was to assess and collect the town's share of the imperial tax; the second, which attained in India such perfection of development as it has known nowhere else in the world, made the trades and professions hereditary. The weaver's son succeeded to his father's station, and strove to emulate his accomplishments. In the weaving families each generation, reared to the art, studied to add new worth and beauty to the designs, the fundamental elements of which had been the proud possession of its forebears. There could be only one result of such a system. Mr. Robinson says: " The spread of this manufacture extended over the whole of India, and as late as the middle of this century was practised, very much in its integrity, from Kashmir to as far south as Tanjore."

It is almost inexplicable that a system so strongly grounded, so literally and figuratively inwoven with the family and civil life of the people, could in so brief a time have been destroyed; but such seems to have been the case. The apparent first cause was the desire of the Indian government to furnish occupation for its prisoners in jails throughout the empire, and incidentally to neutralize the expense of maintaining the corrective system. Brought thus into competition with prison labor, the caste weaver was undersold, and had no resource save to cheapen his product and increase its volume. The jail manufacture was at first looked upon as a splendid invention, since the singular aptitude of the prisoners enabled them to master the weaving readily, and when they were herded together their work could be overseen and orders enforced. Originality in design was discountenanced, forbidden, and chemical dyes were introduced.[1]

The lack of wool had always been a drawback to carpet-weaving in parts of India. In fact, the only carpets made there prior to the Mohammedan domination were wholly of cotton, or cotton mixed with silk. The support of the nobles, who had no need to spare expense in securing materials, had for a long time overcome the difficulty, and wool was brought in quantities from the grazing countries to the north, as it is to some extent to-day. When the new system supplanted the old, cheaper materials were introduced. Hemp and

---

[1] " Take, for instance, such a common thing as the black dye of Kanchipuram, and the red dye of Madura in the Madras presidency, which was famous throughout the world. European black has taken the place of the one, and that rich russet red which delighted the eye of the painter is replaced by magenta."—*Georgiana Kingscote: " The Decline of Taste in Indian Art."*

jute took the place of cotton in the foundations, and the general decadence of the native product was complete. In an article in *The Nineteenth Century*, in 1891, on "The Decline of Taste in Indian Art," Georgiana Kingscote, speaking of the spontaneous native industry, says:

"At one time there were more than two hundred houses where there are now twos and threes, and the famished inhabitants cannot even afford to keep a stock of carpets on hand, and as soon as one is finished are only too ready to sell it, at a loss even, simply as a means of subsistence; and the trade is at such a low ebb that if you want an Indian carpet you must advance the money, and wait until they can get through it, as they cannot afford to employ many workers.

"The coloring of the Indian carpets originally came from Persia, and these colors, especially reds and blues, were as beautiful as those of that country still are. Now, unfortunately, the revival of carpet manufacture is principally carried on in the jails, under English supervision, and the patterns are decidedly English, and the texture thick like English pile, thus encouraging the loss of that extremely fine work peculiar to the Persian carpets. Here, again, magenta, being a cheap English color, plays a great part, and spoils the harmony of the coloring. One drop of water is enough to spoil the carpet by making the magenta in it run into the white ground. French and English machine-made carpets and Brussels carpets are invading India, and the carpet trade is sinking fast as, if not faster than, any other."

The same verdict was pronounced at about the same time, and in a much more authoritative manner, by Mr. Robinson. After thirty-five years spent in actual endeavor to uphold and latterly to save the ancient art of carpet-weaving in India, he closes in this wise his review of the subject: "Every encouragement was thus afforded, and the way smoothed for Trade versus Art; and notwithstanding all the protests made by those who became aware of threatened dangers, the manufacture went on in the jails, and the art languished. It is now no exaggeration to say that in India, from the Himalayas to Cape Cormorin, no means exists for the fabrication of art carpets like those found in most of the places here enumerated, nor can the art element in this industry ever be resuscitated until means are found for restoring the conditions under which the originals were produced."

It is a new and, it must be confessed, wholly commercial manufacture that has sprung up in India on the ruins of the art industry which had its splendid beginnings with Akbar. Availing themselves of the fabulously cheap labor to be had without limit in India, the English, French, and latterly American houses have established there factories for the making of rugs according to their own conceits, or following in some sort the characteristic designs of Persia. Provisions of the law interfere with the importation of the prison-made fabrics to America, but the output of the prison looms at Lahore, Agra, Jabalpur, Benares, and Bangalore has fairly flooded the English market for years, being sold for a price which defied all honest competition. Even there, however, it is likely the fabrics will be excluded before many years shall have passed. But that, it is plain, will not restore the art.

Two dealers in New York, both interested in the Indian manufacture, have summarized the whole matter in statements made to the writer. The first said: "There is not a rug-making town in all India to-day where the native patterns are used." The second said: "An effort was made to introduce some new shades at Mirzapur; but although careful search was made throughout all the district, not a dyer was found who knew how to dye *pukka*,— the Hindu term for the old vegetable dyes,— and dyers had to be brought from Amritsar to do the work."[1]

---

[1] It is only fair to say that another well-known rug man, to whom these declarations were repeated, denied them vigorously.

INDIA

And yet Mīrzapur, up to 1850, was one of the greatest manufactories of art carpets in India.

The bold offers made by certain India carpet concerns, principally in Amritsar, of large monetary forfeits to any person who shall find evidences of aniline color in their fabrics, and, in fact, the personal declaration of American dealers interested financially in the Indian manufactures, lead inevitably to the conclusion that the use of vegetable dyes is being resumed, or, at any rate, that by some means greater stability is being sought in the coloring.

In many respects, however, the methods of manufacture now pursued are identical with those in vogue in the prisons. The chief feature of the prison system which recommended it for commercial purposes was that all the weavers employed upon a particular contract were herded together, where supervision was easy and obedience to orders imperative. Here, too, the personal equation was eliminated. Individuality in design was suppressed, an advantage which the contracting firms have never been able to obtain in dealing with the Turkish, Persian or Caucasian weavers, save in Sultanabad, Kirman and Tabriz, and more recently in Meshhed, where huge carpets are made. In all the other weaving districts in the Mohammedan countries the weavers have stubbornly refused to work *en masse*, but weave upon looms reared in their own houses, where, free from superintendence, they often exercise their own ingenuity, and give to the fabrics a touch now and then of the true Oriental character, which accords so ill with the demands of the Western firms.

This lesson was learned from the jail system, and although in some towns of India home looms are retained, the weavers of the great carpet centres work in droves, within walls and under guard. They are searched when they quit the workshop, and upon the completion of the carpet every atom of the wool remaining from its construction must be returned to the owners. Under the old system the workmen and workwomen kept these leavings, and used them in other and altogether different fabrics, to effect the variant note so potent in warding off ill luck.

In India the women do no weaving. The great majority of the weavers are boys, ranging in age from six to fifteen years, and most of them under twelve. They are under the absolute sway of the native masters, a sort of padrones, and when, from one reason or another, the "boss weaver" leaves a factory, he takes his entire following with him. This is an altogether uncomfortable state of things for the firms carrying on the business, since in places like Amritsar the defection of a large body of these tiny toilers can cause incalculable inconvenience and delay. The maximum wage of one of these child weavers is about five cents a day. Skilled adults work by the thousand stitches, and a great day's earning is about twenty-five or thirty cents.

What has been said in another chapter on the transportation of designs from one part of the Orient to another, and their adoption into other ornament systems, applies in its fullest force to India. Considering the illimitable conservatism of the Hindu, it is difficult to understand how the Mohammedan designs could have crowded out those of the earlier races, while the language, religion, and social customs remain. All through the north of India the Persian forms were used almost exclusively, though taking on a rich ornamental character which even in the most finished of the Persianized products suggested the native, half-barbarian splendor. In the south of India there were retained many of the old creations; but even these were of the same ancient origin as the Persian, although altered by centuries of native Indian usage. They had been brought into India by Aryan invasion further back even than the time of Darius, and thus, after long separation, the currents of the primitive and universal symbolism were again united.

INDIA

The treatment in many India carpets of the eighties was little more than a burlesque; but pieces made later on contract looms preserve with comparative fidelity the details of the Persian rugs from which they were copied. In the prison weaving both kinds of knots were used, and in the cheap grades a simple twist, which is no knot at all, but merely a turning of the yarn around the warp, depending wholly upon the tension of the weft to hold it. It must have been rugs of such workmanship which prompted Sir George Birdwood to say in his "Industrial Arts of India," in 1884: "The foundation, as now scamped, is quite insufficient to carry the heavy pile which is a feature of this make, and is, moreover, so short in the staple as to be incapable of bearing the tension even of the process of manufacture. Jabalpur carpets often reach this country, which will not bear sweeping or even unpacking. I know of two which were shaken to pieces in the attempt to shake the dust out of them when first unpacked. The designs once had some local character, but have lost it during the last five years."

There are among the Indian carpets of to-day, nevertheless, some fabrics which are stout, soundly made, quite well dyed, and, being copies of good spontaneous Persian designs, are meritorious in that regard. It is not hard to distinguish the wheat from the chaff. In selecting from among these carpets there is probably no rule other than of personal preference in design, supplemented by the general requirements as to material and texture, and the customary tests for solidity of color.

Amritsar.— Reference has already been made to the natural qualification which tends to make Amritsar a home of carpet-weaving. Most of its water is of good quality, and it is near to the course of wool-supply. In addition it has within easy reach the Kashmir district, where skilful dyers and weavers became plentiful after the decadence of the shawl manufacture. It is, moreover, a centre of trade, and one of the chief stations on the Punjab railway. Thus its manu-factures find easy transportation to the coast.

In a system so purely commercial as is the Indian carpet-making of to-day, all these are ample reasons for the general transfer of fac-tories from other parts of the empire to Amritsar. For a long time it was the custom of the Kashmir shawl-weavers to journey down to Amritsar to weave shawls during the winter months. In this manner the Kashmir methods were brought into vogue here. The manufac-ture of heavy carpets for the trade has outgrown the old industry. Many of the Kashmir customs have been abandoned, but one impor-tant feature still prevails. A rug, or pattern, is divided into sections, as many as there are weavers at work upon the looms, and in a book are written down in Kashmiri characters all the stitches in each sec-tion, with the colors, and the exact sequence in which they must be put in, from the beginning to the finishing of the rug. Each weaver has a number corresponding to that of the section upon which he is employed. It is the task of one boy to read off these stitches, day in and day out, through the making of many carpets. While he reads, the loom masters, each having three or sometimes four looms under their control, go about and inspect the work, for errors. When such are found the weavers are compelled to pull out all the faulty knots and replace them. There are many thousands of men and boys employed in the carpet industry of Amritsar, counting wool-handlers, dyers and weavers, and the work of so many facile hands makes up a mighty carpet export.

W. S. Caine, in his book on "Picturesque India," says: "Some of the finest carpets in India are woven at Amritsar. One dealer just inside the first gate, entered from the railway station and hotels, em-ploys from seven hundred to one thousand hands in carpet-weaving, at a wage of from three to six annas per day [nine to eighteen cents]. He works mainly for three or four great London firms, and I have

PLATE XXIV. SAMARKAND

16.5 x 7.2

Loaned by Mr. William McLaren Bristol

The old-time weavers of Samarkand made strenuous effort to attain the Persian profuseness in design, but as has been set forth in the text, were hampered by Chinese influence, which dictated the use of the heavy round or octagonal medallion in the field, and of the old Mongol religious emblems. The discovery of this old and in every way interesting carpet was a piece of good fortune.   Here, it will be seen, the entire space in the field is covered with repetitions of the Chinese cloud band (compare Plate I), but the arrangement is in rows, like that of the vases in that purest of Persian designs, the old Kirman shown in Plate XVIII.   Further concession to the Persian—a sign manual, in fact—is found in the minute pear figures thrown in at intervals throughout the ground, apparently without rhyme or reason.   The Turkoman elements are plain here, too, in the broad, striped webbing at the ends, and the border designs, which are merely the tarantula and scorpion devices, with a suggestion of the tree.

seen no worthier results in any of the carpet manufactories I have visited up and down India."

The output of the Amritsar looms, therefore, is perhaps the best by which to judge the present-day carpet product of India. That part of it which is handled by American firms is probably the best which these great factories have to show, better, no doubt, by reason of the fact that the agents dealing directly with India can and do dictate concerning designs, colors and all the points of construction. But the whole system is distinctly commercial, and for the general stock the same patterns are produced in all grades, ranging from three knots by three to twelve by twelve, to suit the needs of the buyer. There is a corresponding variation in the quality of the dyes and the workmanship, and some of the staple stuff would discredit the tepee of a Piute. The designs are taken chiefly from the Persian, and the Feraghan seems to be a favorite. Others are copied in the most impossible of colors from huge, glaring designs of English carpets. Many small mats are made, which suffer sadly by contrast with even the poorest of the *yesteklik* which come from Anatolia.

In the lower grades, whether of mats or larger pieces, there is seldom any effort at artistic finishing of the ends, an enormously heavy and badly bungled overcasting taking the place of the attractive fringes which adorn the ends of the Turkish, Persian and Caucasian rugs. It must be said for Amritsar, however, that since it became the factory of the better class of whole carpets for American firms, the concerns dealing in the wretched low-grade fabrics just referred to have transferred their manufacture to other towns, where labor can be had more cheaply; so that Amritsar probably merits the good word spoken by Mr. Caine.

The best grade of carpets made here are what are known as "pushmina," from the fact that they are made of *pashim* or *pushim*, the fine wool found next to the skin of the sheep. Some of these, in which closeness of texture is aimed at, have a silk warp. The stitches are sometimes as many as fourteen by fourteen. Raw-silk rugs are also made in Amritsar, but the manufacture has not met with great success.

Kashmir.— Since we are dealing with floor-coverings, there is little to be said about Kashmir. Its fame was won in the manufacture of shawls, and although some carpets were made there of old, they showed in colors, materials, patterns and workmanship, even at the best period of their development, the effect of propinquity to the shawl industry. Sir George Birdwood describes one of the older examples as having "grounds of pale yellow and rose color, and floral patterns in half-tones of a variety of colors. The borders were weak and not distinct from the centre, but the coloring and general effect were serene and pleasing."

"Its peculiarities," Mr. Robinson says, "were in some degree due to the use of shawl wool for the fabrics, and to a method of arranging designs quite its own. The width of the borders was nearly as exaggerated as in those of Tanjore in the south of India, but the filling of the design differed from them by being minute in proportion to the space occupied. The scale of coloring also distinguished it from other manufactures and was probably the effect of chemical properties in the water."

Of the modern fabrics of Kashmir, which, though they are quite different, still retain some peculiarities which had their birth in the shawl-making, nothing can be said which has not been said of other varieties of Indian goods. The general run of the staple product is poor, but the carpets turned out to order for English and American firms are of a better style and design, and where the selection of materials is made by the Western agents, and the contractors are fast bound by stipulation, fairly good fabrics are produced.

Mirzapur.— There is probably no city in India whose carpet industry has known a more extraordinary series of ups and downs than has that of Mirzapur. Situated on the south bank of the Ganges, it is in the centre of the richest and most cultured part of India. It is near neighbor to Benares and Allahabad; it is on the railway, and is but half as far as Amritsar from Calcutta. It is fairly populous, has extensive manufactures of brasswork, and is a still famous mart for cotton and grain. The Hindu element is strong here, and the city presents, on the river-front, some remarkable Hindu temples. This atmosphere had undoubtedly much to do with the designs of the old Mirzapur carpets, which, before English commercial manipulation began, showed a pronounced Hindu character in distinction from the Persian forms. Instead of any manner of floral diapers, they displayed medallions, within which all the floral forms were traced.

It was only a little while after the introduction of the Mirzapur carpets into England that English firms began to lower the quality of them. Efforts to restore it scored desultory success, and as late as 1867 the fabrics maintained a fairly good reputation. The jail system, coupled with precipitate trading, finally finished them. The texture became coarse, the materials poor, the colors of such sort as has been indicated in the introductory part of this chapter.

The later development did something to redeem the industry, but merely to the end of securing a satisfactory workshop, and probably not with any view of again producing the fabrics as they were before the great era of decadence began. The modern Mirzapur carpets show round, floral figures, with dark red as the prevailing color, usually arranged in rows upon a pale yellow or cream-colored ground. Dark red, almost maroon, prevails also in the borders, which carry some arrangement of the pear pattern resembling the main borders of the Khorassans, or else a repetition of the floral forms found in the body of the rug, with a connecting vine.

The wool for the present-day Mirzapur carpets comes chiefly

from the western part of Rajputana and is of an inferior sort. The great endeavor on the part of both native and foreign firms engaged in the manufacture has been to secure wool which would give better results when wrought, and yet come within the "near" rates they were willing to pay in their desire to keep the fabrics down to "competition prices," and at the same time widen the margin of profit. One American agent tried bringing wool from Beluchistan, but the local dyers could do nothing with it. They treat the wool with lime, too, to give it brilliancy, which is only adding another ill.

Lahore.— The British capital of the Punjab is one of the places where prison weaving has been done. The central jail there has held as many as two thousand prisoners, and in addition there are district and female jails, a thug jail and a "school of industry," in all of which both woollen and cotton carpets have been made. The manufacture of the old-fashioned fabrics held on there with much tenacity, nevertheless, considering the proximity of so much that tended to demoralize them.

The Lahore carpets were among the first of the Indian products to attract commercial attention in England, and the East India Company's vessels took a great number of the fabrics home to be sold. Records of the company indicate that even in the seventeenth century, while the impulse starting from Akbar must still have been strong, extremely good carpets were by no means so plenty as may be supposed. One agent, writing in 1617, reports the purchase at Agra of thirty fine Lahore carpets. In a letter written only a short time afterward, he says: "It requires a long time to get well-chosen carpets. True Lahore carpets are not so suddenly to be gotten." This declaration seems to have been in answer to some complaint that he had not sent larger consignments, and indicates how quickly the carpets caught the British fancy.

Despite the debauchery of the product by the jail system, a certain amount of weaving, following tolerably well the old models, seems to have been done in Lahore down to a recent time. Even within the past two or three years a few examples of considerable age have been offered for sale in New York, and taken quickly even at the high price demanded.

Weaving outside the jails was extensively revived here at one time, and though the fabrics were in nowise equal to the old ones, some of them, woven in the Persian fashion, were fairly good. The prevailing design is a Persian pear pattern for the fields, arranged like that of the Herat or Saraband, and a border in which the Greek elements are predominant. There are seldom more than forty knots to the square inch.

Agra.—Agra, whither travellers journey to gaze upon the beauty of the Taj Mahal, has its carpet industry too—an industry the early history of which Mr. Robinson recounts in this wise: " The Indus valley had always obtained rugs from the neighboring Afghans on the north and the Beluchee tribes on the south of the river; but as the Mohammedan power became established in central India, the necessity was found for local manufacture of carpets too large to be carried by camels or even by elephants. Thus Agra, Jhansi and other places east became seats of the manufacture."

In point of size and thickness the Agra carpets of to-day are fit successors to those of the olden time. They are of enormous weight and solidity. The designs are similar to those common in the time of Mongol ascendancy, the cone forms playing an important part. For a long time after the establishment of the weaving in jails and the industrial school, the carpets were nearly all in a monotone of two colors, green or blue, with pale cream color. More recently the use of browns and purples was begun. The central field in the later rugs presents an angular form of some Mohammedan device, and the border, very often, the transverse arrangement of the pear shape spoken of as being a feature of certain Khorassans. In the jails, where the manufacture is still carried on, cotton carpets are made, thick and heavy like the woollen ones.

Allahabad. — This beautiful and thriving city, at the junction of the Ganges and Jumna, is a Hindu stronghold, but it is the centre as well of the most thoroughly British influence in the realm. Although not one of the most important weaving cities, there are exported from it a great many carpets, similar in almost every respect to those of Agra. They range in texture from forty-eight to possibly one hundred knots to the square inch.

Masulipatam. — It was here that the first British settlement was established in 1620. Even then the city, though small, was renowned for its fabrics. From fine, closely woven, beautifully designed rugs, they have, under the sweat-shop system, taken on the cheap character of much of the Indian output. These rugs were at one time widely sold in the United States, but have lost caste since the large importation of other and better fabrics began.

Jaipur or Jeypore. — This, the capital of the state of the same name, is the principal commercial centre of Rajputana. It stands in a plain, surrounded on all sides save one by hills which the ancient rulers made sites of remarkable fortifications. Under British dominion the city has progressed greatly. It has fine paved streets, gas lighting, hospitals, dispensaries, almshouses and schools, and a famous observatory, built in 1728. The carpets woven here copy the designs found chiefly in the rugs of eastern and middle Persia. They nearly always present the cypress-tree, and also many animal forms, laid upon ground of dark red, blue or ivory white. The borders have a swaying-vine pattern, with the customary floral adjuncts.

Miscellaneous. — In Jabalpur, Ahmedabad, Ellore, Poonah, Delhi, Bijapur, Madras and Jamu, all seats at one time of considerable carpet manufacture, fabrics are still turned out, but they are not imported in any great number into this country. Velvet carpets from Benares, Patna and Murshidabad once had some fame. Tanjore, Warangal, Multan and Hyderabad all produced remarkable rugs under the old dispensation, but little or no trace of their industry remains.

Rug.	Knot.	Warp.	Weft.	Pile.
Daghestan............	Ghiordes....	Usually gray wool	Wool ; sometimes dyed .	Fine wool, short.. .....
Derbend.............	Ghiordes....	Brown wool or goat's-hair.	Wool	Fine wool ; rather long...
Kabistan	Ghiordes....	Wool or cotton	Usually cotton..........	Fine wool ; usually short.
Tchechen or " Tzitzi.".	Ghiordes....	Usually fine white wool...	Wool	Fine wool ; medium lengt
Tcherkess or Circassian.	Ghiordes....	Wool...................	Wool	Fine wool ; rather short..
Karabagh	Ghiordes....	Stout, wool.............	Wool	Wool ; medium length...
Soumak	Flat weave..	Wool...................	Wool	Nap ; wool ....
Shirvan	Ghiordes..	Wool ; white in antiques ; brown, gray, and sometimes particolored in moderns.............	White wool in antiques ; wool or cotton in moderns	Wool ....
Kazak...............	Ghiordes....	Wool...................	Wool ; often four threads after each row of knots.	Wool ; long in Ilats ; med um in Takhta Kapon...
Mosul	Ghiordes....	Usually wool ; sometimes cotton	Usually wool ; sometimes cotton..............	Wool, filik or camel's hair
Turkman or Genghis...	Ghiordes. ..	Dark wool or goat's-hair..	Gray or brown wool ..	Fine selected wool in ol pieces ; coarser quality i moderns..............
Mosul Kurds.........	Ghiordes....	Dark wool or goat's-hair..	Gray or brown wool	Wool ; rather long ....

Rug.	Knot.	Warp.	Weft.	Pile.
Konieh	Ghiordes ..	Antique, fine wool.. ... Modern, coarse wool, particolored.........	Fine wool	Fine selected wool, medium....
Kir-Shehr............	Ghiordes ..	Wool	Wool	Fine wool, rather long ....
Kaba-Karaman	Ghiordes ..	Coarse wool............	Wool	Fine wool, long.............
Yuruk	Ghiordes ..	Brown wool or goat's-hair.	Wool or cotton	Coarse wool ; medium or rather lo
Anatolian or Cæsarians ..	Ghiordes ..	Usually wool......	Brown wool or goat's-hair	Fine wool, sometimes mixed w goat's fleece ; long..........
Ghiordes Antique.......	Ghiordes ..	Fine wool, cotton, or silk.	Usually wool	Fine wool ; long ....
Ghiordes Modern	Ghiordes ..	Coarse wool............	Cotton, linen, or sometimes single strand wool................	Very fine selected wool, short ; so small figures in cotton.... ..
Kulah Antique.........	Ghiordes ..	Fine wool..............	Usually cotton..........	Wool, varying lengths in differe grades ....
Kulah Modern.........	Ghiordes ..	Coarse wool............	Fine wool	Selected wool, short ....
Demirdji	Ghiordes ..	Coarse wool............	Cotton or wool	Wool, long ....
Oushak..............	Ghiordes ..	Wool	Coarse wool	Wool, medium ....
Bergamo	Ghiordes ..	Fine wool ; usually dyed .	Wool	Wool, varying lengths in differe grades ....
Ladik...............	Ghiordes ..	Very fine wool	Wool ; usually dyed....	Fine wool, medium length......
Ak-Hissar and other Mohairs	Ghiordes ..	Coarse wool............	Wool ; usually dyed....	Fine selected wool, rather short.
Meles or Carian.........	Ghiordes ..	Wool...................	Coarse wool............	Mohair ; sometimes mixed with wo
			Cotton or wool........	Wool, rather short ....

IAN.

Sides.	Ends.	Knots to Inch Horizontal.	Knots to Inch. Perpendicular.
ow selvage ; usually of extra yarns, colored...	Narrow web ; compact knotted fringe	8 to 12......	9 to 15
lly overcast.....................................	Long, heavy knotted fringe ; in some a wide Turkoman web..................................	6 to 9......	7 to 10
cast ; selvaged with extra cotton threads, or ody finish "..............................	Narrow web ; ends loose if cotton, knotted fringe if wool......................................	9 to 14......	12 to 15
lly selvage of added yarns.................	Narrow web ; knotted fringe	7 to 9.......	8 to 10
ge ; usually of wool, sometimes cotton, added.	Narrow web ; knotted fringe (small).............	7 to 9.......	8 to 10
ule ; overcast, selvaged or "body finish"....	One end usually has web turned back; other has fringe or loops of the warp........................	6 to 9	7 to 10
ule....................................	Usually loose, heavy knotted fringe.............	12 to 20...... Warp-threads to the inch.	6 to 12
rule.....................................	Narrow web and long coarse fringe in moderns ; finer finish in antiques...........................	Ant. 7 to 9.... Mod. 5 to 7....	8 to 11 6 to 8
e selvage, sometimes of added yarns ; varies weight..............................	Heavy fringe on one end ; other sometimes has web and thick selvage outside it, or web turned back and hemmed........................	6 to 8	7 to 9
ally overcast	Narrow web ; fringe if warp is wool ; stout selvage if cotton....................................	6 to 8......	8 to 9
sually selvaged with extra yarns of brown wool.	Web, sometimes of Turkoman width, and shaggy fringe.........................	6 to 8......	7 to 8
rcast ; or an added selvage, with color changed very few inches after Kurdish fashion	Warp woven in thick selvage ; outside of that triangular mats and rope's-end fringe...	6 to 7......	6 to 7

SH

Sides.	Ends.	Knots to Inch Horizontal.	Knots to Inch Weft.
arrow selvage (added).....................	Web and selvage ; sometimes fringe.............	7 to 9....	8 to 10
rule......	Usually web and loose warp....................	5 to 7	7 to 8
vage (sometimes added).................	Usually colored web ; short fringe......	7 to 10......	7 to 10
rule	No rule....................................	4 to 6.....	4 to 6
eavy and peculiar goat's-hair selvage.......	Narrow brown web and short fringe or braids	6 to 7.....	7 to 9
eavy extra selvage.....................	Colored web, warps made into fringe or braid....	7 to 10.....	9 to 12
lk selvage (added).....................	Sewed silk fringe, or narrow web and loose warp .	9 to 12	10 to 12
o rule................................	Web, usually, with loose warp ends	4 to 8.....	4 to 9
sually narrow colored selvage (added).......	Narrow web, usually yellow ; warp ends loose....	8 to 10.....	8 to 12
o rule..................................	No rule....................................	4 to 7.....	4 to 7
o rule..................................	No rule....................................	6 to 8.....	6 to 8
o rule..................................	No rule....................................	4 to 9....	4 to 9
sually wide selvage.....................	Broad red web, usually striped or figured ; short fringe ; some have narrow selvage	8 to 10.....	10 to 12
ide selvage (added).....................	Broad red web, short fringe ; some have narrow selvage	10 to 12.....	10 to 12
vercast ; sometimes heavy selvage	Narrow web ; warp loose....................	6 to 9.....	6 to 9
elvage ; added if warp cotton, of weft threads if wool..............	Narrow web ; loose fringe of colored warp.......	5 to 9.....	5 to 10

Rug.	Knot.	Warp.	Weft.	Pile.
Tabriz.............	Ghiordes...	Cotton; sometimes linen or silk.............	Cotton, single-strand wool, linen..........	Selected wool, short.......
Herez [1]	Ghiordes, rarely Sehna.	Usually cotton..........	Cotton, sometimes brown wool...............	Wool; quality and length with grades...........
Kara Dagh	Ghiordes....	Wool................	Wool	Wool, medium.........
Sehna.............	Sehna	Cotton, linen, or silk	Cotton, single-strand wool, linen..........	Selected wool, very short..
Kurdistan proper	Ghiordes....	White or gray wool.......	Wool; also extra filling between warp-threads.	Wool, medium..........
Kermanshah.	Ghiordes....	Wool or cotton	Wool, natural brown or dyed	Wool, medium..........
"Sarakhs" or Bijar....	Ghiordes....	Wool................	Wool	Wool, rather long; thick a upright; hard surface....
Koultuk or Zenjan.....	Ghiordes....	Cotton; sometimes wool ..	Wool	Wool, medium ....
Souj-Bulak..........	Ghiordes....	Wool................	Wool	Wool, medium, doubled; p thick and upright........
Feraghan	Sehna	Cotton.............	Cotton; rarely wool.....	Wool; short in antiques, n dium in moderns.........
Saruk..............	Sehna	Cotton; sometimes linen..	Cotton; sometimes linen	Selected wool, short.......
Saraband	Sehna	Cotton	Cotton; sometimes colored	Selected wool, short.......
Selvile	Ghiordes....	Wool; sometimes gray....	Wool; usually colored ..	Wool, medium............
Hamadan [3].........	Ghiordes ...	Cotton.............	Cotton or wool..........	Wool, camel's-hair or fili sometimes mixed........
"Jooshaghan" or Djushaghan............	Ghiordes....	Wool	Wool	Selected wool, medium......
Kirman.............	Sehna	Cotton	Wool	Selected wool, short........
Shiraz	Ghiordes, or Sehna	Wool; sometimes goat's-hair in coarse moderns..	Wool	Wool, medium............
Niris	Ghiordes....	Wool................	Wool	Wool, medium............
Khorassan proper......	Sehna	Cotton.............	Wool	Wool, medium............
Meshhed	Ghiordes....	Wool or cotton	Wool	Wool, medium............
Herat	Ghiordes, rarely Sehna.	Wool or cotton	Wool	Wool, medium............

[1] Includes Bakhshis, Herez, Görevan, "Serapi," q. v.   [2] See reference in description to embroidered line across the web.   [3] Includes also other ru

Rug.	Knot.	Warp.	Weft.	Pile.
"Bokhara" or Tekke....	Sehna	Wool................	Wool	Fine wool, short; sometime goat's-fleece.............
Yomud.............	Sehna or Ghiordes..	Brownish wool or goat's-hair	Wool or goat's-hair.....	Fine wool, medium. ....
"Afghan" or Bokhara ..	Sehna	Goat's-hair or dark wool...	Black or gray wool or goat's-hair..........	Fine wool, or goat's-fleece, me dium or long.............
Samarkand	Sehna	Coarse cotton or silk; occasionally wool	Cotton or wool; in most old pieces four threads after each knot-row ..	Wool, or sometimes wool and raw silk, medium..........
Beluchistan	Sehna	Wool................	Wool	Wool, or goat's-fleece; medium
Yarkand and Kashgar....	Sehna	Coarse cotton........ ..	Cotton, as in Samarkands.	Wool, rather long; some silk.

N.

SIDES.	ENDS.	KNOTS TO INCH. HORIZONTAL.	KNOTS TO INCH. PERPENDICULAR.
cast, wool or silk ; rarely selvage........	Narrow web ; sometimes striped ; warp ends loose.	10 to 20......	10 to 20
ally overcast	Narrow web ; warp ends usually loose, but sometimes knotted............................	5 to 12......	7 to 14
ally selvaged....................	One end selvaged and turned back; the other selvaged and fringed............................	8 to 11......	9 to 12
cast	Narrow web ; warp ends usually loose............	10 to 20......	10 to 20
rcast, usually with brown wool	Narrow web, knotted fringe ; one end sometimes selvaged or turned and hemmed [2]...............	8 to 11......	8 to 11
rcast, usually with brown wool	Narrow web, knotted fringe ; one end sometimes selvaged or turned and hemmed...............	8 to 12......	8 to 12
rcast	Narrow web, knotted fringe ; one end usually selvaged	7 to 10......	8 to 10
rcast or selvaged......................	One end plain selvage ; others selvage and loose ends.....................................	7 to 9......	8 to 10
rcast	One end plain selvage ; other selvage and loose ends.....................................	7 to 8......	10 to 11
rcast	Narrow web, warp-ends loose....................	5 to 12......	6 to 14
rcast	Narrow web, warp-ends loose...............	9 to 20......	9 to 20
rcast	Narrow web, warp-ends loose	8 to 12......	9 to 14
rcast	Narrow web and knotted fringe one end ; twisted warp-loops on other........................	7 to 9......	8 to 10
rcast	One end usually selvaged ; other loose warp-ends or knotted fringe........................	7 to 9......	9 to 11
rcast	Narrow web, loose warp-ends..................	8 to 11......	9 to 12
rcast	Narrow web, loose warp-ends..................	10 to 20......	10 to 20
rcast, sometimes variegated and heavily tufted............................	Web ; usually peculiar checked selvage ; warp-ends may be loosely tied.........................	6 to 12......	7 to 14
rcast	Web ; usually short fringe of warp ; checked selvage frequent	6 to 8......	7 to 9
rcast	Very narrow web, or none ; warp-ends loose........	8 to 11......	9 to 13
rcast	Narrow web, fringe of warp, sometimes knotted....	8 to 11......	9 to 11
rcast	Narrow web, fringe of warp, sometimes knotted....	8 to 10......	9 to 11

ontributory districts, Kara-Geuz, Oustri-Nan, Burujird, Bibik-abad. which show only slight variation in texture, though the designs have a wider range.

MAN.

SIDES.	ENDS.	KNOTS TO INCH. HORIZONTAL.	KNOTS TO INCH. PERPENDICULAR.
sually overcast	Web—white, red, or striped ; sometimes very wide ; in some plain piled surface ; fringe...............	8 to 20......	8 to 20
lvage, often checked in yarns of two colors..	Usually wide, reddish web ; long, loose fringe of warp-yarns	7 to 12......	9 to 14
sually heavy selvage of goat's-hair, added....	Wide colored web or plain pile ; loose warp makes shaggy fringe	6 to 9......	7 to 10
sually narrow selvage, added ; overcasting in moderns....................	Narrow web or stout selvage, and fringe	6 to 8....	5 to 7
arrow selvage ; overcasting in some moderns.	Usually wide web, patterned....................	5 to 12......	6 to 10
elvage, two threads of warp, added yarn	Warp ends loose	5 to 7......	5 to 7

INDEX

A

Afghan-Bokhara rugs, description, 235–238

Afghanistan, native name for Khorassan, 225; nomad rugs of, 237; rugs, *see* Bokhara rugs; wool-growing in, 34

Agassiz, on Greek key pattern, quoted, 70

Agra rugs, 265

Ahmedabad rugs, 266

Aidin, "Smyrna" rugs made in, 132

Aiyin rugs, 225

Akbar, Emperor, 252

Ak-Hissar mohair rugs, 39; description, 157

Alizarin, decline in value of, 27

Allahabad rugs, 266

Amritsar, 257; rugs, description, 259

Anatolia, method of carding wool in, 38

Anatolian, rugs, 35; brown shades in, 54; description, 142; mats (Yestiklik), description, 95, 141–143

Angora goat's-hair, 34, 39

Anilines. *See* Dyes

Animal forms in Bokhara rugs, 228, 232; in Genghis rugs, 130; in Meshhed rugs, 224

Apple design (Sihbih), 76

Arabic influence, in Djushaghan rugs, 205; in Kir-Shehr rugs, 139

Ardebil, mosque carpet of, 171

Arras, French factories at, 19

Arshin, Persian unit of measurement, 24

Asia Minor, antique rugs of, copied in Tabriz, 172; mode of cleansing wool in, 36

Assyria, rug designs in, 15

Asur-Banipal, 15

Aubusson, factories at, 19

Azerbijan, 166; rugs, description, 167

B

Babylonian designs. *See* Assyria

Babylonica peristromata, 16

Baghdad, fabrics of, 15

Bakhshis rugs, description, 175

Baluk-Hissar, fair at, 22

Bandhor rugs, origin of name, 6

Barber-pole stripe, in Farsistan rugs, 110; in Kabistan rugs, 110; in Konieh rugs, 137; in Laristan rugs, 110; in Mosul rugs, 128; in Yomud rugs, 110, 234

Barter, system of, 23

Basra. *See* Bassorah

Bassorah, school of painting, 12

Beaumont, A. de, "Les Arts Decoratifs en Orient et en France," quoted: on the superiority of antique art products, 14

Beauvais, factories at, 19

Bellew, Dr., "From the Indus to the Tigris," quoted: on Khorassan rugs, 220; on shrine at Meshhed, 223

INDEX

INDEX

INDEX

INDEX

INDEX

INDEX

Milassa, market for Meles rugs, 158
Mills, steam, 38
Mina Khani designs, 75, 166
Mir design in Saraband rugs, 197
Mirzapur rugs, description, 262–264
Mohammedan restrictions on animate forms in art, 11
Mongol influence in Niris rugs, 215
Mordants, 48
Morocco, 64
Mortlake, Surrey, looms at, 20
Mosul, 126
Mosul Kurdish rugs, 130
Mosul rugs, 3, 40, 63; description, 127–129; why classed as Caucasian, 103

N

Namazlik. *See* Prayer rugs
Neolithic Age, pottery designs, 17
Newton, C. T., on Greek key pattern, cited, 69
Niris rugs, description, 214
Nishapur, 219
Nomad tribes of the Caucasus, 112
Norseland. *See* Scandinavia
Novi Varos rugs, 30

O

Odjaklik (hearth rug), 29; description, 95; Kazak, 114; Konieh, 136
Ornament forms, derivation of, 62
Oushak, dyers, 43; grade names used for modern Koniehs, 138
Oushak rugs, 35; compared with big Anatolians, 143; description, 152; loose knotting, 89
Oustri-Nan, 201

P

Palermo, rug manufacture in twelfth century, 19
Palm. *See* Pear
Parsa, 212

Pashim, 36
Patterns. *See* Designs
Pear, 63; in Genghis rugs, 130; in Ghiordes, 147; in Herat, 225; in Kabistan, 109; in Kermanshah, 188; in Meles, 158; in Meshhed, 223; in Mosul, 128; in Persian, 109; in Saraband, 109, 197; in Sehna, 183; in Shiraz, 109, 213; in Teheran, 203; origin, 68
Peloton rouge. *See* Filik
Pergamos. *See* Bergamo
Persia, animal figures in designs, 12, 15; deterioration of rugs in, 7; bazaars, 7; berries, 53; blue in Kurdistan rugs, 181; lost art of making blue, 53; influence on other rug-making countries, 60
" Persia and the Persians," Benjamin, S. G. W., 53
Persian khilims (doru), 250
Persian knot. *See* Knot, Sehna
Persian provinces, best rugs made in, 161, 163, 165
Persian rugs, 160–166, 173; manner of selling, 133; reciprocal trefoil design in, 119
" Pick," Turkish unit of measurement, 24, 133
Pile, substitution for primitive web, 82; trimming of, 89
Pliny, 16, 93
Polish carpets, 119
Poona, 266
Prayer rugs, 15, 36; Asia Minor, 145; Bokhara, 40, 230; Daghestan, 106; description, 94; Ghiordes, 88; compared with Kulah, 149; description, 145–147; Kaba-Karaman, 140; Kulah, 137, 155; description, 149; Tcherkess, description, 114; tree forms in, 115, 147
Pushmina rugs, 261

R

Raphael, Persian students under, 19
Reclus, on Kirman rugs, quoted, 208

INDEX

INDEX

INDEX

"Tzitzi" rugs, 30, 63; description of, 111–113; marketed in Shemakha, 120

Tzoul, 251

U

United States, manufacture of rugs in, 2, 8; as a market for rugs, 1

V

Vambery, cited, 25

Venice, rug manufacture in, 19

W

Warp, arrangement on looms, 82; dyed at the ends, 84; -fringe, 92; in antique rugs, 83; silk, 83

Water, solvent quality, essential in washing wool, 37; in Angora, 138; in Demirdji, 151; in Oushak, 153; in mixing dyes, 44, 45; supply for dyes, 45

Weavers, Armenian, 143

Weavers, boy, in Azerbijan, 167; in India, 258; in Kirman, 170, 209; in Tabriz, 170; profession hereditary in India, 253, 257; Karabagh, 117; guild of, 25; nomad, 25, 60; Persian, 163; superiority of Eastern, 30, 143; superstitions of, 92; Turkish, 133; wages of, 24, 134

Weaving, 80; ancient and modern methods compared, 14; Assyrian, 16; in Kulah done by men, 150; done by women, 25; in Herez, 178; in Indian jails, 5, 254, 256; method of, 83; process of 82–87, 89, 93; tools for, 86

Wilson, Thomas, on the origin of the Swastika, quoted, 70–72

Women, as designers, 25; as weavers, 25, 163, 178; in Christian settlements, 31; social conditions, 25

Wool, Afghan, exported to Europe, 34; Anatolian, 35; combing of lambs for fine, 35; Farsistan, 34; foundation for rugs, 83; preparation, 36; quality required for rugs, 35; scarcity in India, 254; Spanish, 34, 35; superiority of Eastern, 34; Transcaucasian, 116; Uzbek Tartar, 39

Y

Yaprak rug (Oushak), 152, 153

Yaprakli, fair held at, 22

Yarkand rugs, 64; description, 243–245; tree forms in, 66

Yarn, purchase of, 39; spinning of, 38; supply for weaving, 85; treated with lime, 47

Yesteklik (Konieh), 136; description, 95. *See also* Anatolian mats

Yomud rugs, 40; barber-pole stripe in, 110; description, 233–235; latch-hook design in, 105

Yourdes. *See* Ghiordes

Yucatan, 13, 70

Yule, on Afghan wool, cited, **34**

Yuruk people, 26, 140

Yuruk rugs, description, 140

Z

Zenjan rugs, 192

Zoroastrians, pear pattern traced to, 68